THREE ACRES AND A COW

This is the photograph of Eli taken circa 1890, which he used as the frontispiece of the 1892 edition of his work.

To Albert

THREE ACRES AND A COW

The Life and Works of
Eli Hamshire

Written, Edited and Published by
David Stemp

Best Wishes,

David Stemp.

27 Netley Close,
Cheam, Surrey SM3 8DN

To Ben
for his patience and devotion

First Published in Great Britain 1995
by David Stemp, 27 Netley Close, Cheam, Surrey SM3 8DN
Tel: 0181-641 5765
Copyright © 1995 David Stemp
ISBN: 0 9525910 5 7
Printed in Great Britain
by TTP International, 123 Westmead Road, Sutton, Surrey SM1 4JH
Tel: 0181-715 9957

Contents

Acknowledgements

I would like to thank the following people for their help which enabled me to produce this book:-

Matthew and Mary Alexander of Guildford Museum.

Nigel and Janet Balchin of 'Hullbrook Cottage', Ewhurst.

Richard and Sue Brocksom of 'The Wicket Gate', Ewhurst Green.

Winnie Browne (née Warrington) of Brook Lane, Albury.

John and Belinda Burt of 'The Fields Cottage', Ewhurst Green.

Ivy Cornes of 'Durdle Dore', Rowly Drive, Cranleigh.

John Daniels of Gellatly Road, New Cross.

Kevin Evans of Carshalton Beeches, Surrey.

Mrs Jane Griffiths of Wroxall, Isle of Wight.

Alan and Rose Hamshire of Gadbridge Lane, Ewhurst Green.

Carol Hamshire of Gadbridge Lane, Ewhurst Green.

Edie Hughesdon of Connaught Road, Teddington.

Tony Humphreys of New Malden, Surrey.

Janet Kelsey of Auckland, New Zealand.

Michael Miller of 'Faverton', New Park Road, Cranleigh.

Cecil and Monya Muggeridge of 'Parliament Farm', Ewhurst Green.

Shirley Pidgeon of 'Green View', Ewhurst Green.

Mr. A. Rosenberg of 'Square Leg Cottage', Ewhurst Green.

Mrs. Prue Rumens of Christchurch Park, Sutton.

Mr. Harold Stemp of St. Thomas's Road, St. Annes, Lancashire.

Mrs. H. N. Stemp of St. Thomas's Road, St. Annes, Lancashire.

Freda Vincent of Gadbridge Lane, Ewhurst Green.

Mr. and Mrs. R. Weller of 'Fair View', Ewhurst Green.

Foreword

Ifirst became aware of Eli Hamshire when I was two or three years old, and I was taken into the inner sanctum of my grandparents' front room, which was dominated by a large oak-framed, sepia-tinted picture of the very gentleman. To a young child he was an awe-inspiring sight, being a cross between a benign ogre and Father Christmas. This feeling of awe was further enhanced in my formative years as I sat and listened to tales of his often larger-than-life exploits, many of which were gleaned from his writing and some from the personal recollections of my grandfather, who, although he was only nine when Eli died, could remember him vividly.

As I became older I can remember being given copies of his books to read in the long summer holidays which I often spent with my grandparents in Cranleigh. I found the books heavy going and only resorted to looking at them when I had exhausted my copies of the 'Hotspur' and 'Wizard'. Nevertheless, I can remember being impressed by the ingenuity of his poem on the evil of corsets and by the cautionary account of the death of Samuel Kimball, 'A Boy Killed by Cigarettes'. His correspondence with the likes of Gladstone and Bright impressed me less.

I renewed my acquaintance with Eli Hamshire many years later, when, having been redeployed, I found myself having to teach nineteenth century social history to reluctant fifteen year olds. It was as I searched for relevant source material for my pupils that I remembered and rediscovered the works of my great-great-grandfather. As I re-read his writing, I began to fully appreciate the original genius of the man, who, despite having been born the seventh son of a farm labourer, and, despite having, to a large extent, been self-educated, highlighted the major social issues of the day in a series of pamphlets, and often suggested his own brand of unconventional and down-to-earth remedies for these problems. The most famous of his suggestions, and the one for which Jesse Collings usually takes the credit, was that most of the evils of the day could be allayed if every man was allotted 'Three Acres and a Cow'.

Eli's writings were a boon to me as a teacher as they helped me both to understand a period with which I was far from au fait, and also provided my pupils with a first-hand account of the sufferings of the poor in the second-half of the nineteenth century.

As several of my friends had asked me if it were possible to obtain a copy of his book, I decided that 1992 was the ideal time to start work on reproducing his book as it was the hundredth anniversary of the publication of the fourth and complete edition of 'The Source of England's Greatness and the Source of England's Poverty', and 'The Three Great

Locusts'. I aimed to have the book ready for publication by 1996, the centenary of Eli's death.

I have tried to make his writing more palatable for the modern reader by occasionally reorganising and reducing the length of his paragraphs, by eliminating some of the repetition, and by interspersing Eli's table of Contents into the text, thereby breaking up his continuous prose into more manageable sections. I have also left his sometime eccentric spelling and occasional use of dialect untouched as, I feel, they reflect the man, the largely self educated rustic.

It was a great temptation to axe the whole of his poetry, which, I felt, made his contemporary William McGonagall appear to be a poetical genius, as it rarely scans and usually repeats what has been said more effectively elsewhere in prose. I was stopped from taking this draconian course of action when it was pointed out to me by an erudite nonagenarian, that she had often sat outside pubs as a child and listened to poetry of this ilk being recited. It was, after all, written by the 'Unadulterated Radical' for the working class-man for whom the message was more important than the method of delivery.

At the request of my bridge partner and proof reader, Prue Rumens, who wanted to know more about the man himself, I decided to introduce the book with a short section on Eli Hamshire, his family, and the village of Ewhurst in which he appeared to have lived all his life. This was not as easy as I thought it would be, as very little has been written on the man himself which can not be read in his book, and family anecdotes are not always reliable.

Even his book, 'The Source of England's Greatness', which he said was going to be a history of his life, provides little positive record of the major events in his life, although it does present the reader with a very good picture of the caring character of the man himself and his views on life in general. My search for further information upon the man and his roots led me into the fascinating and ofttimes musty world of the County Record Offices, where crumbling wax-sealed wills and deeds compete with the marvels of the latest in data retrieval systems. Although I failed to find out everything I wanted to know about Eli himself, I did uncover a vast store of information about the family as a whole which, I feel, helps to put his life and writing into greater perspective.

I would like to thank the staff at the following establishments for their patience in the face of my often inane questions: the County Record Office, Kingston; the Muniment Room, Guildford; the County Record Office, Chichester; the Greater London Record Office; the British Library; Somerset House; Matthew and Mary Alexander of Guildford Museum; the Business Press International Library and Archives; the Domestic Buildings Research Group (Surrey); and, last but not least, John Janaway and the staff at the Local Studies Library in Guildford who bore the brunt of my questions and who pointed me in the correct direction whenever I became lost.

I would also like to thank all those residents of Ewhurst Green who welcomed me, a complete stranger, into their homes and allowed me to examine documents appertaining to their properties and also gave me access to a variety of previously unpublished pictures.

Finally, my thanks also go to all those relatives whom I pestered mercilessly for information. Eli's granddaughters, Ivy Cornes and the late Winnie Muggeridge, and his grandson, Allen Hamshire, who still lives in Gadbridge Lane, were probably the most helpful as they formed the closest living link to Eli himself. Others, such as my father, grandmother, Cecil and Bonny Muggeridge also added to the store of anecdotes and information about the man and his family. In particular I would like to thank Janet Kelsey of Auckland University for helping me to unravel the genealogical data, which, when combined with the facts obtained from the Record Offices, help to complete the picture of one of nineteenth century England's greatest, original, rustic thinkers and characters.

D.A.S.
July1995.

The tiny engraving above, which I found in the very first edition of Eli's work in the British Library, was the only illustration which Eli used in either of his books. It probably depicts Ewhurst itself at harvest time and features the village's most prominent landmark, the windmill, on Ewhurst Hill.

HAMPSHIRE FAMILY– ALBURY

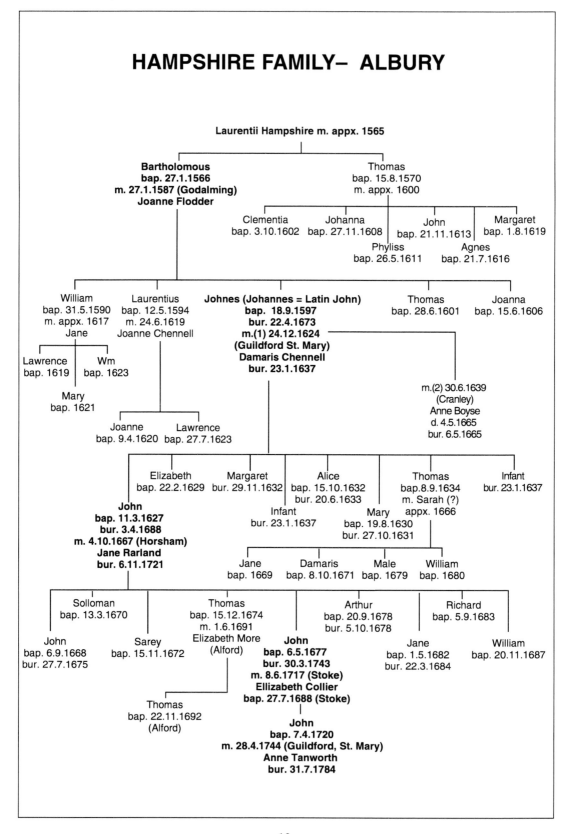

Laurentii Hampshire m. appx. 1565

Bartholomous
bap. 27.1.1566
m. 27.1.1587 (Godalming)
Joanne Flodder

Thomas
bap. 15.8.1570
m. appx. 1600

Clementia
bap. 3.10.1602

Johanna
bap. 27.11.1608

Phyliss
bap. 26.5.1611

John
bap. 21.11.1613

Agnes
bap. 21.7.1616

Margaret
bap. 1.8.1619

William
bap. 31.5.1590
m. appx. 1617
Jane

Laurentius
bap. 12.5.1594
m. 24.6.1619
Joanne Chennell

Johnes (Johannes = Latin John)
bap. 18.9.1597
bur. 22.4.1673
m.(1) 24.12.1624
(Guildford St. Mary)
Damaris Chennell
bur. 23.1.1637

Thomas
bap. 28.6.1601

Joanna
bap. 15.6.1606

Lawrence
bap. 1619

Wm
bap. 1623

Mary
bap. 1621

m.(2) 30.6.1639
(Cranley)
Anne Boyse
d. 4.5.1665
bur. 6.5.1665

Joanne
bap. 9.4.1620

Lawrence
bap. 27.7.1623

Elizabeth
bap. 22.2.1629

Margaret
bur. 29.11.1632

Alice
bap. 15.10.1632
bur. 20.6.1633

Thomas
bap.8.9.1634
m. Sarah (?)
appx. 1666

Infant
bur. 23.1.1637

John
bap. 11.3.1627
bur. 3.4.1688
m. 4.10.1667 (Horsham)
Jane Rarland
bur. 6.11.1721

Infant
bur. 23.1.1637

Mary
bap. 19.8.1630
bur. 27.10.1631

Jane
bap. 1669

Damaris
bap. 8.10.1671

Male
bap. 1679

William
bap. 1680

Solloman
bap. 13.3.1670

Thomas
bap. 15.12.1674
m. 1.6.1691
Elizabeth More
(Alford)

Arthur
bap. 20.9.1678
bur. 5.10.1678

Richard
bap. 5.9.1683

John
bap. 6.9.1668
bur. 27.7.1675

Sarey
bap. 15.11.1672

John
bap. 6.5.1677
bur. 30.3.1743
m. 8.6.1717 (Stoke)
Ellizabeth Collier
bap. 27.7.1688 (Stoke)

Jane
bap. 1.5.1682
bur. 22.3.1684

William
bap. 20.11.1687

Thomas
bap. 22.11.1692
(Alford)

John
bap. 7.4.1720
m. 28.4.1744 (Guildford, St. Mary)
Anne Tanworth
bur. 31.7.1784

The Hamshire Family Background

Eli Hamshire was born into a typical farming family which had obtained a living from the land in the Ewhurst/Cranleigh area, with varying degrees of success, for over two hundred years. At the time of Eli's birth, however, the family fortune was at a low ebb when compared to that of previous generations.

To a large extent, it was quite difficult to discover any new and original information about Eli's predecessors. The majority of them were illiterate and left no first hand accounts of their lives. Most of my information, therefore, had to be gleaned from the legal terminology of deeds, wills and manorial records, or from the barest of entries in the surviving parish records.

Although the records are rather scant and often confusing, I was lucky to discover a reference in the Cranley Parish Register, for May 3rd 1749, to the house in which the family lived. The record stated that James, who was being baptised, was the son of Eli's great-grandfather, John Hampshire of 'Thornsflask', which was a corruption of 'Thornsflush', a small farm which still exists on the Guildford Road, Cranleigh, about three or four miles from Ewhurst.

The name 'Thorn's Flush' probably derived from the fact that, until this century, it was situated beside a rather muddy pond which was surrounded by thorn trees. A written agreement of 1728 between the then owner of the farm, Richard Chandler, and his tenant, John Tickner, describes it as being more or less eight acres of arable land and undergrowth.

Armed with the name 'Thornsflush' I was able to discover a series of deeds in the County Records' Office which led me back to the arrival of the family in Cranley, on October 20th, 1624. On that date one John Hampshere, a husbandman of Albury, bought for the princely sum of £145, a small farm called 'Thornest', on the Cranley/Wonersh border, together with a lease for ten thousand years, from Edward Smallpiece, a tailor of Cranley.

The farm at that time was comprised of a messuage, or farm building, a barn and four acres of pasture land, orchard and undergrowth. As part of the same deal John Hampshere also obtained two other closes of pasture called 'Hollies' and 'Hollickes' which brought the farm up to about twelve acres in size. The land was probably quite heavily wooded and the Wealden soil difficult to cultivate.

I think that it is safe to assume, however, that the Hampshires must have been an extremely resourceful and successful family of yeoman farmers to have survived the occasional plagues, famines, poor harvests and fluctuating agricultural prices of the early seventeenth century, and still to have been able to pay £145 for 'Thornest'. The relative size of this pay-

This is one of the earliest photographs of 'Thornsflush', taken about 1890 - 1900. Initially it had been a simple two up and two down cottage with an outhouse and dairy at the back. The pond can just be seen to the right of the wall, whilst in the background the drying sheds for the brick works are visible. The narrow white flint road is the current B2128.

ment can, I feel, be best appreciated when it is compared to the shilling (5p) a day an agricultural labourer might hope to earn at that time.

Indeed, the Hampshire family of Albury figure quite prominently upon the Lay Subsidy Rolls of the area which registered for a special tax only the wealthier members of the community. William Hampshire, John's eldest brother, for example, having to pay a tax of £5, appeared to be considered the sixth wealthiest person in the village in 1620.

The Hampshires are called 'yeoman' farmers in several of the entries in the Parish Registers, and as such would have had a social status only a little below that of the local gentry. This feeling of social superiority was probably responsible for John Hampshire's decision, two months after the acquisition of 'Thornest', to marry 'by virtue of a licence' his sweetheart from Albury, Damaris Chennell, on Christmas Eve, 1624, at the lovely and already ancient church of St. Mary the Virgin in Guildford.

The fact that John obtained permission to marry in this prestigious church again tends to suggest that the family must have had a certain amount of wealth and influence. It is also rather interesting to note that for appearances' sake John and Damaris were prepared to travel across eight miles of muddy tracks to Guildford in the middle of winter, rather than marry in one of the local parish churches.

An early print of Saint Mary's Church in Guildford, where John Hampshire married Damaris Chennell in 1624.

The cryptic entries in the Parish Registers provide some record of the births, marriages and deaths within the family which followed the marriage of John and Damaris. These records, however, are far from satisfactory as they are often incomplete and are contained in at least four separate Parish Registers: Cranley, Wonersh, Guildford and Ewhurst.

The picture became even more difficult to decipher when I realised that the eldest son of the family, for the next two hundred years, was always called John. It was only as my search continued into Eli's ancestors that I began to realise how fortunate I had been to discover, in the County Record Office, at least twenty-five documents which related to the family and their property. This additional information allowed me to unravel the dates of the string of Hampshires and to discover that occasionally a long-living John Hampshire would be succeeded as owner of the property by his grandson, the son having died early.

In a way, the task of deciphering the Parish Registers was also hindered by the often eccentric spelling of the surname. The Cranleigh Parish Register, for example, gives at least ten different spellings of the name: Hamsheere (1627), Hampshiere (1639), Hamsher (1661), Hampsher (1665), Hamshier (1668), Hamsheir (1673), Hampshere (1675), Hamshire (1749), Hampshire (1753) and Hamshere (1772). The most extreme form of the name, however, had to be the Hamptheschyre, which I found on a deed of 1387 in Kingston. As the Registers indicate that most members of the family were unable to write their names, it is not surprising that there were so many variations in the spelling of the name. It was Eli himself as the first truly literate member of the family, who finally decided on the 'Hamshire' version for his own family.

Several quite fascinating facts still survive, from a variety of sources, concerning John and Damaris and their descendants, and indicate that life in the seventeenth century was often a lottery even if one had money. They had at least six children, John, Elizabeth, Alice, Thomas and the twins, Margaret and Mary. Alice and the twins all died before reaching the age of three, and Damaris herself died in childbirth in 1637 and was buried with her infant child. John himself remarried, an Anne Boyse, within eighteen months and continued to farm 'Thornest' for many more years.

In 1661, he was virtually compelled to donate a 'Free and Voluntary Present' of 5 shillings to the newly restored monarch, King Charles II, to help him out of his financial predicament. Although this payment was called 'voluntary', pressure was exerted upon landowners, such as the Hampshires, to contribute. Failure to pay could lead to social ostracism.

The local Manorial Rolls mention that John was fined for not looking after the local highway and, in July 1665, the records of the Guildford Quarter Sessions show that John had to appear in court for allowing his watercourse to overflow in rainy weather. Perhaps it was this court appearance, the death of his second wife in August 1665 and his advancing years which made him decide to relinquish the property to his son the following year. One of the deeds of 'Thornest' shows that he allowed his 'son and heir aparant' to rent the land for £4 a year as part of his wedding present.

On November 11th, 1671, the Parish Register for Wonersh provided the interesting fact that his son, John, had to pay 6d. to the churchwardens of that parish *for redemption of English captives taken by Turkish Pyrates.'*

Not all the Hamshires stayed on the farm or remained in farming. In a release document of 1712, Thomas, James, Richard and Soloman Hamshire relinquished their interest in the property of John Hamshire deceased in favour of John Hamshire of Cranley. Thomas was a weaver at St. Giles in Middlesex; James was a corn-chandler at St. Martin's-in-the-Fields; Richard was a carpenter in West Grinstead; and Soloman, whose occupation was not recorded, also lived in West Grinstead.

This photograph of the Manfield family and 'Thornsflush' was taken about 1910 from just beyond the pond. The section of the house nearest the road is the oldest part of the house. Both downstairs' rooms had hearths. The chimney nearest the camera houses an inglenook fireplace. Note that the shutters have been removed from the downstairs' windows.

This is a photograph of 'Thornsflush' in the 1990's. The pond no longer exists and has been replaced by an electricity board sub-station.

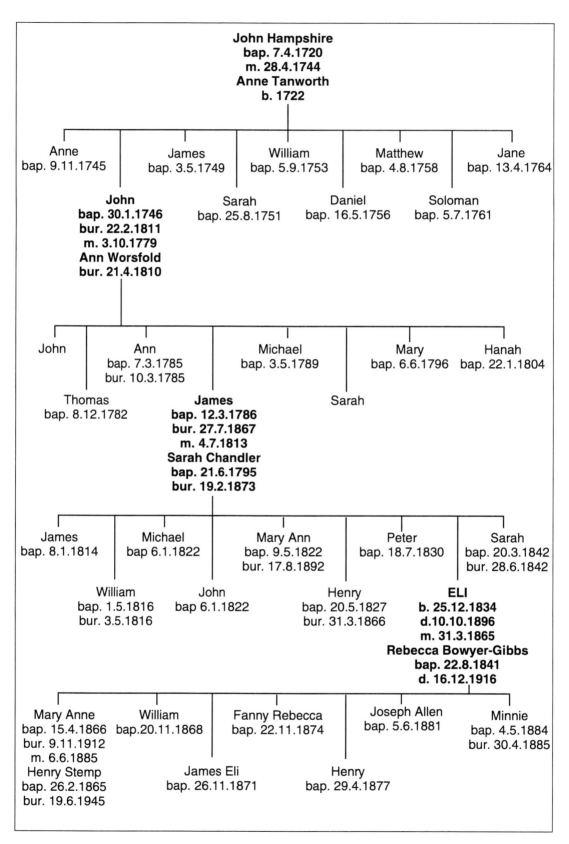

John Hampshire
bap. 7.4.1720
m. 28.4.1744
Anne Tanworth
b. 1722

Anne
bap. 9.11.1745

James
bap. 3.5.1749

William
bap. 5.9.1753

Matthew
bap. 4.8.1758

Jane
bap. 13.4.1764

John
bap. 30.1.1746
bur. 22.2.1811
m. 3.10.1779
Ann Worsfold
bur. 21.4.1810

Sarah
bap. 25.8.1751

Daniel
bap. 16.5.1756

Soloman
bap. 5.7.1761

John

Ann
bap. 7.3.1785
bur. 10.3.1785

Michael
bap. 3.5.1789

Mary
bap. 6.6.1796

Hanah
bap. 22.1.1804

Thomas
bap. 8.12.1782

James
bap. 12.3.1786
bur. 27.7.1867
m. 4.7.1813
Sarah Chandler
bap. 21.6.1795
bur. 19.2.1873

Sarah

James
bap. 8.1.1814

Michael
bap 6.1.1822

Mary Ann
bap. 9.5.1822
bur. 17.8.1892

Peter
bap. 18.7.1830

Sarah
bap. 20.3.1842
bur. 28.6.1842

William
bap. 1.5.1816
bur. 3.5.1816

John
bap 6.1.1822

Henry
bap. 20.5.1827
bur. 31.3.1866

ELI
b. 25.12.1834
d.10.10.1896
m. 31.3.1865
Rebecca Bowyer-Gibbs
bap. 22.8.1841
d. 16.12.1916

Mary Anne
bap. 15.4.1866
bur. 9.11.1912
m. 6.6.1885
Henry Stemp
bap. 26.2.1865
bur. 19.6.1945

William
bap.20.11.1868

Fanny Rebecca
bap. 22.11.1874

James Eli
bap. 26.11.1871

Joseph Allen
bap. 5.6.1881

Henry
bap. 29.4.1877

Minnie
bap. 4.5.1884
bur. 30.4.1885

Eli's Great-Grandfather

By the time Eli's great-grandfather, John, had inherited the farm in 1744 it had grown to about twenty acres with the acquisition of the eight acres of 'Thornsflush', and all the evidence points to the fact that the family were highly respected and still regarded themselves as petty gentry. His father, indeed, had been an Overseer of the Poor and a Way Warden for the Parish of Cranleigh on several occasions between 1710 and 1717.

John, like his forefather, also went to the trouble, on the 28th of April, 1744, to marry in the still prestigious church of St. Mary the Virgin, Guildford. His wedding, however, was not recorded in the Parish Register but fortunately has survived in the Bishop's Transcripts for the Diocese of Winchester for that year. This document describes him as a twenty-four year old 'yeoman, bachelor of Cranley', who married the twenty-two year old daughter of a lime burner, Anne Tanworth of Cranley.

John and his wife Ann(e), had at least nine children between 1745 and 1764: Ann, John, James, Sarah, William, Daniel, Matthew, Solomon, and Jane. The strongly religious flavour of the children's names, although quite common in eighteenth century rural communities, does tend to suggest that the family was quite heavily influenced by the Bible. Indeed Eli mentions in his writings that Dissenters regularly held meetings in his grandfather's barn in Cranleigh. An undated booklet, issued by the Cranleigh and District Chamber of Commerce at least forty years ago, states that the first records of Nonconformity in the parish date back to 1750 when services, conducted by John Harris, an author of some repute, were held in a cottage on the Common.

As it was only a short step from 'Thornsflush' to Cranleigh Common, it is highly likely that the Hampshires attended these early meetings and volunteered the use of their barn for future gatherings. It is, however, impossible to ascertain which John Hampshire allowed these meetings to take place and when.

Another indication of the relative success and prosperity of the family is, I feel, shown by the fact that the land was put up as security for a loan of £200, probably to acquire more land, at four and a half percent interest, in 1760. The loan was from one William Martin, a writing master, of Cranleigh. The interest on this loan, however, was not paid, and the whole of the property was sold to John Bonsey (or Bousey) for £300, on August 7th, 1762. William Martin received £218.16s. and John Hampshire £81.4s.

This, I felt, was the end of the family's association with 'Thornest', 'Thornflush', 'Hollies' and 'Hollickes'. I was wrong! As a matter of curiosity I read the last will and testament of John Bonsey written in 1758. At the end of the will there was a codicil, dated November

5th, 1762, which considerably altered the provisions of the will.

The first beneficiary of John Bonsey's will was his wife, Margaret, who was to have the rents and profit from his Estate. The next to benefit was his nephew, Richard, who could only have the property, *"during his life only with power to cut timber for the necessary repairs of the said Estate and no other use,..."* Finally, and most surprisingly, *"and after his decease I give and devise the said Estate to John Hampshire, son of John Hampshire of whom I purchased the same and to his heirs for ever."*

It would appear from an additional proviso to the will that John Bonsey was probably an extremely close friend of the family, and not merely motivated by compassion for the family he had dispossessed. He stated that when John Hampshire junior or his heirs re-acquired the property, they should pay £5 per annum to Daniel Greenfield and William Martin, both of Cranley, who would use the sum to bring up, maintain, educate and apprentice the other children of John Hampshire senior, as they thought best. It was highly likely, however, that these children would be too old to benefit from this bequest by the time John junior acquired the property.

John Bonsey's acts of Christian charity in returning the land to the Hampshires and providing for the welfare of the children, lend credence to the thought that he may have been a fellow Dissenter and perhaps worshipped at their house. It is also possible that William Martin and Daniel Greenfield were of the same religious persuasion.

John Bonsey died early in 1764 and his nephew, Richard, according to the Shere, Vachery and Cranley Court Rolls, acquired the property on the death of John's widow on October

This is one of the final photographs of the old barn at 'Thornsflush', taken in about 1980 before the barn was converted into a cottage, where John Hamshire allowed the Dissenters to meet. The barn had probably altered little in the previous two hundred years.

22nd, 1766. Richard may also have married a member of the Hampshire family in Albury, as the Parish Register shows that a Richard Boncey married a Mary Hampshire on November 21st, 1762.

According to the records of the local Manor Court, Richard was still alive in 1777 as he is recorded as having served upon a jury. By 1780, however, he must have died, as the local Land Tax returns show that the property had reverted into the ownership of the Hampshire family, although it was to be another two years before they were to live there again.

From 1762 until about 1780 the whereabouts of the family is rather vague. An article issued by the Ewhurst History Society in March, 1981, claimed that the family came from Lurgashall in Sussex. I could find no record of them having settled in Sussex, however, in the West Sussex County Record Office. Personally I feel that they probably used the proceeds of the sale to buy a few acres of land to the south of Cranley, in the parish of Alfold. The first of the Land Tax records for Alfold in 1780 tends to indicate that two pieces of land had been held until shortly before that date by the Hampshire family. One William Eager was charged 9s.6d. for Hamshiers Land, and Mathew Hill was charged £1.10s.4d. for 'land late Hamshier'. Areas of land in the Wonersh tax returns, however, were also designated as being 'late Hamshier'.

The Cranleigh Land Tax returns for 1780 and 1781 list Eli's great-grandfather, who was still alive, as being the proprietor of the original estate, but that a Robert Stedman was the occupier, paying a Land Tax of £1.12s. By 1782, however, John Hampshire had returned and remained at 'Thornsflush' until the property passed into the hands of his son, John, in 1785.

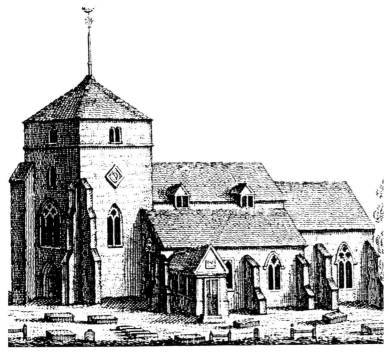

This is an engraving of Cranley Church from the 1760's. It was engraved by James Peak from a drawing by H. Hill. It was here that most of the Hampshires were baptised and buried. (Reproduced by kind permission of the Surrey Local Studies Library).

Eli's Grandfather

Eli's grandfather appears to have farmed the estate quite successfully and to have fulfilled the wishes of John Bonsey regarding the payment of five pounds a year to his brothers and sisters. In 1799, however, he made a final payment of £31.10s. to them to terminate this provision.

The increased profits to be obtained from farming, as a result of the Napoleonic Wars, probably motivated the family in 1805 to expand into the neighbouring village of Ewhurst, and led them into a period of even greater prosperity. Although Ewhurst was about three miles away from 'Thornsflush', Eli's grandfather must have been quite familiar with the village as he was a witness at the wedding of Thomas Harrison and Rachel Holt in Ewhurst in 1772, and also married his wife, Ann Worsfold, there in 1779.

During his lifetime the parish records for Cranleigh show six children being baptized by John and Ann between 1782 and 1804, including Eli's father, James, in 1786. There was no trace of the eldest son, John, (nor his daughter, Sarah) in any of the local Parish Registers, and I was not entirely sure of John's existence until I found that he claimed his inheritance in 1812. Working backwards from the 1851 Census, however, it would appear that John had been born in 1778 in Wonersh, although the 1861 Census gives the place of birth as Albury. The fact that he was illegitimate may have led to his not being baptised.

The Land Tax returns for Ewhurst from 1805 to 1810 show that John Hampshire rented the sizeable 'Old House Farm' from Thomas Goldhawk and had to pay a tax of £6.5s., besides being assessed at £10.10s. for the parish tithes. It seems likely that John left much of the running of the Cranleigh estate to his two eldest sons, John and Thomas, whilst he relied heavily upon his nineteen year old son, James, and the rest of the family to tackle the new venture in Ewhurst.

This is a modern day photograph of 'Old House Farm'. It looked nothing like this in 1805.

Eli's Father and Family

The death of Eli's grandmother in 1810 and of his grandfather in 1811 appears to have started a slump in the family fortune, particularly for Eli's father, James. His grandfather's Cranley estate was claimed by John, 'the eldest son and heir of John Hampshire, late of Ewhurst', who capitalised on the period of agricultural prosperity by selling it, within a year of his father's death, for £1,206.

As his father had died intestate, James, by the Divine Permission of the Bishop of Winchester was made the administrator of his property. His task of administration was made even more complicated, however, by the fact that John had died in the very same year as the owner of the property, Thomas Goldhawk, and for the next six years the Land Tax records show that the property was owned and occupied by the respective executors. The length of time the property was in the hands of these executors suggests that there were legal complications, which might have been expensive, and could have been the motivation for Eli's dislike of the legal profession and for his recommendation that everyone should write a will. The fact that James was illiterate would not have helped matters.

Having lost both his father and mother in such a short space of time, having the farm to run and two young sisters, Mary and Hanah, to look after, must have been a strain on the young James. In 1812 he advertised for a housekeeper and on July 4th, 1813, he married the successful applicant, Sarah Chandler, from Holmbury in the local parish church of St. Peter and St. Paul. According to Eli's grand-daughter, Winnie, Sarah's mother was a school mistress, but the fact that her daughter could only make her mark in the wedding register tends to discount this idea.

This engraving, by Charles Thomas Cracklow, shows how the Parish Church in Ewhurst looked in 1823. (Reproduced by kind permission of the Surrey Local Studies Library).

Although life was probably quite difficult for James and Sarah, they seemed to have maintained a reasonable standard of living in the first years of their marriage whilst they remained at 'Old House Farm'. The baptisms of their sons, James and William, in 1814 and 1816 respectively, and the burial of William in the same year, record the father as being a farmer of 'Old House Farm'. By the time the twins, Michael and John, were baptised in 1822, however, and for the remainder of his children's baptisms, James is merely recorded as being a labourer.

In 1817 the legal problems concerning 'Old House Farm' were resolved and the ownership passed to Mr. Goldhawk junior, the Hampshires relinquishing their tenancy. The next fifteen years were ones of relative hardship for the family and coincided unfortunately with the period of agricultural depression which followed the onset of peace in 1815.

This reduction of the family to poverty from a position of relative wealth undoubtedly had a strong influence upon Eli's philosophy. It is difficult to imagine him being so critical of the landed classes, or having such a strong social conscience, if he had been brought up in the comfort and security of 'Old House Farm'.

During the next seven years the Hampshires are only mentioned in the Land Tax returns for the years 1819-1821, when they were the tenants of a Mr. Cheeseman and paid 8s.4d. tax. For the remainder of the time they must have relied on the generosity of friends and relatives. Between 1821 and 1825 James is occasionally mentioned in the Ewhurst Vestry Book as receiving help from the Parish. On March 4th, 1821, for example, he was allowed a pound on account of a bad hand, whilst on June 2nd, 1822, he was allowed another pound towards his rent *'he being unable to make reserves.'*

By 1825, however, the family fortune seemed to be improving and the Land Tax Returns show that James was now the tenant of a Richard Hills and paid a sum of 12s.6d. on a property described as a farm. This was probably the very same property, designated a homestead, as he was shown as occupying at Ewhurst Green, on the 1842 Tithe map, and which he rented from one Edward Hills. This particular property, and presumably the one in which Eli was born, consisted of a cottage and garden, two meadows and a strip of underwood, totalling about three and threequarter acres. The fact that James could provide for his family from such a modest sized homestead, was probably the inspiration for Eli's 'three acres and a cow' policy, which he recommended as a cure for the poverty of the agricultural classes.

'The Fields Cottage' dates from the last quarter of the sixteenth century when it would have been a timber-framed, smoke-bay house. The house faces westwards towards Ewhurst Green and the farm pond. To the south the barn has now been converted into a cottage. There is still evidence of the original wattle and daub to be found within the cottage. A chimney was probably added to the smoke bay in the seventeenth century. By the time Eli was born, the main living quarters in the cottage were two downstairs rooms which had backing hearths between them. Their ceilings were quite low whilst the ceilings in the upstairs rooms were within the roof space. The cottage would probably have been quite warm and snug although a little overcrowded.

This sketch shows the rear of 'The Fields Cottage', the oldest visible part. The original cottage would have extended from the right-hand edge of the extension on the left to just beyond the door. Just under the eaves and above the central window can be seen one of the original beams. (Reproduced by kind permission of "The Domestic Buildings Research Group".)

Any thought of an improvement in the family fortune, was cruelly curtailed in 1828-1829 when James suffered an illness which incapacitated him for at least a year. It was Eli's mother, Sarah, who held the family together during this period of deprivation, although she undoubtedly leant heavily upon her eldest son, James, who was aged fourteen at this time.

Their combined efforts, however, were not enough to stave off the threat of the landlord selling their furniture, as Eli so dramatically describes in 'The Source of England's Greatness'. Sarah was reduced to sitting on a stone-lump by the roadside to cry to her Maker for protection. As if in answer to her prayers, their problems, at that time, were partially alleviated by a payment of five pounds from a group of Dissenters in Guildford, who had used their house for meetings. Eli, however, failed to mention in his book that the family were reduced to receiving Poor Relief from the parish. Indeed, it might have been the suffering of his parents at this time which made him so sympathetic to the plight of the poor, so generous to the needy and so scathing about the relief of the poor.

The Ewhurst Vestry Minutes of December, 1828, show that the officials of the parish, meeting as usual in the 'Bull's Head', awarded James 5 shillings poor relief. In March, 1829, he received a pair of shoes, whilst in May he received a further 3 shillings. In July the payment had dropped to 2 shillings *'and for his boy a round frock and breeches and shirt'*. The final payment was another paltry 2 shillings in December of that year, although he received another pair of shoes the following February. These payments appear a veritable pittance when compared to the £5 payed to the Hampshires by the Dissenters. James's fortunes and health had recovered sufficiently, by 1835, for him to purchase a local carrier's business for £15. The manner of his acquisition of this business is laced with intrigue and violence, and was fortunately recorded for posterity by a thwarted business rival of Eli's father in a letter to his son. This letter was preserved in the Dollar papers of the Eager Collection in the Lady Peake Institute in Cranleigh. The whereabouts of this letter is now a mystery, but its contents were fortunately recorded by Mary Alexander of the Guildford Museum. The relevant part of the letter which is dated December 15th, 1835 states:-

"In 2 or 3 weeks after you left on a Thursday Night as Old Peter was a coming Home from Guildford between Hound House Hollow & the Direction Post where the Road turns off to Horse Block Hollow Two Men came up to him and askt him the way to Rudgwick & then one struck him across the Arms with a Stick & the other fired at him & the Bullet graz'd his left Eye lash as he was sitting on the front of his Cart & passed through the Tilt on the other side if it had been an Inch farther back doubtless he would have been kill'd but his Old Horse took fright at the Report & set off at a Gallop & got away from them as the old man told me the next Morning his frock was very Bloody when I saw him & his Eye tied up it so alarmed him he did not go for some time but sent his Sons George and Wm. when he went again he had one of George's Boys with him & some Man to meet him as far as Shere every Night which was so Expensive & the Dread when Night came on caused him to give up I did not like to go till he gave up to hurt him & what did he do instead of offering me his Concern he sold it to Hamshire for 15£ & had he with him before he gave up & Introduced him to all his Custom & his Yeast Trade & all, but Immediately the first time as Hamshire went I went also & went a Tuesdays & Saturdays to Guildford & Thursdays to Dorking but it did not Answer my Purpose by no means a Tuesdays, Saturdays is something better, & I had no time for nothing at Home but if I had like to got Custom enough to pay I would kept on but as I was not like to it I have given up Tuesdays & goes only Saturdays to Guildford & Thursdays to Dorking as usual."

Winnie Muggeridge recalled being told the story many times by her mother over eighty years ago. Apparently the horse careered down Mill Hollow until it reached the 'Windmill Inn' public house where Old Peter regularly drank. It pulled up in front of the pub and when Old Peter did not appear for his drink, the locals came out and discovered him lying semiconscious in the wagon.

Old Peter may have fallen foul of the smugglers who were reputed to travel regularly inland from Shoreham, their pack mules loaded with luxury articles such as tea and tobacco. One of their bases, near the route which crossed Pitch Hill, was reputed to be the 'New Inn', or the 'Windmill Inn' as it later became known. This isolated inn in the hills to the north of Ewhurst was supposedly a favourite meeting place for the smugglers and had a false roof in which the contraband was stored. The smugglers also used the nearby windmill, which stood at a height of over 800 feet on Ewhurst Hill, to guide them to their destination. Nowadays the windmill is almost completely obscured by trees. The encroachment of the trees could have been the reason why the last miller, Caleb Coldman, left the mill and moved down to the 'Windmill Inn' in the valley below.

Caleb Coldman and his wife outside the 'Windmill Inn' where they lived in the 1870's.

The Windmill at Ewhurst in the nineteenth century, from the 'Charm of Old Surrey' by H.M. Alderman,

Although it is now impossible to trace the author of the letter concerning Old Peter and the battle to obtain the carrier's business, it could have been the Daniel Mann who, in the 1836 Pigot's Directory, was described as being a carrier between London and Horsham on Tuesdays and Fridays, and in 1839 was listed as being a carrier between Guildford and Horsham on Saturdays. A Daniel Mann lived in Shere in 1835 at the time of the attack on Old Peter, but had moved by 1841, perhaps to pursue a carrying career elsewhere.

I also found it difficult to trace Old Peter who sold the business to James, until I realised that Peter could have been his surname. The 1841 and 1851 Census returns show that one James Peter, an agricultural labourer, who lived to the north of the parish at Pitchill was the most likely candidate. He would have been 64 in 1835, whilst his sons, who were bricklayers, were both aged 34.

The letter is of interest, however, not only because of the graphic depiction of the attempted highway robbery, but also because it gives the reader an insight into the life which James and Eli, in his turn, were to follow for approximately the next thirty-four years.

A modern traveller would drive from Ewhurst to Guildford on the more direct route through Cranleigh. The first part of this route, in the early nineteenth century passed over the thick Wealden Clay and would have been virtually impassable for a cart in winter, until one reached the Guildford to Horsham Turnpike Road which had been opened in 1794. Even there the journey would have been impeded by the four or five toll gates, to be encountered between Cranleigh and Guildford, at places such as Gaston Gate and the Leathern Bottle. The charge of 6d. for a cart at each of these toll gates was another deterrent from using this route.

William Cobbett, in his 'Rural Rides' in 1823, aptly described the difficulties a traveller had to encounter; *"From Ewhurst the first three miles was the deepest clay that I ever saw....I was warned of the difficulty of getting along....it took me a good hour and a half to get along these three miles.....now, mind, this is the real 'weald', where the clay is 'bottomless'."*

It was often necessary in winter, according to a visitor in the last century, to increase the number of horses on a coach from four or six to eight to combat the clay. Oxen also proved a popular means of transport for those less interested in speed, as their cloven hooves gave a better purchase on the steep, muddy, winding tracks.

Because of the problems the clay posed, the carrier tended to travel northwards over steep, narrow, winding passes such as Mill Hollow or Horseblock Hollow to the top of the Greensand ridge, where he encountered the sandy, wooded expanses of Hurtwood Common. The unusually named Horseblock Hollow dates back to a small encounter in the 1640's between the Cavaliers and the Roundheads. The Cavaliers had desperately tried to protect their standard by forming a block only to be cut to pieces by the surrounding Roundheads. This battle was re-enacted, as Eli mentions, every Whit Monday at the 'Boy and Donkey' in Cranleigh in a fight between the Cranleigh Diamond Tops and the Ewhurst Roundheads.

From Hurtwood Common the route passed along narrow tracks such as the romantic sounding Hound House Hollow until it arrived in the valley of the Tilling Bourne at the beautiful and ancient village of Shere. From there the carrier would turn westwards, sometimes travelling along the dry routeways of the North Downs, through villages such as Albury and Merrow, where he would find additional customers for the vital yeast trade. Although this route added two or three miles to the overall journey, it was obviously quicker than the more direct route through Cranleigh.

As Ewhurst had not had a decent road since the Romans, the railway would not arrive in Cranleigh for another thirty years and the Wey-Arun canal was rather distant, the local people, must have depended to a large extent on the carrier for their supplies, and as a result the job must have been quite lucrative. It did not appear from James's rival's letter, however, that there was enough trade in the mid-1830's for more than one carrier, providing that that carrier was conscientious in carrying out his work. By the 1840's, however, the financial climate must have altered and the amount of trade increased, as the local Russell's, Andrew's and Kelly's trade directories (1842-1857) show that a rival carrier and part-time mealman, John Jones of 'Badcock Cottage', Ewhurst, operated the same route on the same days.

Most of the early directories of the period state that James visited Guildford every Tuesday, Thursday and Saturday, and Horsham on Monday. The Post Office Directory for 1845,

This engraving of Guildford High Street is probably just as recognisable now as it would have been to Eli in the 1890's.

however, states that he only traded on Wednesday and Saturday. Whatever the truth of the matter, James and Eli must have found very little time to relax. The other days were probably taken up with distributing goods locally, carrying out necessary maintenance work on the wagon, or in helping the rest of the family around the farm.

Carrying was not without its physical dangers, however, as Old Peter had discovered, and there could sometimes be hidden overheads as one of Eli's brothers found to his cost when he was fined a pound for allowing the wagon to get stuck by the roadside. The most unpleasant feature of the job, undoubtedly, was the constant exposure to the elements. The long winter months, with their limited daylight hours, would often have been extremely unpleasant, the carrier having to put up with a combination of wet, windy and freezing conditions. Snow would have made the steep, winding passes over the hills, which are often referred to locally as 'Little Switzerland', impossible. The detrimental effect of the weather upon the health of the carriers was probably one of the reasons why there seemed to be quite a turnover in their names which are listed in the different directories, and it was undoubtedly one of the contributory factors which led to Eli's early demise.

Carrying was, nevertheless, an ideal additional source of revenue for James to supplement the little he must have earned from his three acres, particularly as he still had a rather large, young family to support. At the time he acquired the carrier's business in 1835, his sons James (21), John (14) and Michael (14) would have been able, on the whole, to fend for themselves, and to provide a valuable source of help around the farm. The other children, Mary Ann (13), Henry (8), Peter (5), and Eli (1), would have still been very dependent upon James for their welfare.

James's hours as a carrier, however, would have been remarkably long, as the 10 to 12 mile journey to Guildford probably took at least three hours each way in favourable conditions. The 1853 Russell's Directory reveals that he used 'The Star' public house in Guildford, which was the rendezvous of many of the country carriers and errand men who maintained communications with the surrounding villages. It was probably there that Eli obtained much of his information on current affairs: he would have met traders from all parts of the county and would have had access to a wide variety of local and national newspapers, which he appeared to read avidly.

James's customers would have known where to find him, as he would arrive at Star Corner each working day at 11 a.m., and stay there until he left at 3 p.m. Before his day began, however, the wagon would have had to be loaded and further goods picked up in transit. Upon his return he would have had to distribute some of the goods which he had acquired, and then, having taken care of his horse's needs, he might be able to retire for the evening, providing that there were no outstanding tasks to be performed on the farm.

It is not surprising, therefore, that he decided in 1859 to reduce his work-load by axing the Tuesday journey to Guildford. His local rival, John Jones, must have also found the job extremely onerous, for by 1858 he had ceased to trade as a carrier and in the 1861 Census is listed as a mealman and baker. Jones (69) probably sold his carrying business to a younger man called Charles Daws, who operated from 1860, like Jones, from the 'Jolly Butcher', over the same route as the Hamshires every Tuesday and Saturday.

James could have been influenced into branching out into the world of carrying by the success of his cousin, William Hampshire, who is listed in the London Postal Directories, of 1832 to 1838, as being a carrier operating on Mondays and Fridays from the 'Catherine Wheel' at Borough to Guildford and Bramley. He might even have borrowed the necessary £15 to set the business up from William or from his own brother John, who had fared so well from his father's death.

Whether James saved or borrowed the money the carrier's business seemed a sound investment and the family began to prosper and expand in a modest fashion. The Tithe Map of Ewhurst for 1842 shows that in addition to the small homestead which he rented off Edward Hills, he also rented a small cottage and garden on the opposite side of the Green from William Longhurst to house his growing family.

The Ewhurst Vestry Book for 1844 shows James as being assessed at £84 for local rates. When one considers that this was the ninth highest rateable assessment out of the 33 householders listed, it would appear that the family had staged a marked recovery in just over a decade. James would probably have been called upon to make quite a sizeable contribution to local taxes, as the records of the meeting on the 29th of November show that, although the Poor Rate was only 10d. in the pound, it was the third such rate since Lady Day; similarly, the demand of 9d. in the pound for the Highway Rate was the second such levy since Lady Day.

The Vestry Book of 1844 also shows that James employed two men and a boy to run his growing business. It appears highly likely that his employees were members of his own family. His eldest son, James, who was already married to his first wife, Sarah, was probably one of the men, and lived in the small cottage across the Green. The 1841 Census shows that Michael (20), Henry (14), Peter (10) and Eli (6) were still living at home. As a man was classified as being over 18 years old, Michael could have been the other man working on the farm, although he was later to become a builder. The boy could have been Peter, aged 13 in 1844, who was still living at home in 1851, although he was then classed as being a sawyer. Eli, who was aged 9 in 1844, also probably spent many hours a week, helping his parents with the lighter chores, such as feeding the chickens and helping to tend to his father's horse.

The Censuses also reveal that the family supplemented their income by taking in the occasional lodger. In 1841, one Daniel Edward (50), a cordwainer or shoemaker, lived with the family, as did Lucyar Robinson (17), a relative from Billingshurst in Sussex, who probably helped Sarah around the house for her keep. In 1851, Lucyar's brother, Job (18), worked as an agricultural labourer for James, and was to remain a lifelong friend of Eli. Eli's granddaughter, Winnie, could remember going to stay with Job in Billingshurst in the early years of this century.

The Hamshire influence at Ewhurst Green increased dramatically in 1848 when the records of the Manor of Gumshall Towerhill show that James's son, Henry, who was a servant at Hampton Court Palace, purchased from Henry Aylward a cottage and two and a half acres of land, which were situated next to the small cottage where his eldest brother, James, lived. The following year he also rented a further four acres of neighbouring waste land. It is rather surprising that Henry, who was only 21 years old at the time should have been able to raise the £60 necessary for the transaction. He was, however, educated and obviously had the initiative to acquire a reasonable post at the palace. I feel that as he no longer lived in Ewhurst, and as he built a stable and carthouse on the property, he probably bought it as an investment and sublet the land to his father and brothers both to cultivate and to use as a base for their carrying business.

This copy of an old 'Forest Stores' postcard, taken in about 1920, shows David Tidy and his grandson, Reg, in front of the pond on Ewhurst Green. 'The Fields Cottage' is just out of sight to the left of the photograph. The cottage to the right of the horse is the one which used to be the barn of 'The Fields Cottage'.

The overall impression that one obtains about Eli's family is that it was extremely tightly knit, and that the children cared considerably about their parents and one another. Even when Eli's sister, Mary Anne, married Moses Botting of Alfold in 1842, she did not move far away. The 1851 Census shows the couple, and their three children, living in the cottage next door, which had probably originally been the barn of 'The Fields Cottage'. Her brother, Peter (16), probably worked with her husband as he was also classified as being a sawyer. Further evidence of this concern for one another is also provided by the fact that the eldest son, James, having remarried a widow, Elizabeth Broomer, returned to the family home, to look after his widowed mother in her advancing years, when all the other children had married and moved.

Eli's birth and early years

Eli was born on Christmas Day, 1834, and lived his early life in 'The Fields Cottage', at Ewhurst Green. The house must have been alive with people and bustling with activity, and although it had seen hard times, it was by then feeling the benefit of an economic recovery. Eli was the seventh son, and the eighth and youngest child, of Sarah and James, although it is possible that they may have had, in 1842, a further child, Sarah, who died at the age of fourteen weeks. As he was the youngest in the family, and was twenty years younger than his eldest brother, James, he probably received more attention than the others, particularly from the sister he adored, Mary Ann, who was twelve years his senior, and after whom he named his eldest daughter.

His father, James, however, was a strange, brooding, melancholic figure who seldom spoke to the boys. He must have been severely scarred by the problems and responsibility of his early life. When he spoke, however, it seems that his sons listened and respected his advice. Eli describes his words as having 'weight with my conscience'.

The only picture which survives of Eli's parents may have been taken at the time of their Golden Wedding in 1863, although it could be much older. The faded print shows James to be a well-built, dignified looking figure with rather handsome features. He is wearing the traditional countryman's smock, and sits with his arm around his wife's shoulder. Sarah, for her part, wearing a white bonnet and woollen shawl, looks a rather plain and homely character, with sad and predictably care-worn features.

In contrast, however, his mother, Sarah, appeared to have been extremely lively, religious, resourceful and considerate to those less fortunate than herself. It was she, after all, who had kept the family together in the deepest days of James's illness, not only through her deeds but through her 'heart and brain' prayers.

Eli mentions his mother several times in his book and seems to have regarded her with genuine love and admiration. She is first mentioned in the short poem with which he introduces the 'Source of England's Greatness'. Even the prospective birth of her son, apparently, did not prevent her from thinking about the other members of the family, as she vainly strove to cook them a goose for Christmas Dinner.

It was Sarah, moreover, who was the person responsible for Eli having had what appears to be a happy, sheltered, protected childhood; and it was she who made sure that he obtained an education, that he read the Bible, and, moreover, that he developed a social conscience. Eli recalls her admonishing her boys for imitating the afflicted, and when a neighbour became ill she took it upon herself to look after the neighbour's step-daughter for a week. Eli, who was only thirteen at the time, seemed to have already developed a desire to help those in need, and assisted his mother by providing the young child with an egg to eat. The following year, he even dissuaded a young pregnant woman from drowning herself in the village pond as she had been disappointed by her lover.

Apart from these incidents, we actually know very little about Eli's early life, for although he says that his book is to be a history of his life, he devoted most of his writing to describing the suffering of others. He would, however, like all farm children, have been expected to help with the farm chores from an early age, his education being sporadic and having to be fitted into lulls in the agricultural calendar.

He was more fortunate than many of his contemporaries in that he did receive a limited education. Before the local church school opened in 1840 there had been a charity school in the village since about 1820, where a local lady taught a dozen village children to write with a stick in sand. There is, however, no record of Eli having received any formal schooling. The book 'Bygone Cranleigh' by B. Seymour and M. Warrington suggests that he taught himself to read from the family Bible. Whilst the Bible was obviously the most important book in the house and exerted a great influence upon Eli and his family, I feel that he must have received some form of education to read it in the first place.

Eli's granddaughter, Winnie, claimed that he attended a Dame School, where he would have paid 2d. a day for a basic education. Seymour and Warrington say that there were at least five Dame Schools in nearby Cranleigh in 1846. As anyone with a limited amount of education was allowed to open one of these schools it seems probable that there would have been one or two of these schools in Ewhurst. It, therefore, seems likely that if Eli did not attend the newly opened local church school, then he would have visited someone such as Mary Stenning (62), who was listed in the 1841 Census as being of independent means and living locally at Ewhurst Green. Another possibility was Mary Child (45), who was listed as being a schoolmistress. As later records show that the school tended to employ

This is a photograph of Mr Holloway and Group 2 at Ewhurst School in 1884. Eli's daughter, Fanny, is the second from the right in the middle row. To her left is a friend of the family, George Weller, who was sacked by Eli for playing around whilst chicken plucking. Eli's granddaughter, Ivy Cornes, on seeing the photograph, said George Weller had a harelip and farmed at 'Rumbeam Farm'. On close inspection of the original photograph, one can see the harelip.

married couples - William and Jane Head in 1851, and James and Frances Richardson in the 1860's and 1870's, Baldwin and Jane Downs in 1881, Mr. and Mrs. Austin in 1887 and Herbert and Alice Brooker in 1891 - Mary Child may not have been employed by the school. This post may have belonged to the young married couple, Mr. and Mrs. Henry Jenkins, Henry being listed as a schoolmaster, living within the parish at Cox Green, in 1841.

Before looking a little more closely at Eli's later history, however, I feel that it is necessary to examine in more detail another strong influence upon his life - the village of Ewhurst.

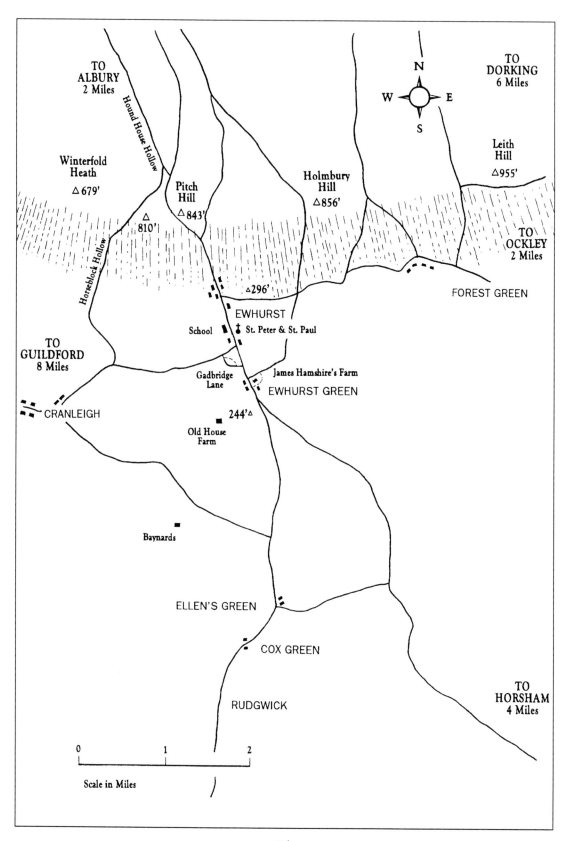

TO
ALBURY
2 Miles

TO
DORKING
6 Miles

N

W   E

S

Leith
Hill
△955'

Winterfold
Heath

△679'

Hound House Hollow

Pitch
Hill
△843'

Holmbury
Hill
△856'

△
810'

Horseblock Hollow

TO
OCKLEY
2 Miles

△296'

FOREST GREEN

EWHURST

School   ✝ St. Peter & St. Paul

TO
GUILDFORD
8 Miles

Gadbridge
Lane

James Hamshire's Farm

EWHURST GREEN

CRANLEIGH

244'△

Old House
Farm

Baynards

ELLEN'S GREEN

COX GREEN

RUDGWICK

TO
HORSHAM
4 Miles

0   1   2

Scale in Miles

The Village of Ewhurst

As Eli spent most of his life in the village of Ewhurst, it is not surprising that his writing and philosophy were so strongly influenced by the rural nature of the community in which he lived; nor that he criticised so vehemently the divisive social structure which led to the wealthy landowners enjoying a life of comfort, whilst many of their neighbours often lived in abject poverty.

He was born in a village which had probably not altered much for hundreds of years. Louis Jennings in his 'Field Paths and Green Lanes' called it *"a one horse place."* Cobbett, on the other hand, thought that it was *"a very pretty village ... the Church of which is most delightfully situated."*

There had been a settlement in the Ewhurst area since at least Roman times, as the remains of a villa have been discovered to the north of the parish, not far from the Roman road which ran to the west of the village. At the time of the Norman Conquest, the area was a very sparsely inhabited section of the Royal Manor of Gomselle, and as such failed to merit an entry in the Domesday Book. Whilst the church contains evidence of Norman workmanship, Ewhurst is not referred to as a parish until about 1290.

According to the Rev. Owen Manning and William Bray in their book 'The History and Antiquities of the County of Surrey', which was published in 1804, Ewhurst was *"probably so called from the unusual quantity of Yews with which the Hurst or Woodland thereabout abounded."*

Ewhurst was the ideal place for a settlement as it lay on, and to the south of the Greensand hills, which provided wood and stone for building materials, at a point where numerous small streams issued forth to meander across the lush, undulating lowland. Oaks flourished on the deep soil and stiff clay, and, where they had been cleared, wheat, barley, oats and turnips were grown in abundance.

The parish itself is quite large and roughly rectangular in shape, stretching from the steep, sandy, wooded upland of Winterfold Heath, Pitch Hill, and Holmbury Hill in the north, southwards for five miles over the gently rolling, forested Wealden Clay to neighbouring Rudgwick. From east to west it is about one and a half miles wide and contains approximately 5,000 acres. (figures seem to vary from 4,390 acres in Kelly's Post Office Directory for Surrey in 1846, to 5,634 acres in the Ewhurst Vestry Book of 1844).

As far as trade and communications are concerned, the village is conveniently situated with regard to its larger neighbours, lying approximately 35 miles south of London, 12 miles to the southeast of Guildford, 11 miles southwest of Dorking, 4 miles west of Ockley, 8 miles northwest of Horsham and 3 miles northeast of Cranleigh. Although its position appears ideal, the stiff clay and the hills made communications difficult and led to a greater sense of isolation than one would at first imagine.

Despite its size, however, the population at the time of Eli's birth would have still been rather sparse, totalling only about 850 people, most of whom either lived on small isolated farms or in tiny hamlets such as Ewhurst itself, Ellen's Green, Cox Green or Ewhurst Green. Although the population and amount of dwellings did increase significantly over the century, as the following Census figures from the 'Victoria County History of Surrey, Vol. 4 (1912)' show, Eli probably wouldn't have seen too great a change to the village in his own lifetime.

	Inhabited	Uninhabited	People.
1801	115	1	644
1811	N/A	N/A	706
1821	N/A	N/A	821
1831	N/A	N/A	828
1841	178	0	942
1851	166	5	872
1861	174	7	881
1871	185	10	959
1881	184	20	892
1891	205	15	1,021

These figures show a steady upward trend, despite minor fluctuations, both in the number of dwellings and in the total population. The seemingly large jump in population in 1841 was partially due to a group of 26 travellers who were living rough as they passed through the village on their way to the Rudgwick Fair.

In 1801, 511 out of the 644 people in the village were directly dependent on agriculture for a living, whilst, of the remainder, 31 were involved in trade, manufacture and handicrafts which were probably based on agriculture. Therefore, at least 85% of the population appeared to be dependent, in one form or another, upon agriculture for their survival.

The abundant woodlands around Ewhurst would have provided a ready source of fuel for the glassworks at Somerbury Wood and Ellen's Green, and for the iron furnace at the Vachery Pond near Cranleigh. The iron masters and glassworkers were not popular with the ordinary villagers as they depleted the local woods and made fuel more expensive and difficult to obtain. The changes which did occur within the village over the rest of the century, were slow, and the overall picture of a community dependent upon agriculture remained. The Kelly's Post Office Directory for 1846 lists only 22 tradesmen within the village, but their occupations paint a truly rural picture. There were 4 blacksmiths, 3 mealmen, 2 bakers, 2 wheelwrights, a tailor, a carpenter, a grocer, a harness-maker, a miller, a cooper, a butcher and a publican. The publican of the 'Bull's Head', Mrs. Charlotte Child, was probably the very person with whom Eli had had an altercation in his youth, and into whose pub he had sworn never to set foot again.

The old 'Bull's Head' in the 1890's. (Reproduced by kind permission of the Surrey Local Studies Library.)

The Censuses reveal a great social contrast in the quality of life available for the different classes within the village. Many of the villagers had large families and probably experienced periods of great hardship in times of agricultural depression when food was scarce and the Workhouse beckoned. At times when the harvests were plentiful, however, one can imagine their lives as being idyllic.

Some of those recorded in the Censuses, however, were even less fortunate as they lacked any permanent home. Eli probably knew the three villagers who were recorded in 1851 as living in barns. One of these, George Gravett, was still living rough at the time of the next Census. At the same time, another parishioner, Henry Smith, an umbrella maker, was also recorded as living in a barn with his wife and two children.

Many of those who lived rough in the hills to the north of the village were probably never accounted for. Those who followed trades such as tree felling and charcoal burning, proba-bly lived an itinerant life, moving from one makeshift shack to another. Louis Jennings said that the people on the hills were known as the *'Heathers'* and were *'a terror to the peaceful villagers'*. Eli's brother, Peter, lived on Pitch Hill amongst this community for several years.

If these unfortunate people received no Poor Relief from the parish, they might have been eligible to receive Smith's Charity. The Henry Smith, whom Eli eulogized in his book, died on January 30th, 1628, and bequeathed varying amounts of money to the numerous parishes in the southern counties where he had been favourably received in his days as a tramp. This money had to be spent in a specified way for each particular parish on poor persons who received no alms from the parish. In Ewhurst the money had to be used to provide bread and clothing for the needy. The amount of aid varied and increased from £6.15s. in 1712 to £50 in 1891.

Eli would have been only too aware of the almost obscene life of affluence and comfort enjoyed by the clergy and the landed gentry who lived in luxury in houses such as 'The Rectory', 'Maybanks', 'Garlands', 'Malaquoits' or 'Baynards'. Although the landed gentry were often the butt of Eli's scathing comments, his most scurrilous criticism, however, was reserved for those members of the clergy who cared more about their own comfort than the souls of their parishioners.

The local Rector was a prime target for Eli's reproach. In 1841, for example, the incumbent Rector of the parish, Charles Stewart, received an income of £755 p.a. from his parishioners, and must have spent most of it on the upkeep of the simply palatial Rectory. The magnificence of the building with its ornate and intricate facade, its mock cloisters, its numerous towering spires and chimneys, can be seen in the print on the opposite page, which was taken from the 'History of Surrey' by Brayley and Britton (1850).

The print was presented to the authors by the Reverend Stewart and by the architect of both the Rectory and of the newly renovated church (1839), Mr. R. Ebbels. The final touch of exoticism is undoubtedly added by the peacocks roaming freely through the grounds.

The needs of the Rector's wife, his son and any guests could easily be met by the ten servants he employed. His successor, John Mount Barlow, who was the Rector of Ewhurst for forty-seven years, between 1845 and 1892, appears to have led a more austere life as only three servants were recorded as living in the Rectory in 1851. By 1861, however, and for the next thirty years, the censuses show that this number had increased to six.

The lifestyle of another clergyman, Thomas Thurlow, was even more open to attack by Eli. Thurlow appeared to be a retired clergyman as he is listed in the 1851 and 1861 Censuses as being a clergyman *'not having care of souls'*. To add to his sins, in Eli's books, he was also a magistrate and a gentleman farmer, who farmed 140 acres on the Baynards Estate. To tend to his wants and to those of his wife and son, Thurlow engaged no fewer than fourteen servants. The description of their positions in the household, as found in the Census of 1851, gives, I feel, a particularly good picture of the magnificent style of life enjoyed by the Thurlow family. There were six male servants: a butler, a footman, a page, a coachman, a groom and a helper; and eight female servants: a housekeeper, a kitchen maid, a scullery

maid, an undermaid, a lady's maid, a house maid, a laundry maid and a dairy maid.

The old rectory burnt down in 1861. This is an architect's drawing of the building which replaced it and which is now used as a nursing home.

Eli's relationship with the gentry appears to have been quite ambivalent. On the one hand, he tended to dislike and criticise them as a class, because they were often high-handed, and appeared to be only interested in pursuing a life of comfort and pleasure at the expense of the working classes. He also felt that they held a disproportionate percentage of the land, which could have been more profitably used to support the poor. On the other hand, Eli seems to have taken a great delight in mentioning the fact that he was personally acquainted with several of the gentry and often spoke of individual members, such as the Earl of Onslow, as though they were close friends.

As the 'Carrier's Boy', Eli probably found it safer to attack the gentry as a class rather than to attack individual members and risk being sued for libel. His readers, however, would be fully aware of the identities of the main offenders. Many of the unidentified subjects of Eli's vitriolic criticism can probably be found in Kelly's Post Office Directory of Surrey 1881, which lists the principal landowners in the village as being ; P.J. Locke King; Thomas Lyon Thurlow esq.; Reginald Bray (principal Lord of the Manor); the Earl of Onslow; J. Braby esq. J.P. and the Hon. Leveson Gower.

Although Eli had witnessed, during his sixty-one years in Ewhurst, a growth of approximately 25% in the number of dwelling places and in the total population, this increase was small when compared to the 100% growth nationwide. As a result of this way below average increase, the village and the way of life of its residents had probably altered little. The most important physical changes which occurred during Eli's lifetime were probably the almost complete reconstruction of the local church of St. Peter and St. Paul in 1839 with

The old Ewhurst Post Office, formerly the 'Bull's Head' at the beginning of this century. (Reproduced by kind permission of Surrey Local Studies Library).

stone dug from Pitch Hill, the opening of a National School in Ewhurst for 120 children in 1840, and a smaller one in Ellen's Green in 1870, the construction of a proper metalled road, and the building of several, often pretentious, new houses upon the hills, where well-to-do immigrants to the area often settled.

The picture on the previous page, taken again from Brayley and Britton, shows the newly reconstructed, picturesque church viewed from the southeast. It has changed very little in the last one hundred and fifty years, since Eli was a child.

Eli was intensely proud of the village in which he lived and wrote several tracts in his book where he compared the facilities on offer in Ewhurst, such as the allotments, with those on offer in the slightly larger village of Cranleigh. One can imagine him in his youth taking part in the annual fight which used to be held outside the 'Boy and Donkey' every Whit Monday, between the Cranleigh Diamond Tops and the Ewhurst Roundheads.

The construction of the road through the village in the middle of the century, and the opening of the Horsham to Guildford Railway in 1865, helped to expose the village to change. The later Censuses reveal a greater spread of occupations among the workforce: the fact that an engine driver is listed in 1881 reflects the inexorable shift away from a dependency upon agriculture. The outside world was at last beginning to impinge upon the sleepy village, but the fact that the village was still a place of tranquil rustic charm is probably best emphasised by the fact that it attracted several artists to settle there.

The most prominent of these artists was undoubtedly the landscape painter, George William Mote, who painted several local scenes, one of which, entitled 'The Charcoal Burners on Pitch Hill' (see left), graphically illustrates the squalor in which the lowest echelons of society lived in the hills to the north of the village.

It could have been one of the artists living in the area whom Eli persuaded to produce the delicate engraving with which he concluded the first edition of 'The Source of England's Greatness' (see Foreword).

After 1865, the village became accessible for commuters who could catch the local trains from either Baynards or Cranleigh Stations to Guildford, and from there on the regular service to London. There was also an increase in this period of the number of people listed in the Censuses as being independent, which tends to suggest that the village was beginning to attract people who had retired and wanted to live in a pleasant environment, within easy reach of the City if necessary.

Even today, with a population of 2,339 (1991), large areas of Ewhurst maintain the simple rural charm which led Cobbett to describe it as *"a very pretty village"*. This feeling of timelessness is particularly true of Ewhurst Green, where Eli spent most of his life, and where the twentieth century appears to have been held at bay.

This picture portrays the tranquility of Ewhurst Green at the turn of the century. The old cricket pavilion is to the right of the photograph.

43

Eli - the Youthful Entrepreneur

From his photographs and writings one can imagine that by the time Eli was fourteen, he had acquired a reasonable education and was physically well developed for his age. This, combined with the fact that he must have worked with his father and brothers, from an early age, both on the farm and in the carrying business, acquiring experience in the general principles of farming and business practice, lead to a maturity one would not expect in a modern teenager.

He obviously felt confident enough in his own ability to rent a field, in 1849, from a local landowner, William Eager of Whipley, for £4 per annum. In a way he may have been trying to emulate his elder brother, Henry, who had just acquired two parcels of land by the Green. He does admit in his book, however, that the initial payment he made for the land was too much, as the only crops that he could produce that year were horse-mint and clover. By harvesting the horse-mint and clover, and by mixing it with pig-manure, he was able to improve the quality of the land to such an extent that it would produce, in later years, two tons of hay per acre over a two month period.

The fact that a fourteen year old could raise the considerable sum of £4 supports the theory that he had worked from an early age and that he had also developed a very thrifty nature. This thriftiness was a trait which followed him through life and, in a way, seems at variance with his undoubted acts of generosity to those in need. The most popular story in the family which illustrates these qualities is taken from his days as a carrier. Whenever Eli came upon a tollgate he used to unhitch the horse from the wagon and take them through separately. Instead of paying 6d. for a horse and cart, the horse would pass through free and the cart, which he pulled through, would be classified as a truck, for which he paid a fee of a halfpenny. The money he saved he would give to the first needy man he next met on his journey.

The field Eli rented from the Eager family was slightly to the north of Ewhurst Green village at a place called Goodbridge on the 1842 Tithe Map, although it was more universally known as Godbridge. In total area it measured 2 acres, 2 rods and 33 poles. With the adjoining underwood, which he appears to have annexed, at a later date, he farmed roughly 3 acres. This was approximately the same size as his father's smallholding by the Green. The fact that both he and his father could obtain a living from such a small acreage, undoubtedly inspired his 'three acres and a cow' philosophy.

Eli gives several examples in his books, such as the purchase and eventual resale of his first cow for a tidy profit, which show that he was an extremely capable farmer and astute business-man. The three acres and the little livestock he tended, however, would have still given him plenty of time to help his father on the carrier's route. He may even have been called upon to take the wagon out by himself and carry on his father's trade from his early teens.

When the 1851 Census was taken on the evening of Sunday, April 30th, there was no trace of Eli in Ewhurst. His father and mother were at home in the cottage by the Green with his brother, Peter, and a relative of Sarah, Job Robinson. A search of all the Census returns for Surrey in 1851, reveals no trace of Eli, although it did turn up a three year old namesake in Shamley Green. As the following day was one of those when the Hamshires traded in Horsham, I feel that his absence from the Census could indicate that he had taken the wagon out earlier that day and was either sleeping rough or staying with friends in Sussex. As his father was aged 66 by this time, and as the only other of his siblings to still live at home was Peter, who was recorded as being a sawyer, it is perhaps not all that surprising that Eli should take such an active role in running his father's business, even at sixteen years of age.

Eli's lifelong friend and drinking companion, Job Robinson, pictured in Billingshurst in 1910.

I may be trying to read too much into Eli's omission from the 1851 Census as it could be just another genuine mistake. His brother's age, for example, was given as sixteen, when it was at least twenty-one. His absence could also be another example of Eli's strong individual nature. He might have felt that the Census was an intrusion into his privacy and, as a result, he might have deliberately disappeared for the evening. He could, however, have been simply visiting one of his numerous relatives. His mother, for example, came originally from Itchingfield in Sussex and her relatives, the Robinsons, lived in Billingshurst. On the other hand, he could have been visiting his brother Henry, who according to an indenture of August 5th, 1855, on behalf of himself and his brother-in-law, Moses Botting, worked as a gentleman's servant at Hampton Court and lived at St. Mary-le-Strand in Middlesex.

Another early example of Eli's financial astuteness occurred the following year when he began dealing in poultry. The area, according to Brayley and Britton in their 'History of Surrey', was one where *"poultry of the Dorking kind is raised in abundance."* Daniel Defoe, in 1724, had also commented in, 'A Tour through the Whole Island of Great Britain,' that the town of Dorking was famous for its geese and capons, and said that it was the business of the region to the south of Dorking, *"to breed and fatten them up, inasmuch, that 'tis like a manufacture to the country people; and some of the capons are so large, as that they are little inferior to turkeys."*

Eli and his father often used to carry crates of a dozen chickens to Guildford at 6d. a crate. On May 8th, 1852, Eli bought some chickens for himself at 'Coneyhurst Farm', to the north of Ewhurst, whilst he was travelling to Guildford. Once he arrived at the market he sold them at 3d. each, making a profit of 2s.6d a crate. He re-invested this profit and set himself up as a dealer.

As it was not always worthwhile for Eli to take the horse and cart into Guildford, he often walked the nine or ten miles there, carrying whatever goods needed to be taken, on a wickerwork frame strapped to his back. The strength and fitness of the young Eli can be seen by the fact that he often carried back, for one of the shops in the village, a hundredweight sack of sugar, for the princely sum of 6d. When walking, he tended to take a short cut through Brook and down Blackheath Lane into Albury.

By the time he was twenty, therefore, he had at least three strings to his bow: he was a carrier, a smallholder and a chicken dealer, and as such must have been relatively prosperous and extremely busy. The pressure of work, however, did not repress his naturally extrovert character and there is plenty of evidence to suggest that he pursued his social life with the same vigour as he approached his work.

Eli claims in his book that he used to go drinking three evenings a week and that he regularly spent 9d. per evening on drink. He gives a graphic account of one drinking session that makes him sound like a nineteenth century lager lout. After an evening drinking and singing in the beer-house, he, and nine of his friends, rolled along to continue their evening's merriment in the taproom of the 'Bull's Head' at ten o'clock. On this particular occasion, however, his rendition of 'The Troubador Touched his Guitar' did not go down particularly well with the landlady, Mrs. Child, nor with a party of gentlemen, who were enjoying a hunting feast, in the parlour. As a result of the ensuing argument he swore that he would never again frequent that particular public house.

His own account of his evening's drinking in the beer-house and at the 'Bull's Head', paints a picture of an extremely loud and jovial character who could be the life and soul of any party. He had all the attributes to be popular: he could sing and play the concertina and probably regaled his audience with tales of the wide variety of characters he had regularly met on his travels to and from market. He had a loud, deep singing voice, which by his own admission was enough to 'set the tea trays on the jar'. He even composed his own songs, one of which, 'I am an Honest Country Lad', is far superior to any of the poetry he wrote. Another song, 'The Golden Wedding', he might even have composed to sing at his parents' golden wedding in 1863.

In a way, Eli must have been seen as quite a trend setter and innovator among his contemporaries. In the beer-house that evening he claimed that his concertina was the first ever seen in Ewhurst. My grandmother can still remember seeing 'Grandfather Hamshire's' concertina being played over seventy years ago by his son-in-law. He must also have impressed his friends with his attempt to build a clockwork horseless carriage, which was powered by a huge spring, which would be rewound when the carriage went downhill. Unfortunately, he could not find anyone to make such a huge and powerful spring.

Two of Eli's drinking companions at that time would have been his cousin, Job Robinson, who was quite a heavy drinker for over fifty years, and his brother Peter, who was described by Cecil Muggeridge as being a *'drinking, running man'*. He often used to run from Shere over the hills to the 'Bull's Head' and then back again. On one occasion, on the return journey, he spotted two policemen he did not know, sitting by the roadside. Peter decided that it would be good fun to find out if they could run. He circled round them in the woods and then burst out of the trees and looked at them in a furtive manner. When challenged, he began to run away from them and they, in their turn, began to chase after him. Although the elderly Sergeant soon dropped out of the race, the young constable stayed in pursuit for several miles. Peter eventually shook him off but his identity was revealed the following day when the policemen made enquiries at the 'Bull's Head'. They apparently gave him a hard time in the questioning, as they were far from amused at being made to look foolish.

This photograph of Eli's brother, Peter, would appear from the clothes of the workmen to have been taken in the 1870's (according to Matthew Alexander, the curator of the Guildford Museum). Perhaps the well was being dug on one of Eli's properties. If so, Job Robinson is probably one of the other labourers.

Unlike Eli, Peter did not pay heed to his father's words on the evils of drink and public house company. He is reputed to have been a very strong man with a rather wild streak and a love of danger and drink. The only photograph of him is a very faded one of him sitting in a bucket, about to descend a well that was being dug in Ewhurst in about the 1870's. Well-digging was fraught with danger and it probably took a rather reckless man to do this type of work. He would also have had to be skilled at bricklaying, as they lined the walls with bricks as they descended. The well behind Eli's ten roomed house is 32 feet deep and bricked for most of its depth.

Peter appears to have had a variety of jobs and to have been rather nomadic. The 1851 Census shows him as being a sawyer who still lived at 'The Fields Cottage' with his parents. His marriage certificate in 1858 shows him as being a timber buyer who lived at Stoke-next-to-Guildford, as did his wife Emma Inwood. He also appears to have lived at Hanwell in Middlesex as his Bible was presented to him by the curate of that parish.

Peter moved to Shere with Emma after their marriage, but he does not really appear to have settled down. He still drank heavily and in his later years he even lived rough among the charcoal burners on Pitch Hill before ending his days in the Hambledon Workhouse.

Eli, however, thought long and hard about his father's words and decided instead to save the 2s.3d. that he spent on drink each week. To this he added 3d., and put half-a-crown aside each week until he had saved £17.10s. He does not say what he did with the money in the book, but it does show remarkable will-power to alter ones lifestyle so dramatically by ceasing to drink for almost three years, after socializing on a regular basis.

Although Eli stopped drinking at the 'Bull's Head' he still drank elsewhere and in particular enjoyed a jar of his own beer. As he made 40 gallons of his home-brewed beer at a time, his own home probably served as a beer-house on more than one occasion. Eli had a great sympathy for the ordinary publican and beer-house owner, whom he felt were at the mercy of the local magistrates and the powerful breweries. Part of Eli's sympathy for this class of person probably stemmed from the fact that one of his father's cousins, another James Hamshere, ran the 'Sawyer's Arms', a beershop in Guildford, for over twenty years. Eli probably drank there quite regularly and would undoubtedly have heard James's tale of his being fined £2 by the local magistrates, in 1843, for selling beer before the permitted hour of 1 p.m. on a Sunday.

By his mid-twenties, however, Eli must have become a much more sober and responsible character. The earliest photograph of him, however, taken about 1860, shows a rather rakish, burly, handsome figure, clutching the lapels of his jacket in a slightly aggressive fashion. With his waistcoat half-buttoned, his cravat casually tied around his neck and his long curly brown hair, he appears to be the epitome of a typical roguish dealer. Only a slight smile playing about the corners of his mouth, the strength of his jaw and a sincere look about the eyes lessen this impression.

The 1861 Census shows Eli as being the only child still living in the cottage at Ewhurst

The earliest photograph of Eli taken circa 1860 by W. Bassett of Guildford.

Green with the ageing James (78), who is described as being an 'almsman', and Sarah (66), the 'housekeeper'. Whilst most of his family were still living in the locality, his brother, Michael, had returned to the family roots in Albury where, by 1881, the Census shows him as farming a twelve acre farm with his wife Harriet and his four children.

Eli obviously had the dual responsibility of supporting his parents and managing all their business interests. He would have had to see to the upkeep of his father's three acres besides his own, he would have had to run the carrying business almost single-handed, and he was still active as a poultry dealer. The Census describes his occupation in slightly disparaging tones by calling him a 'Dealer and Huxter'. A huckster was a form of pedlar or hawker who traded in petty goods, and to describe Eli as such makes his business appear quite trivial and almost disreputable.

By 1863, the pressure of work must have begun to tell on Eli and he had to reduce the amount of time spent on carrying. The Andrew's Almanack for that year refers to the service which he offered as being irregular. It must also have been around this time that another interest began to impinge upon his work in the shape of Rebecca Bowyer Gibbs.

Rebecca Bowyer Gibbs

Eli probably first met Rebecca in the early 1860's. Her parents, William Gibbs (b. 1793) and Mary Allen (b. 1800) had both been born in Derbyshire and had farmed there for a short while after their marriage on November 10th, 1817, at Snelston. In 1821, they, and their two young children, James and Mary Anne, moved the whole of their property and livestock south to High Ashes Farm, Leith Hill, as according to Rebecca, they thought the *'Surrey stones were made of gold'*. William and Mary, however, must have been quite wealthy in the first place as the Land Tax returns for Ockley show that they rented the property for £90 p.a. from Sir Henry Fitzherbert and paid an annual Land Tax of £17.5s. Both the amount of rent and tax were the largest recorded in the parish and the entry tends to suggest that they rented the whole of Leith Hill.

In 1827 William had a disagreement with Sir Henry over back rent. This disagreement almost broke him and the family moved to Charlwood where he farmed on a greatly reduced scale for over ten years. Eventually, thanks to a loan from a friend, he was able to rent 'Park Barn Farm' from the Earl of Onslow, at Broad Street Common, Worplesdon, in about 1838. It was there that Rebecca was born and she was baptised in the local church on August 22nd, 1841, as Rebecca Bowyer Gibbs. She was the youngest of the nine surviving children, five having died either at birth or in infancy.

One would have thought that William's operation at 'Park Barn Farm' would have been modest as he had had to borrow the money to acquire it. This was far from true, however. The 1851 Census reveals that he rented 280 acres, and, apart from the various members of his family, he also employed ten labourers to work it. With an operation of this size it is not surprising that he was able to pay back his debt so quickly.

William also rented a farm of 100 acres at Dedswell near Send which was farmed by his eldest son, James, and four labourers. His daughter, Louisa Agnes, acted as the housekeeper at Dedswell, where she also looked after the nine-year-old Rebecca.

By 1861, the farm at Dedswell was replaced by the 105 acre 'Vanner's Farm' (in nearby Byfleet) which he rented from James Sparks. This farm was again run by his eldest son, James, and employed three men and a boy. He had also bought a house on Worplesdon Common where his only married son, Richard, lived.

By the time Eli had met Rebecca, therefore, her father had built up quite a sizeable family empire. He was the living example of the type of farmer whom Eli had come to hate. He was a bloated capitalist, who had exploited the poor agricultural labourers in his employ and had acquired enough land to support, by Eli's reckoning, almost 130 families.

In 1861, William's eight unattached children, James (42), Mary Anne Dyas (40, widowed), Joseph (38), Frances Amelia (33), Louisa Agnes (30), Robert (26), Thomas (24) and Rebecca (19), either lived at 'Park Barn Farm' or 'Vanner's Farm', and although they undoubtedly had to work for their upkeep, life was probably relatively comfortable. The Censuses record a total of six servants being employed between the two establishments. Although some of these were obviously employed mainly as farm labourers, others, such as Anne Bonner, who is described as a maid of all work, would have been expected to clean and cook and generally wait upon the needs of the family.

The earliest photograph of Rebecca Bowyer Gibbs circa 1860.

From all accounts Rebecca appears to have been a very strong-willed, dominating and self-centred character. Although early photographs of her show a rather pretty young woman, with a fine taste in clothes, there is a look of strength and firmness about her eyes and the set of her jaw. She was seven years younger than her nearest sibling and as such was probably quite spoilt by both her parents and the rest of the family. Although her mother died when Rebecca was only eleven years old, she had a succession of maids to cater for her whims and she probably made their lives a misery. She developed such an authoritarian disposition that on one occasion, according to family legend, when her father was ill, and she wanted to return to 'Park Barn Farm' to look after him, the rest of the family refused to allow her to enter.

Courtship and Marriage

There is no precise record of Eli's first encounter with Rebecca nor of the courtship which followed. He could have met her on one of the many occasions when she used to take butter and eggs from their farm to Guildford Market. The most popular story of their meeting, however, and the most romantic one is that Eli first met her at Guildford Fair whilst she was looking for a maid. Eli, being a very direct person, upon being asked where she should look for a maid, is alleged to have said, *"I can't find you a maid but I can find you a husband."*

The courtship would not have been very long, according to his granddaughter, Winnie, as the round trip to Worplesdon would have been around twenty-five miles. She claimed that he only went there three times. Whether he ever met William Gibbs on his visits to the farm is debatable, as William died on May 16th, 1864. He might have met him, however, on his regular visits to the market.

We do, however, know that Eli's friendship with Rebecca was frowned upon by her family as he was only a small dealer. Her brothers also resented the fact that they were losing a very competent housekeeper. As Eli visited several large houses in the course of his job, he promised to find them a replacement cook. This offer was not exactly appreciated, and he was told in no uncertain tones, according to Winnie Muggeridge, *"We don't want your greasy cooks!"*

William's death, allied to Rebecca's wilful nature, however, would have removed any obstacles to their marriage and provided the couple with a useful nest egg. His will shows that Rebecca inherited a lump sum of £200 plus an undisclosed amount, which was a sixth share of the residue of the estate. She also inherited a sixth share of the household goods at 'Park Barn Farm', which probably also increased her family's antagonism towards her marriage.

Nevertheless, the money and household items would have proved very useful to a young couple entering into marriage. Pride of place amongst her acquisitions must have been the late sixteenth century wooden family cradle, which by tradition always passed to the youngest daughter in the family. Rebecca, however, broke this tradition by passing it to her eldest daughter, Mary Anne, who reverted to tradition by passing it to her youngest daughter Ivy Cornes. The only other item, of which there is any record, is the Gibbs' warming pan which was passed down to Rebecca's grand-daughter, Winnie.

Eli Hamshire (29), a Dealer, and Rebecca Bowyer Gibbs (23) married on March 31st, 1865, in the parish church of St. Mary's, Worplesdon, their witnesses being her fourteen

Superintendent Registrar's District of ——————

1865. Marriage solemnized at _the Parish Church_ in the _Parish_ of _Weybridge_ in the County of _Surrey._

No.	When Married.	Name and Surname.	Age.	Condition.	Rank or Profession.	Residence at the time of Marriage.	Father's Name and Surname.	Rank or Profession of Father.
235.	March 31st	Ett. Hawkins Gitts	29	Bachelor	Dealer	Colonial	James Hawkins	Farmer
		Rebecca Berger Gitts	23	Spinster		Bread St Weybridge	William Gitts	Farmer

Married in the _Parish Church_ according to the Rites and Ceremonies of the ~~Established Church~~ _Church of England_, or after _Banns_ by me, _Henry Tutul Ade_

This Marriage was solemnized between us,	Ett. Hawkins	in the Presence of us,	Henry Hawkins Witness Mary Gitts
	Rebecca Berger Gitts		

Henry Tutul Ade, Curate — Curate

I _Henry Tutul Ade Curate_ of _Weybridge_ in the County of _Surrey_ do hereby certify, that the foregoing comprising 1 Entry numbered 235 — is a true copy of the Entry numbered 235th in the Marriage Register Books of the said Parish, of _Weybridge_, so numbered, made in the Marriage Register Books of the said Parish, of _Weybridge_, Witness my hand, this 31st day of March 1865 —

Henry

Ade

year old niece, Rebecca Mary Dyas, who was the daughter of Rebecca's oldest sister Mary Ann and her husband, Thomas Dyas, who had died before the birth of his daughter in 1851.

This is a photograph of Rebeccas's favourite sister, Mary Ann Dyas (neé Gibbs) taken at about the time of Rebecca's wedding in 1865. On the back of the photograph it says that she is the daughter of the late William Gibbs.

She was baptised on November 5th 1820 at Snelston in Derbyshire before the family trekked south to find their fortune.

Although Mary Ann's features are rather faded, the sumptuous dress she is wearing gives some indication of the wealth of the Gibbs family.

This photograph which was found with personal photographs of Eli's family, could be his brother Henry taken at about the time of the Wedding.

He has the Hamshire nose and gives the appearance of being a refined, educated and relatively prosperous person, although he does not look as strong and healthy as his brothers.

We know that he was a personal servant at Hampton Court, lived at St. Mary-le-Strand and had purchased land in Ewhurst by the age of 21. He died in March, 1866, at the relatively young age of 39.

The wedding of Eli Hamshire and Rebecca Bowyer Gibbs on March 31st, 1865.

From the above photograph, taken of their wedding by the likeness-takers, it must have been quite an impressive affair. Eli looks a tall, broad imposing character with a neatly trimmed beard and well-groomed hair. His well fitting blue suit and waist coat, the gold fob chain, the spotless white cravat and gloves, and the flamboyant buttonhole, make him look every inch a gentleman. Despite being seated Rebecca looks to be quite a pretty, tall-ish, well-built young lady, whose sumptuous old gold dress, which still survives, and her white scarf and bonnet provide an ideal match for her handsome husband. Of the two, however, Rebecca looks the more at ease being dressed like that.

Married life

Despite any reservations Rebecca's family might have felt about the wedding, and despite their strongly contrasting dispositions, Eli and Rebecca appeared to have had an extremely happy marriage, which lasted for thirty-one years. Whilst Eli remained a jovial easy-going smock-clad rustic, his wife, however, according to members of the family who can still remember her, was a rather severe, domineering and very prim and proper lady, who was always accompanied by her maid in later life.

One example, in particular, tends to show how forbidding a character Rebecca could be. Some time after Eli's death, a tradesman knocked on the door and asked to speak to the master of the house, to which Rebecca imperiously replied, *"I am the mistress and the master of this house."*

Several changes obviously occurred to Eli's way of life following his marriage. The first change of any note was his move away from his parent's home, as, according to Winnie Muggeridge, Sarah and Rebecca were not really compatible. In particular, Sarah disliked her daughter-in-law's extravagance with the fire, a trait which remained with her for the rest of her life.

Eli and Rebecca moved into a small cottage on the western edge of Ewhurst Green. It was there, in what is now known as 'Square Leg Cottage' and what was previously known as 'Greenway Cottage', that the first of his seven children, Mary Anne, was born in early 1866. The cottage had for generations been a shepherd's hovel reputedly dating back to the twelfth century.

This is how 'Square Leg Cottage' looks today.

It was on an adjoining plot of land that he employed Job Robinson to build the ten roomed brick and tiled house, mentioned in his will. The building was quite spacious, having two living rooms and a pantry on the ground floor, four bedrooms on the first floor and two more in the attic. It was there that most of the remainder of his children were born. Over the next eighteen years they were blessed by the births of another six children: William (1868), James Eli (1871), Fanny Rebecca (1874), Henry (1877), Joseph Allen (1881) and Minnie (1884).

Although Eli was referred to as a carrier when he acquired a piece of land in 1867, he had been replaced by Charles and William Daws in the Kelly's Directory for that year. His health had begun to suffer and his service had become rather irregular since the early 1860's. By 1869 he appears to have stopped carrying completely.

His decision to cease carrying may have been partly due to the opening of the Horsham to Guildford Railway in 1865, which probably also led to the demise of the Wey-Arun Canal in 1870. In a letter to Mr. Gladstone he complains about the lack of compensation paid to the share-holders of the Wey-Arun Canal, to the coaches and to the carriers, *"and we poor carriers had to lose our money."* The family, however, maintained the Carrier's Licence to carry goods within 35 miles of Cranleigh Station until the 1950's. Eli, I feel by choice, preferred to concentrate his efforts mainly upon his poultry dealing, although the 1871 and 1881 Censuses refer to him as being a General Dealer.

Despite the overall picture of happiness the couple obviously also experienced periods of great tribulation. They both suffered lengthy illnesses and must have experienced great sadness at the premature death of Eli's brother, Henry (39), in 1866, or the more predictable death of his father, James, aged 81, in 1867, and the death of his mother, Sarah, aged 78, six years later. All three were buried under the shade of the yew tree to the west of Ewhurst Church. No trace of the wooden rails which marked their graves remain. The inscriptions which graced their final resting places, however, are preserved for posterity on microfilm in Guildford Library.

Henry's inscription reflected the shortness of his life,

"Even in the midst of life we are in death."

James's epitaph reflected his character, sombre and brooding,

"For God approves the just man's ways to happiness
But sinners and the path they tread, shall both in
ruin end."

Sarah's epitaph, however, revealed her love and concern for her children,

"Children dear time is past
Love remain'd while time did last.
Weep not for me now I am gone,
But prepare to follow me."

The greatest tragedy, however, was the loss of his youngest daughter, Minnie, aged only fifteen months, in 1885. The epitaph on her tombstone is quite plaintive:

"If love and care could have kept her here,
She would not have gone so soon."

Although the thrifty Eli occasionally used to gently chide his wife for being *"too extravagant with the fire,"* one gets the impression that they were a couple who were entirely devoted to one another. One subject over which they did tend to disagree, however, was religion. Whilst Eli used to attend chapel, his wife was a strict church-goer and ridiculed the handshaking habits of the Noncomformists. Nevertheless, they were happily married, and, as Eli so often remarked to his wife, *"There may have been some mole-hills but there haven't been many mountains."*

Eli's oldest brother, James (b. 1814), was shown in the 1851 Census as living, in what is now known as 'Square Leg Cottage', at Ewhurst Green with his wife, Elizabeth. By 1871, however, he had returned to 'The Fields Cottage' to look after his ageing mother. By 1881 he is shown as being a widowed, agricultural labourer living at 'Baynards Lodge'.

Eli, a man of property

The fact that Eli had married a wealthy bride obviously led to changes in his business affairs. Apart from ceasing to be a carrier and increasing his trade as a poulterer, Eli also became involved in a tangled web of property deals.

On January 19th, 1867, he became the copyholder of a piece of land at Ewhurst Green, which had been used as a garden and measured 93 feet by 60. In the draft Deed of Enfranchisement to that property in September of that year, it stated that he intended to purchase it for £2.10s., with the intention of building on it. It appears that he conducted the legal work himself, as a note in the margin says that it would have cost him twice as much to hire an attorney.

This was Eli's ten-roomed cottage on the western edge of Ewhurst Green. The picture was taken before the Warringtons became the tenants in 1902. The bottles in the window suggest that the cottage probably provided refreshments for the cricketers on the green.

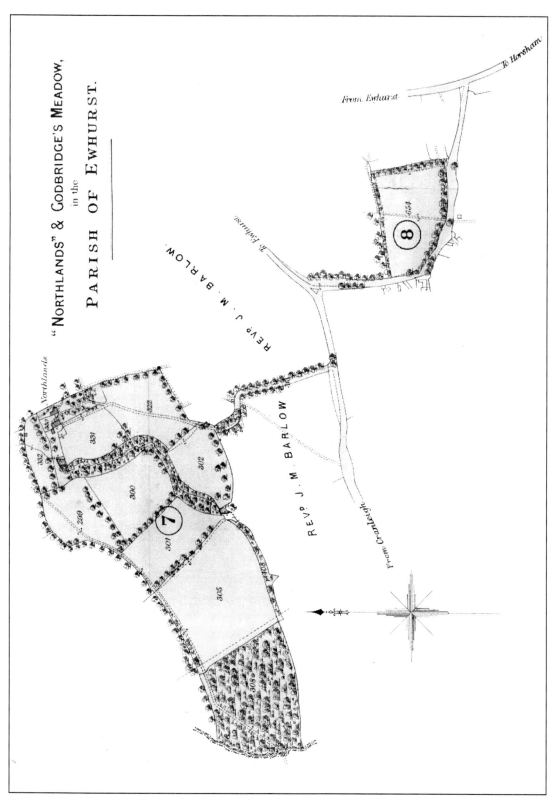

Two parcels of land auctioned in Ewhurst on May 17th, 1881.

In about 1870, according to 'The Source of England's Greatness' (page 172), when the landlord, William Eager, wanted to increase the rental on the piece of land Eli had farmed for twenty years in Gadbridge Lane, from £4 to £15 per annum, he bought the freehold outright. His decision to purchase the land was apparently influenced by the fact that the rector, John Mount Barlow, whom Eli disliked intensely, also had designs upon the property.

It seems rather strange that the property was auctioned for sale by Messrs. Debenham, Tewson, Farmer & Bridgewater on Tuesday, May 17th, 1881, and was bought by Eli for £250. (Either it was some obscure financial exercise, or Eli had made a mistake concerning the time-factor in his book). In the Estate Agents' advertisement the land is described as a

---

LOT VIII.

(*Coloured Green on Plan.*)

FREEHOLD ENCLOSURE OF MEADOW LAND

KNOWN AS

"GODBRIDGE'S MEADOW,"

SITUATE AT

GODBRIDGE GREEN, IN THE PARISH OF EWHURST,

CONTAINING ABOUT

3a.   1r.   27p.

Let to ELI HAMPSHIRE, a Yearly Tenant, at

£4 PER ANNUM.

The Land Tax is redeemed and the Landlord pays the Tithe Rent-charge and the Rates and Taxes.

---

freehold enclosure of meadow land known as 'Godbridge's Meadow' situated at Godbridge Green in the parish of Ewhurst.

The dimensions of the property had grown slightly to about 3 acres, 1 rod and 27 perch. Eli Hampshire was listed as being the yearly tenant, paying £4 per annum, which was not excessive as the literature continued by saying that *the Land Tax is redeemed and the Landlord pays the Tithe Rent-charge and the Rates and Taxes*. It was not surprising that William Eager wanted to increase the rent. Eli had after all rented it for the same sum for over thirty years.

In 1873, he also became the tenant of the copyhold cottage of his deceased brother, Henry, in quite an interesting fashion. In his will dated March 27th, 1866, Henry had stated, *"I devise my property whether in houses, land, funds or in any other property to my Executors to divide as I now direct. My brothers, sister, father and mother to take equal shares, that is to share and share alike after paying my just debts and funeral expenses and four pounds to Elizabeth Colloty for her attentions to me in my last illness."*

After Henry's death in 1867, therefore, his property was divided into eight equal shares between his parents, his four surviving brothers, James, John, Michael and Peter, his sister, Mary Ann, who was by then the wife of a nearby widower, David Inwood and Eli himself. His brother, William, had died in infancy in 1816.

Eli, therefore, held an eighth share of this property which adjoined his own. Upon the death of his mother, intestate, in 1873, he inherited his parents' share in the property, thereby increasing his share to three-eighths. (It was the custom of the Manor of Gomshall that the youngest son should inherit his parents' property.)

He then acquired the other five shares from his siblings for £95, and paid the Lord of the Manor of Gomshall fines totalling £176 for the right to the whole property. He kept this property and had his cousin, Job Robinson, build what now forms two semi-detached cottages upon it.

In 1880, Eli appears to have tried to get this piece of land enfranchised, that is, made freehold. Eli made a great play in his book of the importance of making land freehold before building on it, *"or the lawyers and the lords of the manor will take the advantage of your industry and the money you expend on it."* From a letter which exists in the Bray papers, from the lord of the manor to his steward, it appears that Eli was quite liable to resort to unscrupulous behaviour if he thought he could get away with it. The lord wrote, *"No doubt he has cribbed largely. I hope the dimensions I gave you will be sufficient to guard against further cribbing but I believe there is a road or track which will stop him."*

Another undated entry in the Eager papers, which was fortunately copied by Mary Alexander, also indicates that he was generally considered by many of his peers to be rather a shark when it came to property deals: *"Heckling at a Conservative meeting Hamshire met his match, as he afterwards generously admitted. He had denounced 'the gentlemen' who had ousted the people from their rights by building houses on Pitch Hill and planting laurels and evergreens where there should be useful crops. The candidate Dennis got him to agree that the gentlemen had paid for their land and that he had originally squatted on his three acres. Eli, who had a robust sense of humour, joined in the laugh against himself but undauntedly continued to denounce luxury use of land."*

In 1881, following the birth of her son, Joseph Allen, who weighed 14 lbs., Rebecca was seriously ill and was confined to bed for twenty-one weeks. Thereafter she spent several months in a wheelchair, to which she would sometimes attach a donkey to help her move around the village. As it was feared that she would never walk again, Eli had Job Robinson build a five roomed bungalow with some out-buildings, and a small orchard on the land in Godbridge Lane for £100.

Allen Hamshire still has Job Robinson's invoice for the work which makes interesting reading. He completed the building in ten weeks between July 16th and September 24th, 1881, working a total of 612 hours at 7d. per hour, for which he charged 17 guineas. He was helped by one S. Coushall, who received 3s.6d. per day, apart from two days when he received 5s. for the more arduous and dangerous well work. S. Coushall worked up to 73 hours in a week and received the sum of £10.18s.2d.

It was to this bungalow that Eli and Rebecca moved later the same year, and where they spent the rest of their lives together. It was also there that Rebecca suffered complications after the birth of her daughter, Minnie, in 1884, which led to a long convalescence, dur-

This is a photograph of 'Gadbridge Lodge' taken in the 1920's. Eli's son James Eli, on the left of the picture, had converted it into 'Gadbridge Stores'. James' son, Arthur, who still lives in South Africa, is further to the right of the picture.

ing which time she wrote 'Mrs. Hamshire's Views on Farming.'

Eli gave his bungalow the rather pretentious name of 'Godbridge Lodge,' which was the address he used on most of his correspondence. In later life, however, he mistakenly felt that the name 'Godbridge' was rather irreverent, and changed the prefix 'God' to 'Gad.' Although 'Gadbridge Lodge' has long since disappeared, the road, by which it stood, still bears Eli's amended appellation, 'Gadbridge Lane.'

Eli's detached brick and tiled ten-roomed house was sold at auction at the 'Bull's Head', Ewhurst by Weller & Son on October 7th, 1908, but it was not until August 16th, 1917, following the death of Rebecca, that the remainder of Eli's estate was eventually unravelled and disposed of by Weller & Son at the 'Onslow Arms' in Cranleigh. An Inland Revenue form for that year lists three properties :-

"A freehold meadow containing three acres with a one storied brick built and tile healed cottage of five rooms with pig stye and woodhouse detached in occupation of the deceased." ('Gadbridge Lodge')

PARTICULARS.

All that Desirable

FREEHOLD PROPERTY

COMPRISING, A

Detached Brick-built and Tile-healed House,

CONTAINING

On the Ground Floor
> Two Living Rooms (*one with Chimney corner*),
> Kitchen, and Pantry.

on the First Floor
> Four Bedrooms, and there are also two rooms in the attics.

Detached are brick & tiled Scullery, fitted with copper and sink,
and brick and tiled Wood-house and Privy.

A good supply of water is obtained from a Well over which is a Pump.

There is a Vegetable Garden containing some Fruit Trees.

The property possesses a frontage to the main road of 83 feet or
thereabouts, and a mean depth of about 63 feet.

THE WHOLE IS LET TO MR. H. WARRINGTON ON A WEEKLY TENANCY AT 7/-

The situation of the property is very pleasant as it overlooks the
Green on which is the village Cricket Ground.

Weller & Son's description of the ten-roomed house when it was put up for sale on
October 7th, 1908.

"A pair of semi-detached brick built and tiled healed cottages with small gardens at Ewhurst Green. Copyhold." (These were the present day 'Laurel Cottage' and 'Green View' cottage.)

"A small cottage with outbuildings and garden. Copyhold." (This was the present day 'Square Leg Cottage').

The brochure from Weller & Son divides 'Gadbridge Lodge' into two lots. One and a half acres was sold off as valuable grass paddock. The remainder contained the bungalow and one and a half acres. The bungalow is described as having a living room, 12 foot by 14 foot six inches; a bedroom 12 foot by 12 foot; two smaller bedrooms; a scullery and a cellar. In the grounds were a brick and tiled two-stall stable and coach house, a piggery and two good-sized timber and galvanized sheds. The property is described as having *"a South aspect, and having an altitude of just 300 feet commands extensive and pleasing views."*

The third lot 'Square Leg Cottage' is described as being a freehold old-fashioned cottage facing Ewhurst Green. It was substantially built of stone and brick and was tile healed. The cottage had old oak beams and chimney corners in the living room, a scullery and three bedrooms.

The fourth lot was the pair of semi-detached cottages both of which had two living rooms, lean-to sculleries and two bedrooms. In the grounds were the stable and carthouse built by Eli's brother, Henry. Eli's son, Henry, bought them both for £150 and eventually sold them to his brother, James Eli, in 1931.

If the acquisition of property is any measure of a man's success, then Eli must be deemed successful. After being born into virtual poverty, he had at the time of his death at least four different properties: 'Gadbridge Lodge'; 'Square Leg Cottage'; the pair of semi-detached cottages; and the ten roomed house. He may even have owned 'Weavers' cottage where his eldest daughter lived shortly after her marriage.

'Laurel Cottage' and 'Green View' cottage in 1995. Winnie Browne can still remember Dame Luff using 'Green View' as a sweet shop before the First World War.

Eli Hamshire - the Author

The many years Eli had spent as a carrier, plying his trade in all weathers, had had a detrimental affect on his health, and he suffered quite a serious illness in the early 1880's. He mentions his illness in his will which was dated April 10th, 1884: *"And I give to my daughter Mary Ann Hamshire fifteen pounds in money for her kindness in my illness and her Mother's illness."*

This illness probably brought home to him his own mortality and led him to try to leave a permanent record of his life. He wrote under the pseudonym of 'The Carrier's Boy' and published and sold the books himself. The first hand-written draft of the 'Source of England's Greatness and the Source of England's Poverty', which his family still own, may even have been written whilst he was recuperating.

Although Eli had received an education and appeared to be an avid reader of local newspapers, his actual ability to spell and punctuate was rather limited, and he tended to dictate his later works to his son, James Eli, or to his daughter, Fanny. The extent to which they must have corrected their father's writing can perhaps be best appreciated by looking at the following extract from Eli's will, which he wrote with a purple pencil: *"I GIVE AND BEQUEATH unto To my dear Wife Rebecca Bowyer Hamshire All Property Money in Bank and Stock And chatils of everey diskription and she can seall the ten Romead House situvearted at Ewhurst Green to Pay all my just Deates and if she got marriead againe the Whole of my Property abov specified of Everey Diskription is to goe to my seven Childrin and if thear Mother die ...."*

Most accounts of his life claim that he first published his book in 1884. However, I discovered in the British Library the original slim mauve pamphlet, that was published a

Eli's daughter, Fanny, in 1895, on her twenty-first birthday, proudly holding the book which she helped to write.

year earlier, and which is included in a volume entitled, 'Tracts on Social and Industrial Questions' (1882-83). It shares the volume with such other weighty works as 'Udvandringssporgssmaalet' by C.G.V. Raeder of Copenhagen and 'Die sociale Frage im alten Rom bis zum Untergang der Republic' by Professor Karl Fisch.

The 1883 edition contains only thirty-three pages, and although it mainly includes most of the information that is present in the first section of the 1892 edition, there are some notable omissions. The whole religious section which begins with 'The Old Gentleman's Spectacles', for example, is absent, and was added later. I had thought that he might have added the poetry at a later date, but most of the poetry at the beginning of the book was present in 1883.

Whilst he retained all of the 1883 edition in later editions, he inserted several other articles and re-arranged the order of many of the pages. The arrangement of some of the paragraphs in the original pamphlet did appear rather haphazard. 'The case of Elizabeth Wheeler', for example, occurred on both pages 5 and 33, whilst Sir Roger Tichbourne figured on pages 6 and 32.

By the time Eli published the second edition in February, 1884, the book had almost doubled in size to sixty-four pages. From his letters he seems to have been quite proud of his efforts as an author and with his growing reputation as a 'character' and radical political figure.

This photograph was probably taken in 1892 to celebrate the publication of his book. It is obviously an important occasion as his smock is discarded for the formality of a suit. He definitely looks quite pleased with himself.

Apart from being the author and publisher of the book, he was also in charge of advertising and relentlessly bombarded many of the leading figures of the day with copies of his work, in the hope that he could use their written testimonials to promote further sales. His letters to and from these distinguished figures together with 'Mrs. Hamshire's Views on Farming' formed the backbone of 'The Three Great Locusts'. By taking two or three pages from the 'Source of England's Greatness', a few interesting newspaper cuttings on social issues, and by writing his own views on these subjects in prose and verse, Eli had produced another, slightly longer book, of seventy-two pages. It also included a portrait of the author, and like its predecessor was bound in a soft cover and sold for a shilling a copy.

By that time, he referred to himself as 'The Unadulterated Radical' and was prepared to express himself on any subject from politics to fashion. He continued to write to many of the leading figures of the day in the hope of receiving favourable publicity for his book and was lucky enough in June, 1891, to obtain an interview with Mr. Gladstone, which was recorded for posterity in the 'Pall Mall Gazette'.

With the aid of his latest batch of correspondence he managed to extend 'The Source of England's Greatness' to a round hundred pages for the fourth edition, which was published in 1892. He also published that year a rather grand combined edition of both his books. This particular edition, which cost 3s.6d. for plain edges and 5s. for gilt edges, also included portraits of the author and a large map of the area twenty miles around Guildford.

Although Eli was responsible for writing, publishing, advertising and selling the book, he left the printing to Unwin Brothers of Chilworth and London. It was through a great stroke of luck, shortly before his death, that the original small lead plates of the fourth edition fell into the family's hands. Eli's youngest son, Joseph Allen, was travelling through Chilworth one day during late November, 1895, and noticed that the Unwin Brothers' works had been gutted by fire. Rumaging through the debris he noticed a large undamaged box with his father's name on the side. Inside were the plates of his father's book. Being told that he could keep the two hundredweight box, he carted it home and kept it under his bed in Gadbridge Lane until his death.

This is Eli's youngest son, the fifteen year old Joseph Allen, carrying on the family tradition in Peaslake in 1896.

Eli's Political Views

Within my own family I have heard Eli called a Liberal, a Socialist and a Communist. It is, however, almost impossible to place Eli into any one political slot. He was his own man and based his demands for social reform firmly upon the teachings of the Bible.

In 'The Source of England's Greatness' he claimed to be a Liberal and listed thirty-six reasons why he supported them. He was an enthusiastic supporter of Mr. Gladstone and in his interview with him stated that he wanted to see him back at the helm of the country, *as there was not another man capable of doing it like him."*

In 'The Three Great Locusts' he seemed to have moved further to the left, and called himself 'The Unadulterated Radical.' Basically, he backed those political figures who publicly supported the labouring classes. One of these politicians was Joseph Chamberlain, the champion of the New Radicalism, a man who, in his own words, preached *"the gospel of political humanity."* Eli was also an ardent admirer of Joseph Arch, who, in 1872, had founded the National Agricultural Labourers' Union, which had enrolled over 100,000 members within the first year.

Eli probably even supported Keir Hardie, who (along with three others) became the first Independent Labour Party M.P., when he was returned to Parliament in 1892, although W. McG. Eagar, in an article in the 'Surrey Advertiser' of January 19th 1957, claims that, *"He was no Socialist, but a sturdy individualist who wanted to see the country intensely farmed by God-fearing unurbanised smallholders."*

Despite his support for the working classes and his swingeing attacks on landowners, the Conservatives and their supporters, he approached his own business and life with an almost capitalist mentality. He appears to have had a variety of business interests, he thrived on hard work, he was thrifty and acquired several properties by the time of his death. Perhaps, however, he merely saw these properties as a personal security against having to end his days in the Workhouse, an institution which he loathed and which filled him with dread.

Another example of his desire for security is shown by the fact that he belonged to the Ancient Order of Foresters, a mutual benefit society whose members paid a regular sum of money as insurance against ill health. He was initiated into the 'Prince of Wales' lodge of the brotherhood in Cranleigh, on the fifth of September, 1867, and made regular quarterly contributions of six shillings into the sickness and funeral fund until his death in 1896. Eli says of the Foresters that they were, "a very industrious class of people who try while in health to avoid becoming chargeable on the Poor rates."

Whatever his true political colours, Eli was a tireless crusader for the rights of the oppressed, and although of humble origins, he seemed to thrive in the charged atmosphere of a political meeting where, attired in his slate-coloured smock he feared no man, no matter what his rank or status. He criticised the power of the gentry, the clergy and the lawyer, and bemoaned the poverty of the labourer, the system of poor relief, and the treatment of women and children. He not only criticised the system, but he also suggested his own highly individual solutions to the social problems of the day, most of which were based upon the 'Three Acres and a Cow' doctrine.

He was not a revolutionary, however. I feel that W. McG. Eagar aptly sums up Eli's political position when he says: *"He voiced the countryman's grievance and made demands on behalf of the agricultural labourer which then seemed Utopian but would now be universally recognised as just and reasonable."*

⟶ A. O. F. ⟵

COURT "PRINCE OF WALES,"

No. 4213,

CRANLEIGH

CONTRIBUTION CARD.

No...*5*......Brother *Eli Hamshire*.

Initiated...*5*....day of...*April*...186*7*.

N.B.—No Money to be received without this Card, and every Subscribing Member of this Court must pay one penny for the same, and for losing or defacing it twopence for a new one.

Eli's membership card for the Ancient Order of Foresters.

The Issue of the 'Three Acres and a Cow'

If Eli were alive today I feel that he would have been rather disappointed to discover that most books of quotations do not even mention 'three acres and a cow', and that not one of them, as far as I am aware, mentions Eli Hamshire. Those that include the phrase, tend to attribute it to Jesse Collings M.P. (1831-1920), who had close links with the Agricultural Labourers' Union and used the phrase as a slogan to help rally support for his radical allotment and smallholding policies in the 1880's.

Eric Partridge in his 'Dictionary of Slang and Unconventional English' is one of the authors to point out that he became known as 'Three acres and a cow Collings', and that he was a 'henchman' of Joseph Chamberlain (1836-1914), a powerful figure who had made a fortune in a Birmingham screw factory by the age of forty, and by 1880 had become a member of the Cabinet as the President of the Board of Trade. Within the next few years he was to become regarded as the leader of the extreme Radical party in Parliament. During the campaign for the 1886 general election, amongst his many controversial suggestions was one that compulsory purchase should be used to create more allotments. Some authors (see 'A Dictionary of Catchphrases' by Eric Partridge) even suggest that Chamberlain coined the phrase himself.

The phrase was also partially responsible for the overthrow of Lord Salisbury's First Ministry in 1886. The government resigned after Jesse Collings had carried an amendment, which regretted the omission of measures for the relief of agricultural labourers in the Queen's Speech. It was called naturally enough the 'three acres and a cow' amendment.

Although Chamberlain and Collings probably realised the political value of the slogan, I feel that Eli is a more realistic candidate to be its originator. Whilst Chamberlain had thrived in the industrial heart of Birmingham, Eli had grown up on his father's three acres, before renting a farm of similar size. He, therefore, realised from practical experience that, with careful management, a family could survive on three acres and a little livestock.

Eli claims in 'The Three Great Locusts' that he wrote to Chamberlain on the topic and, *"it was made known throughout the country."* As the letter and its reply are undated it is impossible to say definitely that Eli wrote to Chamberlain before the idea became a national catch-phrase. Eli did, however, send Chamberlain a copy of Mr. Spurgeon's letter, dated September, 1884, which would tend to suggest that their correspondence took place in December of that year, thus giving Chamberlain and Collings time to adopt it for their land reform propaganda of 1885. He did not exactly use the words 'three acres and a cow' in the letter, but his words, *"let any industrious man have two or three acres of land to keep a cow.....*" could easily have been the inspiration behind their battle-cry.

Eli makes numerous references to the 'three acres and a cow' policy in his book and states quite dogmatically, particularly in his letters, that he was the originator of the phrase. He starts off his letter to the Editor of the 'English Labourers' Chronicle', for example, by saying, *"As I am the founder and originator of the Three Acres and a Cow..."*; he also states in the 'Three Great Locusts' that, *"I want the masses of people to see I am the originator of the 'three acres and a cow'..."*; and the map which accompanies the 1892 edition of Eli's book claims that it is by *"A Carrier's Boy, Originator of 'Three Acres And A Cow'."*

According to J. Redding Ware in the 'Passing English of the Victorian Period', Mr. George Smith of Coalville, whom Eli mentions in his book, claimed the invention of the phrase in a letter to the 'Daily News' on August 27th, 1887, and stated that he had brought the subject before a Select Committee on Canals in 1883. This date, however, would still appear to be several years after Eli had first made his views on the issue known.

On several occasions he mentioned a meeting which he attended in Guildford in about 1869, where he first claims to have spoken on the subject. In the introduction to 'The Three Great Locusts' (1889) he said it was twenty years ago that he had spoken on the topic of the three acres and the cow. At that meeting, where Dr. Stallard was present, he told the audience, *"if we could get three or four cottages built upon every hundred acres of land, and two or three acres of land attached to every cottage, so that the labouring class could keep a cow and pigs..."* This meeting was clearly mentioned in the First Edition of 'The Source of England's Greatness' (1883), and would tend to scupper George Smith's claim.

His claim to be the originator of the phrase did, however, cross the Atlantic. An issue of the 'West Surrey Times' in 1889 mentions an article by Dr. Parker, in the 'New York Herald'. The article, describing a meeting in England at which Eli was present, mentioned that amongst the audience was, *"The stalwart figure of Eli Hampshire, the author of 'The Source of England's Greatness and Poverty,' who claims to be the author of the 'Three Acres and a Cow' experiment."*

The 'West Surrey Times' asked, *"Is it the case that this now well-known phrase had its origin from a Surrey man, and can Mr. Hampshire or his friends enlighten us on the accuracy of the statement in the 'New York Herald'?"* Eli replied in typical fashion by sending the editor a copy of his book.

Although Collings was undoubtedly responsible for the popularity of the phrase in the mid-1880's, I believe that Eli had a right to feel aggrieved that his own contribution was never recognised. He never had to suffer, however, the embarrassment Collings must have felt in his later life, when the phrase became a satirical one used more to denote illogical and excessive optimism. The 'three acres and a cow' doctrine was supposed to benefit the agricultural labourers and solve all the country's agricultural problems, but as Ware points out, *"no one discovered where the money was to come from to meet the expense."*

Eli and the Tichborne Claimant

Probably the most unusual topic which Eli included in his book, and one which he loved to raise at meetings, was the questionable legitimacy of the Tichborne Claimant. Apart from the intrinsic interest of the story, it seems strange that Eli should appear to be so concerned with the problem, as it had nothing to do with his own life, agriculture or the plight of the poor. In a way, I feel that Eli's support is merely another example of his concern for the underdog in the unequal fight against bureaucracy and the legal system.

The case started in 1854, when Roger Charles Tichborne (1829-1854) was lost overboard off the South American coast. In 1866, following the death of his younger brother, Sir Alfred Tichborne, his mother (the dowager Lady Tichborne, who nourished the hope that Roger might still be alive) made a well publicised effort to find him. The following year a claimant, Thomas Castro, otherwise known as Arthur Orton, was discovered working as a butcher in Wagga Wagga, Australia. At a meeting which was arranged in Paris that year, Lady Tichborne acknowledged Arthur Orton as being her son. Apparently he resembled Roger Tichborne and had a similar physical disability. This reunion was not greeted favourably by other members of the family who claimed that he was the son of a Wapping butcher.

In 1871, Arthur Orton tried to claim 'his' inheritance and brought an ejection order against the trustees of the Tichborne estate. Although over a hundred people swore that he was the rightful heir to the property, the jury were not convinced and the case collapsed on its 103rd day in 1872. Following a retrial, which lasted 188 days, Arthur Orton was found guilty of perjury and was sentenced to fourteen years' hard labour.

The interest in the case did not abate with this sentence and public debate continued on the question for numerous years. Eli was firmly convinced that there had been a miscarriage of justice and wrote to that effect in the first edition of his book in 1883. He also included in his book his correspondence with a fellow supporter, Guildford Onslow, who was going to visit the Claimant in prison.

Eli must have been somewhat pleased when Arthur Orton was released from prison in 1884 after serving only ten years. It is a shame, however, that he had to find out the truth in 1895, the year before his own death, that he had made a serious error of judgement, as Orton admitted that he was an impostor.

Eli's Smock

The photograph, used as the frontispiece for the later editions of Eli's work, shows the rather burly figure of the jovial-looking author, with his bushy beard and slicked-down hair, sitting upon an ornate garden wall, wearing his traditional working clothes of smock, corduroy trousers and gaiters.

According to Mary Alexander in her article 'The Surrey Round Frock' the smock (or frock) was a rather copious garment which the agricultural labourers of the eighteenth and nineteenth century often wore to protect their more normal coats, waistcoats, shirts and breeches. The smocks tended to be made out of linen, a strong, durable fabric, which is naturally quite waterproof, but could be made even more weatherproof by soaking in linseed-oil. Besides being easier to wash than the more normal heavy woollen, cotton or corduroy garments, it made economic sense for the labourers to protect their other clothes which constituted a major item in their annual budget.

In some regions of the country the amount of smocking and embroidery to be found on the smock was quite extensive and often ornate. Eli's smock, however, was of the typical Surrey style, which had only a small area of smocking on either side of the front and back opening, and lacked heavy ornamental stitching on the side panels. The smock which he wore in the picture, could be the dark brown one the family still own and which would have been the one he wore when working. It would probably have been made by his wife, as was the custom, although ready-made ones were available. It looks stiff and shiny, which tends to suggest that perhaps it had indeed been treated with linseed-oil. Guildford Museum possesses one of Eli's white smocks which he would have worn for Sunday best, weddings or on other important occasions.

It is possible that Eli is wearing his white Sunday best smock in another photograph, which shows him seated besides his favourite picture, showing Jesus delivering the woman taken in adultery. Although the photograph is rather faded, the smock appears plainer, much lighter in colour and nowhere near as shiny as the smock he wore for the picture used as the frontispiece in his books. A rather battered, wide-brimmed hat lies at his feet.

By the late nineteenth century the status of the farm labourer had declined and the wearing of smocks was becoming quite rare and was often viewed with contempt. For Eli, however, the smock was his trademark, the symbol of the oppressed agricultural labourer: *"Now the labourer has to work and toil to uphold those that will not listen to him, but who looks upon his smock with high disdain."*

His smock would have made him easily recognisable at the many political meetings he attended. He describes being at a meeting where several notable figures were present, and questions were invited from the floor: *"and I, with my old round frock on, was the first called upon to speak."* His smock even gained a reference in 'The Pall Mall Gazette', following his meeting with Mr.Gladstone: *"He is remarkable for his appearance - always, Sundays and week-days, is his burly form seen encased in a quaint smock frock."*

This faded photograph is of a be-smocked Eli, circa 1894, sitting beside some of his most treasured possessions. The photograph is dominated by his favourite painting of 'Jesus with the Adulteress in the Temple' which he mentioned in his book as being kept in the kitchen. In front of that is his book, propped up by the Family Bible, whilst photographs of his children are at the bottom left of the picture frame.

Eli, the Loving Father

From the recollections of his grandchildren, Eli appears to have been an excellent father. He spent most of his free time with his children, he was loving and attentive, fun to be with and above all made sure that they all obtained a sound education. He wrote with great pride of their mathematical ability, a skill which would be appreciated by a dealer and huxter. He encouraged them to be literate and records that James obtained extra pocket money by making and selling copies of some of Eli's correspondence. James, in particular, in his role as Boswell, must have spent hours by the great man's side, recording his father's thoughts.

This rather charming photograph of Eli's two eldest children, Mary Anne and William, was taken in about 1872, outside the ten-roomed cottage where they lived at Ewhurst Green. Both look thoroughly healthy and well cared for.

It must have been with great anger and shame that Eli found himself, on one occasion, summoned for neglect. One day, according to family legend, he combined herding three cows along a lane with pushing his youngest child in a pram, whilst accompanied by several of the other youngsters. Upon spotting a gamekeeper across a neighbouring field he halted the procession and went to buy some rabbits. Whilst he was thus engaged a local policeman came along and booked him.

As they became older the children probably helped him with his poultry business, which

This photograph of Mary Anne was, according to her daughter, Ivy Cornes, taken when she was fourteen years old in 1880. It was obviously taken outside the same ten-roomed cottage which had been built by Job Robinson on the plot of land adjoining the present day semi-detached cottages, 'Laurel Cottage' and 'Green View'.

The wedding of Henry Stemp and Mary Anne Hamshire on June 6th, 1885.

had outgrown his other interests to such an extent that he was listed in the 1891 Kelly's Directory as being a poulterer although the Census still referred to him as a General Dealer and Farmer. He tended to employ youngsters to help him with the plucking and would elicit their help by saying, *"If you do some work for me I'll give you some bullseyes."* The family paint a wonderful picture of him sitting, surrounded by his youthful workforce, up to his knees in feathers. He could, however, be strict as George Weller found out to his cost when he pushed a chicken's rear end into another boy's face and was sacked on the spot.

Probably the biggest disappointment Eli had to face from his children was the marriage, against his wishes, in 1885 of his eldest daughter, Mary Anne (19), the girl who had nursed Eli and Rebecca through their respective illnesses. Although she was pregnant, Eli still opposed her marriage to an old school friend, Henry Stemp (20), as he thought they were too young. Privately he disliked Henry and said, *"We've got one Stemp in the family, and don't want another."*

Although Eli refused to allow Henry into the house, the young couple found an ally in Rebecca. She contacted the Rector, John Mount Barlow, who said that he had no objection to them being married in church. The couple married on June 6th, 1885, and moved into a cottage at 'Chapel House Farm', Oakwoodhill, which was about three miles away from Ewhurst Green. The baby, Albert, was premature and died when only a few days old, his body being buried in the grounds of Oakwood Chapel.

This is an engraving of Oakwood Chapel in 1848

Perhaps the death of his first grandson tempered Eli's anger against Henry, as, when my own grandfather, Alfred, was born on March 6th, 1887, the couple were living at 'Weavers', which could have been another of Eli's cottages to the west of Ewhurst Green.

The Stemps, a local farming family, were great Conservative supporters and, as such, were instantly worthy of Eli's dislike. Henry wore a small yellow flower to indicate that he was a member of the Primrose League, a Conservative organisation, founded in 1833 by Lord Randolph Churchill et al., whose objectives were, 'The maintenance of religion, of the constitution of the realm, and of the unity of the British Commonwealth and Empire.'

If Eli had not died so prematurely he would probably have grown to dislike Henry even more. Although Henry was only classified as being a labourer, a tree feller, at the time of their marriage, he quickly became a successful farmer, and by 1908 he had become the owner of the 134 acre 'Utworth Manor' in Cranleigh, besides owning several cottages in Cranleigh, Ewhurst and Alfold, and renting land to farm elsewhere.

This photograph shows Mary Anne in 1888 with Eli's eldest grandson, Alf Stemp, who, with his brother Harry, and Fred Weller, went on to found Stemp & Weller, the agricultural and haulage contractors.

This is Eli's son, Henry, at the beginning of the twentieth century. He was a builder who bought the semi-detached cottages at Ewhurst Green.

This is James Eli, circa 1890, who helped his father write his book, and later became a grocer in Gadbridge Lane.

William Hamshire, Eli's eldest son, became a tenant farmer at the remote 'Hill House Farm', to the south of the parish.

On the whole, however, Eli appears to have been very supportive towards his children as they grew up. He lent his eldest son, William, £170 in 1894 to acquire 'Hill House Farm', which lay in an isolated spot to the south of the village. William also borrowed £25 each from his brothers, James and Henry, and £17 from his sister, Fanny.

In 1894, Eli's youngest daughter, Fanny, also went to live at 'Hill House Farm' as William's housekeeper, before she married, on November 12th, 1901, Moses Muggeridge, a grammar school educated machine proprietor from Rudgwick. She returned in later years to farm 'Hill House Farm' which has since passed into the hands of her grandson, Cecil.

Eli's son, James Eli, became a successful baker and shopkeeper in Ellen's Green before returning to start a shop in Gadbridge Lane, in an extension he added to Eli's bungalow, 'Gadbridge Lodge', in about 1920. Another son, Henry, became a builder and bought the semi-detached cottages overlooking the Green in 1917. His youngest son, Joseph Allen, continued to live at home with his mother after Eli's death and took over the running of the chicken dealing, until he passed the business on to his son, Allen, who still lives in Gadbridge Lane.

On the death of his landlord, Lord Abinger, in 1914, William Hamshire had to leave 'Hill House Farm'. He went to work as a farm labourer for John Cobb, the racing driver, at Lower Green, Esher. A few months later he moved to Ditton Hill, Surbiton. In the above photograph William, is standing beside the horse whilst a retired policeman is helping him to harvest the crop.

This is Fanny, her husband, Moses Muggeridge, her daughter, Winnie, and her son, Eli, sitting in front of the remote 'Hill House Farm' circa 1915. They took over the lease from William in 1914 and bought the farm outright in 1921.

This was the seventeenth century cradle in which all Eli's children were rocked to sleep. Rebecca had inherited it from her mother, Mary Gibbs (née Allen), and she passed it on to her daughter, Mary Anne.

Eli's Death

Eli's health had undoubtedly suffered from the years spent carrying and the exposure to the elements which the job entailed. He was particularly prone to bouts of bronchitis, and it was this complaint, complicated by dropsy, that led to Eli's admission to the Royal Surrey County Hospital, Guildford, in early October, 1896. After failing to recover from an operation to tackle the dropsy, he died on October 10th, at the early age of 61.

Eli was buried four days later in the northwest corner of Ewhurst churchyard, near the grave of his daughter, Minnie. The rather plain headstone, which was carved out of local sandstone, is now quite eroded but its fascinating epitaph can still be deciphered:

IN LOVING REMEMBRANCE

ELI HAMSHIRE

OF GADBRIDGE LODGE, EWHURST

WHO DEPARTED THIS LIFE

OCTOBER 10th AND WAS INTERRED

HERE OCTOBER 14th, 1896

AGED 61 YEARS.

A SINCERE KIND FRIEND AND AFFECTIONATE

FATHER WHO FELL TO SLEEP IN JESUS

———————

THE WISH OF A WAYFARING MAN

MY HEARTY WISH TOWARDS YOU IS THAT

A SUPREME POWER MAY EVER REIGN OVER

YOU AND THAT THE SUN OF GLORY MAY

EVER SHINE AROUND YOU AND THAT THE

GATES OF PARADISE WILL BE OPENED

UNTO YOU, TO THE HIGHEST DESIRE OF

TRUE HAPPINESS.

In a way it is appropriate that the final words upon Eli's headstone should belong to one of the underprivileged, whose lot Eli had striven, throughout his life, to improve. He had been so impressed by the words of gratitude of one particular tramp to whom he had given money, that he recorded these words for posterity and had them engraved upon his own tombstone.

His devoted wife, Rebecca, never re-married and so, according to the terms of his will, inherited the whole of his property. She continued to live in comfort at 'Gadbridge Lodge', with her maid, until her death on December 16th, 1916. Her body lies in an adjacent plot to her husband, under an identically shaped, but even more eroded, headstone.

Winnie Browne, who used to live at Ewhurst Green before the First World War, can remember Rebecca's geese and ducks going down to the pond on the green every day. In the evening Rebecca used to appear at the end of Gadbridge Lane clapping her hands and calling *"Dilly! Dilly! Dilly! Dillies!"*. They would at once leave the green and go up Gadbridge Lane where she shut them away for the night. The mess left by the geese led to Gadbridge Lane being known locally as 'Goose Turd Alley'.

It was after Rebecca's death, however, that Eli's sons ran into problems disentangling his will, particularly with regard to the copyhold cottage at Ewhurst Green, which he had attempted to make freehold in 1873. It is rather ironic, after Eli had urged his readers to make their own property freehold and to make proper wills, that it took so many solicitors' letters, after the death of his wife, to unravel the ownership of his property.

Despite these flaws in his own affairs, his rather jaundiced opinions on issues such as vaccination and machinery, and his often sweeping generalizations about the society of his day, Eli Hamshire was a truly remarkable character. He combined being a self-educated, hard-working, God-fearing, musically-talented, well-loved family man, with being probably the greatest, most pic-

This is a photograph of the formidable Rebecca circa 1910.

turesque, unsung, rural philosopher of nineteenth century England. He spoke on behalf of the agricultural labourer and the oppressed, and although his 'Three Acres and a Cow' doctrine might have seemed too simplistic, he voiced the fears of the down-trodden classes and tried to offer a solution to their problems.

The extent to which he was regarded locally is probably best reflected in the following words, which are taken from his obituary in the 'Surrey Advertiser' of October 17th:

"The deceased, who was 61 years of age, was an ardent believer in the Claimant, and held somewhat extraordinary opinions on social and political questions, which he expressed in printed pamphlets issued under the nom de plume of 'The Carrier's Boy'. He made no pretence that these effusions possessed any literary merit, but the original way in which the deceased expressed his views, could not fail to express amusement to those who perused them. The deceased was of a genial and cheery disposition, and his stalwart figure, always clad in a slate coloured short smock, will be much missed."

Whilst it does not compare in eloquence to the tribute given, in the same issue, to the late Dr. Benson, the ninety-second Archbishop of Canterbury, I think Eli would have appreciated it; although it failed to mention what might have been his most important contribution to the history of the nineteenth century, the fact that, in his opinion, he was the originator of the 'Three Acres and a Cow.'

Rebecca's and Eli's gravestones in the graveyard at St Peter and St Paul's church, Ewhurst.

THE

SOURCE of ENGLAND'S GREATNESS,

AND THE

SOURCE of ENGLAND'S POVERTY;

WITH CORRESPONDENCE ON THE LABOUR QUESTION

FROM THE

RIGHT HONBLE. JOHN BRIGHT, M.P.

AND ARTICLES ON THE FOUR GREAT STANDING EVILS:
VACCINE, NICOTINE, YOUNG WOMEN PINCHING THEIR WAISTS IN, AND INTERMARRYING.

BY

A CARRIER'S BOY.

FOURTH EDITION. WITH A PORTRAIT OF THE AUTHOR.

PUBLISHED BY
ELI HAMSHIRE, EWHURST, NEAR GUILDFORD, SURREY.
1892.

I was born on Christmas Day,
I was the seventh son, my mother say.
My mother had to cook a goose, and I came and put the
goose-cooking out of the way.
I was born at half-past seven in the morning on the
25th December, 1834, this is what my mother say.

THE SOURCE OF ENGLAND'S GREATNESS

and the

SOURCE OF ENGLAND'S POVERTY.

By a Carrier's Boy.

I intend to write this book as the history of my life, with the source of England's greatness and the source of England's poverty, hoping that no jealousy or ill-feeling will arise from any person's feelings, as I write for the benefit of the lower and middle classes of society.

I myself have no ill-feeling towards any man, woman or child. I have been in the habit of travelling twenty miles per day, Sundays excepted (railway travelling excepted), for the last thirty years, and I have been the instigation of saving little children's lives from the brink of starvation. It has given me a heart to feel and a brain to think different to a great many of my fellow countrymen.

I have lived in the parish of Ewhurst, on the borders of Sussex - which is twelve miles from the union workhouse - all my lifetime, and I have known old people who have worked hard and fared hard all their lifetime, and just at the latter stage of their life have been sent away to the union workhouse, with one foot in the grave and one foot out, there to die, after using the heavy irons of toil all their days, and bringing up a large family of children, when they ought to be together to prepare for eternity. Man's allotted time is three-score years and ten: this gives him ten years' Sabbaths to prepare for his latter end.

Then, again, I have known instances of people who have died broken-hearted through the dread of going to the union, and I have known inquests held over their bodies where the juries have brought in a verdict of "heart disease". Now, this class of people is often called improvident.

The Divisional Sums of the Farm Labourer and Her Majesty.

Take the farm labourer, whose weekly wages has not amounted to more than 12s. per week on an average during the last forty-six years, and which is £31.4s. per annum - supposing him to have a family of eight children, and the two parents, making ten, to be kept. Having three meals each per day would amount to 11/16ths of a penny (just under 3/4d.) for each meal, which would amount to 12s. per week. They want the rich to tell them how to live; we pay the rich very dear to tell us how to die.

I chanced to see an almanack with a representation of Her Majesty, holding a Bible in her hand, which book was stated to be the source of England's greatness. Now when I look into the second chapter of this Book, I read that the Almighty did not see fit for man to live alone, and created woman for a helpmeet for him. The woman is not portioned from a bullock, or a horse, or an ass, but she is the portion of a man.

Then we read at the time of the Flood that they were to replenish and multiply. Then, again, when our Saviour came upon earth, He said: "Whom God hath joined together let no man put asunder." Now these laws were instituted when man's Sabbaths were appointed.

Then we have our bishops, and canons, and Church of England ministers, who have their splendid mansions in each parish, and they have large salaries themselves, and they sit as Chairmen at the Board of Guardians, they lawfully marry people, and they are the first to separate them.

I also read in the 'Echo' newspaper that Her Majesty's income was £385,000. If she had the same number in family as the man who holds the plough her money would amount to £35.3s.2d. and 5/16ths of a penny for each meal for each individual. My motive for writing this - I have never seen it done by any other writer - is to show the contrast between the man who holds the plough and those who have these enormous incomes. And they preach equality in a religious point of view.

Then, I say, which horse deserves the most respect - the horse that draws the Queen's carriage, or the horse that draws the plough? Then surely the human beings who hold the plough ought to be better respected than sent twelve miles to the union workhouse, there to be separated, and there to die, which is wrong in the sight of our Maker!

The New Plan of Building Labourers' Cottages.

The new plan of building the labourers' cottages, is with five rooms, with two rods of ground buried in with timber, the w.c. to empty within nine feet of the well of water, and the drain to empty within eighteen feet of the highway road into an open dyke! Now, God gave man light, and He gave the air to breathe and the water to drink, and said unto them: "Be fruitful and multiply, and replenish the earth;" and why should not the labourer who holds the plough have a piece of land, to keep a cow, &c.?

We have what they call model farms in our parish, and, as Job said, they grow thistles in the wheat and cockles in the barley, and a great many other kinds of rubbish, I am sorry to say, and they monopolise the land; and where there used to be twenty little dairies of butter, and a quantity of other produce, it is almost dormant; and they have their hundreds of acres, and enclose the waste land where the poor man used to keep his cow and his pig; and they plant laurels and what I call evergreen rubbish, instead of planting nice fruit trees, which would be a benefit for mankind.

One man has enclosed the church tow-path in our little parish; and at Cranleigh one man who owns thousands of acres enclosed the Goose-green, and an old farm labourer chopped the posts and rails down. In the parish of Wonersh there is a large piece of land added to the park, and there were a few working men who applied for a piece of land, and they were told that the land was in chancery. The parishes, Cranleigh and Wonersh, belong to the same lord of the manor. You see, these men who have abundance of land could enclose it if it was in chancery, but the working man can't get a rod of ground.

Now in the parish of Shere there are 1,717 people, and there are 1,770 acres of waste land. I believe there are about sixteen million acres of commons and waste lands, and, if honestly held by the government in trust for the nation, and let at small rentals, we should probably in a short time receive eight millions sterling per annum. The rents would be paid into the national exchequer, and the taxation of the country lessened by so much.

The Parish Political Economy.

The Paris Political Economy Society has been discussing the advisability of introducing the Torrens Land Act - now in operation in Australia - into France. In the course of the discussion it was stated that the land in France is broken up into 126,000,000 plots. Surely something can be done in England in this same way.

A Poor Old Man by the Road Side.

Now I saw a poor old man lying by the side of the road, with a handkerchief over his head, and my horse shied at him. I said, "Not well, guv'nor?"

And he said, "No, I am not well, friend. I have got cold congealed upon cold, and I feel almost in despair; and I feel empty. But I have seen better days."

"Yes," I said, "there are many high trees fall to the ground; and here's twopence for you."

He then took hold of my hand, and he said, "My hearty wish towards you is that a Supreme Power may ever reign over you, and that the sun of glory may ever shine around you, and that the gates of paradise will be opened unto you to the highest desire of true happiness!" And the tears ran down his face when he said it.

There is not one man in a hundred who would pull his horse up and give a poor man twopence by the side of the road. I then gave him another twopence and drove on, and my thoughts were, 'Do those magistrates get that hearty wish who give fourteen days' imprisonment for asking for a crust of bread on an empty stomach?' And as I thought this over in my mind there came a sort of chill over my body, and the tears began to run down my cheeks as I remembered there were so many thousands in the country like him.

I had just read of an inquest, held on a baby four months old. The mother of the child said her husband had been out of work some months, during which time witness and her husband and six children had been almost starving; the poor mother herself not having sufficient nourishment, the child was starved at her breast.

To the females of England: How long will you be crushed down by the ruling powers of this country? We hear much of abolishing the House of Lords. If we could get a House of Females in the room of them, they could then stand up for their own protection!

And then, again, I saw a case in a paper where a poor woman had three months' imprisonment for sleeping in an outhouse, and was so ill when committed that she only lived three days.

FUNERAL OF ELIZABETH WHEELER:

'Sent to Hard Labour for Three Months for being Homeless and Destitute.'
Out in the dark and the danger,
Out in the night and the cold,
Though our Saviour was longing to lead her
Tenderly into His fold.

Oh, where are the mourners? - alas! there are none
In the world now she is gone!
But bear softly her bones over the stones,
Tho' a pauper, she is one that her Maker yet owns!
The foxes have holes, and the birds of the air have nests,
But this young woman in this so-called Christian country had nowhere to rest,
How much there is needed to inquire for the distress!
Or how shall we stand with our Maker in that Great Day of rest?

The CASE of ELIZABETH WHEELER. - Mr. Burt put a question to the Home Secretary (Sir W. Harcourt) in the House of Commons upon this case, Mr. Macdonald inquiring if the right hon. gentleman had communicated with the magistrates at Guildford with regard to three months' imprisonment - a sentence sometimes passed on men for killing their wives - (laughter) passed upon the woman for sleeping in an outhouse.

And when these men, who refuse a glass of water,
Are in the valley and shadow of death,
It will work on their consciences
When they are striving for breath.
On the 27th of January, they took her, helpless and distress'd,
A sentence sometimes pass'd on men for killing their wives
(Laughter in the House of Commons),
And that was all she got for her redress!

And how hard they deal with the little paltry cases with the small tradesmen! For in nine cases out of ten they are perfectly innocent, but they are sure to have to pay £1.18s. I think it would be wise if the magistrates were to read the 19th and 25th chapters of St. Matthew, the 16th chapter of St. Luke, and the 5th chapter of St. James, and see if their Master set that hard example, and ask themselves the question, how are they going to give an account of their stewardship in that Great Day, for it leaves me in a mystery to understand.

And I had been reading in the 'West Surrey Times' that at the Guildford Board of Guardians a lady said the difficulty was that tramps made the excuse to people when they solicited alms that they were sent out of the workhouse hungry. Being a lady I know well (and her mother before her), and greatly respect, I must tell her what I saw in the month of December, 1880. I saw a poor man who had just come from the Guildford Union, and he had with him his wife and his four little children. The man's teeth chattered with the cold as he was speaking to me, and he said his little girl cried for food before he got a hundred yards from the union.

Then I saw another poor man with a family of five; the man had a little child on his shoulder asleep, and three little ones stood shivering with cold. The poor mother cried and said her feet were wrung rough beneath her, and that she had only been confined five weeks, and was then very ill. I gave her sixpence to get some refreshment, and told her she was in danger of losing her life. This was at seven o'clock one Saturday night. In this case I leave the females better to understand.

Another member said he believed the master of the house would tell the Board that ninety-nine out of a hundred of those applying for relief were rogues and vagabonds. To the reader: Were these little infant children rogues and vagabonds?

The next speaker regarded the circular which had been distributed as perfectly useless, as people would forget all about its contents in a week. He had given instructions to his servants not to supply tramps with anything, not even a glass of water; and in this he was supported by police authorities. This is quite true, as I knew one poor man who had fourteen days' imprisonment for asking for a drink of water. Inhumanity is what I call a monstrous great sin.

Men born to titles and fortunes attend but little to the cultivation of the mind. Pleasure, monopolising the land, and cruel sport are the idols to which they sacrifice. We read in the Bible, "Whoso hath this world's goods, and seeth his brother have need of them, and shutteth up his bowels of compassion from him, how dwelleth the love of God in him?" Job the stranger did not lodge in the street, and I opened my doors to the traveller.

And therefore I think, whatever difference there is among men in their outward condition, in their capacity of mind or strength of body, or place in the world, He that made the one made the other also, which is a good reason why we should not mock at men's natural infirmities, nor trample upon those who are not so well-to-do as ourselves, but in everything do as we would be done by.

The Old Gentleman's Spectacles.

I remember hearing of an old gentleman who lost his spectacles upon which he set great value, and for nearly a year they could not be found; but one day, on taking down his bible, to his great surprise he found them where he had left them for nearly twelve months.

And I once heard of a poor woman who had a Bible given her by one of the Royal family, and in which was placed a five pound note; and when she had had the book nearly a year, one of the Royal family paid her a visit and asked if she had read the book, when she said that she had read it through and through; her visitor then asked to see the book, and as soon as she opened it she saw the note exactly where she had placed it, which proved at once that the reading of the Bible had been neglected; and I think there are many of us who are guilty of neglecting our Bibles, especially some of our magistrates, and for such as these I quote the following parables:-

"There was a certain rich man which was clothed in purple and fine linen, and fared sumptuously every day. And there was a certain beggar named Lazarus, which was laid at his gate, full of sores, and desiring to be fed with the crumbs which fell from the rich man's table; moreover the dogs came and licked his sores.

And it came to pass that the beggar died, and was carried by the angels into Abraham's bosom: the rich man also died, and was buried; and in hell he lift up his eyes being in torments, and seeth Abraham afar off, and Lazarus in his bosom. And he cried and said, 'Father Abraham, have mercy on me, and send Lazarus, that he may dip the tip of his finger in water, and cool my tongue, for I am tormented in this flame.'

But Abraham said, 'Son, remember that thou in thy lifetime receivedst thy good things and likewise Lazarus evil things: but now he is comforted, and thou art tormented. For I was hungered and ye gave me no meat: I was thirsty, and ye gave me no drink: I was a stranger and ye took me not in: naked, and ye clothed me not: sick in prison, and ye visited me not.'

Then shall they also answer him, saying, 'Lord, when saw we thee an hungered, or athirst, or a stranger, or naked, or sick, or in prison, and did not minister unto thee?'

Then shall he answer them saying, 'Verily I say unto you, inasmuch as ye did it not to one of the least of these, ye did it not to me. And these shall go away into everlasting punishment'.

Go to now, ye rich men, weep and howl for your miseries that shall come upon you. Your riches are corrupted, and your garments are moth-eaten.

Your gold and silver is cankered, and the rust of them shall be a witness against you, and shall eat your flesh as it were fire. Ye have heaped treasure together for the last days.

Behold, the hire of the labourers who have reaped down your fields which you have kept back by fraud, crieth: and the cries of them which have reaped have entered into the ears of the Lord of Sabaoth. Ye have lived in pleasure on the earth, and been wanton: ye have nourished, as in the day of slaughter. You have condemned and killed the just; and he doth not resist you. But after thy hardness and impenitent heart, treasurest up unto thyself wrath against the day of wrath and revelation of the righteous judgment of God, who will render to every man according to his deeds. Be ye also patient, stablish your hearts, for the coming of the Lord draweth nigh."

And the book says deliver us from evil; and thy will be done.

> *From the first step on earth*
> *To the brink of the grave,*
> *They will not put their hand*
> *To the plough nor the spade.*

Mr. Ichet on Illegitimate Children.

The late Mr. Ichet, the guardian, said to me, "You are a thinking man, I know;" and he put his hand upon my shoulder, and said, "We have a woman in the house who has had three bastard children, and she is about to have the fourth. What should we do in a case like that?"

I said, "It is a rather hard question to answer. But I have a picture in my kitchen which will resemble your question. There are twenty-four Scribes and Pharisees, and a young woman in a sitting posture, with one hand holding her head and the other with a rope around her wrist, and our Saviour stands pointing towards her, and, looking round at the Scribes and Pharisees, He says, 'He that is without sin among you let him first cast a stone at her'. Now, I think this is a picture which would suit you guardians, if you were to look at it in the right light, for perhaps you were not quite innocent in your younger days, if you are now.

And we read in our Bibles that they are the weaker vessels; and a great many calamities attached to childbearing, and the pains and sorrows the fair sex have to contend with, we know nothing about. Then why should they be taken advantage of so much? Then, I say, let the poor woman go free, and assist her as well as you can, and punish the fathers of the children well, and instead of paying 2s.6d. per week, make them pay 5s., and that would check them in taking the advantage of the weaker vessels."

The young men, as a rule, will lead the young women along 'the green pasture of Love,' and after they have taken advantage of them will turn them into 'the sandy desert of Forgetfulness!'

Then it says: "In sorrow thou shalt bring forth children." And we read in our papers daily of young women concealing the birth of their infants. Then they are liable to be hanged or sent to prison. Now, where are the fathers of such children? Why should they go scot free? Then, again, we see cases where young women bring young men before a bench of magistrates, and the man will employ a solicitor, and he will perhaps cross-question her, and the young woman being confused, will perhaps make a blunder, and the father will get away scot free. Now it seems unreasonable for a young woman to bring a young man before a bench of magistrates if there had been no connection between them. I think we should try to ease each other's burdens.

This was the large pond on Ewhurst Green where perhaps the young girl intended to end her life. To the right of the Hamshire geese one can see the stacks of faggots and a small figure in a smock.

I well remember, when I was a lad of fourteen, meeting with a young woman who had been disappointed by a young man, and she was pregnant by him. I found she was in a distressed state of mind, and I went home with her. There was a large pond in the field, where she was going to put an end to her existence. I then told her the serious consequences, and that she was to let it come open to the world. The result was, she took my advice, and the young man had to pay 2s.6d. per week for twelve years, and the young woman then got married, and she is the mother of ten children, I am told.

I once knew a working farm bailiff who had a daughter come home in the family-way. The parents did not dare take her in, or the father would have to leave his house and his situation. The result was, the young woman had to go to the union workhouse to be confined. She there caught a fever and died. The mother of the young woman often cried, and told me what a trouble it was on her mind. I instance this case as a caution to young women

Now, we often hear about abolishing the House of Lords. If we could get a House of Women in the room of them, the fair sex could then go in and stand up for their own protection. I believe they would be the instigation of bringing our land into a better state of cultivation. They would not want to own the land to make a god of the sport, as the House of Lords do - I mean the game laws and stag parks - but they would be more for putting cottages on the land, and they would make it more comfortable for the great matrimonial institution.

We have a duke who has figured in the Divorce Court as an adulterer, a wife beater, a ruffian, who struck her when in the family-way - a man odious, obnoxious, bad, and infamous. There is scarcely a day when the Divorce Courts are not filled with such cases. We have a House of Commons filled with lawyers, and these, like every one else, like to see their profession well patronised. Those who wish to divorce their wives for every offence would do well to consider what would become if God should deal with them in like manner.

Mr. Cobden and Mr. Gladstone have given a few very good reforms, but nothing what there ought to have been. Our England ought to be like a little paradise by this time, with double the population; but now the land is monopolised, and not one acre of land in a hundred gives its proper produce of vegetation, and I think it is high time to turn our attention to it.

And we have rivers, railways, and roads, and every conveyance to supply sewage on the land. It is not the fault of the English labourers. Look at the improvements that have been made during the last fifty years in London alone; and then think of all other kinds of industry; and see the millions of tons of coal and iron that the labourer ventures his life for, for the benefit and comfort of his fellow countrymen.

The condition of the outcast poor is a blot on our civilisation, which ought to be removed.

———————

On November 22nd, 1883, at Clapham Congregational Church, the Rev. Munral, in an address on the bitter cry of the outcast in London, said he had found some wretched women who had been wives and daughters of merchants and traders; one of these, formerly the wife of a West-end tradesman who received £1,000 from her father on her wedding day, had gradually sunk to being an inhabitant of one of the lowest lodging-houses in Drury-lane.

The speaker found one of the poor women employed as a paper-gatherer, her ribs had been crushed between two vehicles. A doctor from the hospital had set her ribs, and she lay in bed with scarcely any covering on her but the bandages, trying vainly to suckle her baby of three months old, the cold wind at the time blowing through the broken windows. In another house he found a woman with a baby only a day old, crying because the landlord had given her a week's notice to quit, because she was one week behind with her rent.

———————

Mr. G. Smith, of Coalville, at a meeting of the Church Congress said, in this country alone there are 8,000 canal boats registered as dwellings, and between 40,000 and 80,000 persons living in them; he said that the parents, together with grown up sons and daughters, used the one narrow confined cabin as a living and sleeping room.

Only fancy what a wretched life to live in happy England! Is such a state of things possible? However, spiritually, these people are cared for by no one, and but for persons like Mr. G. Smith, who take a special interest in them, they would be utterly neglected. And my opinion is that the welfare of those that venture their lives on the water and in the mines ought to be studied as well as those who work upon the land.

———————

The Replenishing of the Land, the Soldiers, and Multiplying the People.

Now, what do we have our existence here for? I think to study and think for each other's welfare, and more particularly for those who are unfortunate in procuring a livelihood. For instance, look at our soldiers! They have often been compelled to enlist through being locked from the use of the land, and have been shot down like dogs!

Now, these men have been suckled, and their mothers have a great care for them from the breast, whilst the richer classes have not got their natural feelings the same as the poorer classes have. They are put into a nursery, and are brought up by nurses. Their parents see but little of them. They live on goat's or ass's milk, and I think they become, like their foster-mothers, thick-headed and hardhearted! They intermarry with their own relations, such as their first cousins, for the sake of money and estates, and their children are in some way or other always deficient. I find in the dumb creation - with stock - it is a good plan to cross breed them.

I read in 'The Illustrated Paper', Feb. 26th, 1881, that Sir George Colley, in the Transvaal, left his position on Majuba Hill because the men had neither water nor food all one day, and the cries of the wounded were so painful to hear. The men licked the moisture from the box covers, and chewed the damp grass. The night was pitch dark, and their track was broken. To the reader: Only fancy the agonies that are felt in the battle-field! Besides, look at soldiers' wives and children left uncared for, but only by the union workhouse, and there to be separated. Now, these wars are what a great many call "England's glory," but they are what I call "England's disgrace," to all humanity! It says in our Bible, "Thou shalt love the Lord thy God with all thy heart, and thy neighbour as thyself."

Now, I heard a widow complaining, and she said she lost two shillings every time she had four horses billeted on her, when soldiers were on the march, besides all her labour, cooking, and having to give them clean sheets for their beds, &c. Now, I think this poor widow treated the soldiers well, for when she went to the butcher's for their meat, he would ask if it was for soldiers, and if so, he offered her stinking steak: but no, she would have the same for them as for herself.

Now, this poor widow often had soldiers billeted on her, because she used them well. Now you see the tradesman would take advantage, because the men were only soldiers; they are oftentimes despised. It is forgotten that these are the men who protect our property, or I think they would not be so despised as they often are.

Now, suppose some wonderful being, possessed with the power, were to go to every man, woman, and child, and take possession of England, Ireland,

Scotland, and Wales, and then go to Turkey, and every other nation in Europe; thence to China, where there are over 400 millions of human beings. If this great being obtained one sovereign from each individual, and all this enormous, incomprehensible mass of wealth were poured together, what do you suppose it would represent? Why, as nearly as possible the amount of money the English aristocratic parliament has spent in war since the time of Charles I, nearly 800 millions of which are now unpaid, and a burden upon the people.

Now, suppose the reader will imagine all the fearful disasters that have befallen this country during any period he pleases to take - all the colliery explosions, and all the fearful railway accidents, shipwrecks of our own vessels, accident by fire, water, tempest and lightning, and every other calamity you can think of, and the sum of them all will not equal, I believe, or come anywhere near, the sufferings and misery which the people of this country have endured by reason of its innumerable wars! Besides all this, the higher classes take pensions out of our pockets to support their own class of beings!

The British and Foreign Bible Society circulated 2,846,029 copies of the Scriptures for the year ending March 31st, 1883. Since the foundation of the Society it has circulated over ninety million copies, and has caused the Bible to be translated and printed in 240 languages. Surely our ruling powers ought to settle by Arbitration; our great Master never intended there should be any bloodshed according to his Book.

Finding Civil Employment for the Soldiers.

Were the various roadside plots in the camp allotted out for building houses suitable for the working-classes and military men, having large gardens, say a quarter of an acre each, how much better would it be than erecting houses for those referred to in densely populated localities, say North Town, &c.; were work scarce, the produce of the garden and the poultry, even if the pig was prohibited, would largely aid in the support of a pensioner and his wife. Again, suppose it is as I am informed that a soldier must not marry, and may not take his wife into barracks until he has been seven years in the army, and has money in the bank, what must be the result is beyond guessing.

The Game Laws.

I feel it a duty to enlighten the public a little on the game laws. I have known sales of underwood to take place, when the auctioneer has announced that the owner would want a day's sport in a month's time, and there may have been forty or fifty men kept waiting to go on with this job of work, because the owner wanted a day's sport, with the result, in many cases, of empty cupboards at home, debt incurred with little tradesmen - causing dullness of trade, increasing our paupers, and filling our prisons. I cannot enumerate the evils of this system in this little book. But where there is a law so detrimental to thousands, I think we cannot expose it too much.

Now, pheasants are brought up like barn-door fowls, and they go and shoot them down like soldiers in the battle-field; and to hear the shrieks and cries is something awful! Now, the pheasants are wounded in just the same way, and I think it a great piece of cruelty to our beautiful feathered tribe.

Then, again, the same class of men go fox and staghunting. There was a man who told me he bought some underwood, and the man he had bought it of sent his coachman up one Sunday night to say that he was not to send his men there to work for a week, because the fox was laying in the cover, and they would be there with the hounds to hunt it. Now, these men would be thrown out of employment if their employer had nothing else for them to do.

I saw an old farmer one day in his field, who had been a farmer for sixty years, and he pointed out to me a horse track. He said, "These fox-hunters and stag-hunters want to make me believe that they never do any mischief; but why don't the wheat and seeds grow in that horse footmark as well as all round outside?"

Now, the stagnant water stood in that footmark, which caused the wheat and seeds to perish. He said, "There may be five thousand footmarks; it would make a big piece of ground if you were to put the footmarks together. Besides, it makes the ground work steely the next time we plough it. And that is not all, for they break down our fences and gate-backs, besides letting our stock out into the roads, where the policeman might see them, and summons us before the magistrates - and that costs two or three pounds, as a rule." This is a disgrace. And I know the pasturage is allowed to stand and rot.

I knew a farmer who said the staghounds rode up one land of wheat, and the other land they did not touch. At harvest he reaped the wheat from each land, and laid each by itself, and there was just half a bushel difference on the land they rode and trod down to what there was on that they did not tread. These are facts from practical experienced farmers; - that they ride and tread into the earth that which we ought to have for our sustenance.

––––––––––

Then I think it to be a great piece of cruelty to ride after those beautiful stags. They run through the bushes and the brambles with their tongues hanging out of their mouths, and a stream of blood running from their noses the size of a wheat straw; and then to fall backward from the fence into the dyke, and into the hound's mouth, to be torn about before the huntsman can get to them. They keep them for six or eight weeks, and turn them out again, when they recover their strength. I have also seen the horses' fetlocks bleeding, and the spurs used too much; and often hear of the horses dropping dead beneath their riders. And a great many accidents occur through these kinds of what they call sport.

We read in our Bibles that God created man in His own image; therefore we are monuments of God's sparing mercy; and why should we use the beautiful creatures that are sent for our food with such barbarity? I call it a disgrace to all humanity - the corruption of the times.

The laws nowadays are like the spiders' webs, which holds small flies and suffer the great ones to break through and escape. Now if I were to go into Guildford with my horse's shoulder wrung the size of a shilling, and I had tried all I knew to prevent, the same class of beings who ride after the poor stags would fine the likes of myself from £1 to £5, or three months' imprisonment.

And it is just the same with the small tradesmen. If his scales are just a little deficient, or should he sell a tin of mustard slightly adulterated, and not knowing what it consists of, he is fined from £1 to £5. Why don't they go to the manufactories, and put a stop to it there? I have known as much as forty or fifty pounds paid as fines on bench days; and we, as ratepayers, ought to have a balance-sheet every year in each parish throughout the country, and know what becomes of this money, as there is not one in five hundred who now knows what becomes of it.

––––––––––

And why not choose our magistrates by an election? If a man gets drunk in the borough, he is fined five shillings; but if the county police find a man drunk just outside the borough, he is fined £1 and costs. If a poor old woman accommodates her neighbour with a loaf of bread, and it happens to be half an ounce deficient, she is fined £1.18s. Now there is a great difference about this sort of thing. To cut half an ounce off a loaf would look very mean.

Then if she happens to have a measure in her possession which has not got a stamp on it, she is fined £1.18s., although the measure is correct. It is what I call a genteel way of robbing the small tradesmen, for in nine cases out of ten they have no intention of cheating the public. There are so many paltry things to enumerate, that I think it a disgrace to sit on the magistrate's bench. The county is more than an honour.

My brother once got off the side of the road, and being at night, he could not get the load out; the policeman came that way and saw the wagon stand, and then summoned him, and he had to pay £1, though there was sufficient space for anything to pass or re-pass.

Now I know these same magistrates to have trees of timber standing within five feet of the centre of the road; but this is not noticed, because it belongs to what they call gentlemen's parks; although it keeps the roads wet and the ratepayers have to keep the roads in repair. The roads have no chance to get dry, the leaves making a deal of labour at the autumn of the year. And the surveyor can't get the stones on in the months of October and November, which is the proper time to do the work; and then in the month of April the men have to pick the stones off again, or they would be rolling about all the summer, and often cause the horses to fall down. But now they break the stones very small, and they are soon ground into dirt; the roads are getting very thin in this part of Surrey.

England's greatness no man can nor will deny,
Her prestige the labourer sustains;
The roast beef of Old England the labour supply,
And the glory of England maintain.
Labourers cause the resource to be culled from the land,
Or raise by their toil and their skill;
The malt tax is gone - then be of good cheer:
You can, if you wish, brew a good cask of ale!
The clod of depression will soon pass away
If let into farms of four to one hundred acres
(And no man ought to have more) your rent you could pay,
And the farmer's monopolization be all done away!

Not Sufficient Means.

At the Middleton Cheney petty sessions, on Monday, the 25th, a middle-aged farm labourer, named William Peckover, in receipt of 10s. a week, from which had to be deducted one shilling for rent, was summoned on the ground that he, being possessed of sufficient means, did not contribute towards the maintenance of his father. Evidence of the chargability having been given, the defendant was ordered to pay half-a-crown a week.

George Wade, fifty-nine years of age, and William Wade, his brother, were also summoned on a like charge. The relieving officer deposed that the father was in receipt of 2s.3d. and two loaves weekly, making altogether about 3s.5d.; and as it was shown that George was in receipt of 12s. a week, and only paid 6d. a week rent, whilst William was only in receipt of 10s. a week, and paid 1s. a week for rent, the full amount allowed by the guardians was ordered to be divided between them in the following proportions: George to pay 2s.3d. a week, and his brother 1s.2d.

But perhaps the hardest case of all was that of John Mayo, a stonebreaker on the roads, earning 10s. a week, and sixty-three years of age, paying 1s. a week rent, who was ordered to pay 1s.6d. a week towards the maintenance of his father, 83 years of age.

To the reader: I think these officials ought to break stones all their lives, and only have the same to exist on all their lifetime, and then they would not be so hard-hearted towards their fellow-creatures. I feel myself indebted to the poor hard-working men, and I have sometimes given them twopence to get a pint of beer: but little do those who ride in their four-wheeled carriages ever think of them. I often think what little thought they have for the poor.

Faith, Hope, and Charity.

I recollect the clergyman at the time of the confirmation telling me to remember Faith, Hope, and Charity. If I understand the meaning of these three words, it seems to me like three virgin sisters that came down from heaven to earth to get husbands. Faith soon met with a match, and was married to Abraham, the father of the faithful; and Hope was and is courted by every one - the scholar, the soldier, and the tradesman; but poor Charity wanders up and down, neglected and disregarded by almost all men.

When faith and hope are at an end, charity will burn with its brightest flame. Sixth chapter of Luke, 38th verse: "Give, and it shall be given unto you; good measure, pressed down, and shaken together, and running over, shall men give into your bosom. For with the same measure that ye mete withal it shall be measured to you again." What will those beings meet with who give my fellow-countrymen fourteen days for asking for a crust of bread on an empty stomach?

A Night's Lodging at the Union.

I saw two men who went for a night's lodgings at the union. They were tailors, and their hands were wrung raw through jamming flints. They were kept there till eleven o'clock in the day: but their poor hands were not fit for work if they could meet with employment. How wrong it is to keep them so late in the day! It is not enough to oppress and trample upon the poor!

There will be many of us found unfaithful stewards at the Great Day if we do not relieve them. But let a man get a hole in his coat, and he might travel till his soles dropped from his feet before he could meet with employment. I have seen thousands on the road, travelling in a terribly deplorable condition; and to hear their pitiful tales, and see the little children in arms and round their heels has caused my heart to ache many a time.

Now, we hear much talk of our superiors. I don't believe in them: neither do I in inferiors. We read in our Bibles that we are all one flesh and blood; and if we can act the Samaritan's part, I feel it is our duty to do so. I have seen the parsons give a black look at me, as if I had no right to speak to them.

Now, to ask for a crust of bread on an empty stomach I think is a most serious thing, especially when there is a feeling as if the worms are gnawing the inside. I have seen some of my fellow-creatures bite their food as if they could not get it into their stomach quick enough; and I have known these poor unfortunate creatures come to my door and ask for a crust of bread, or for a glass of water, and for so doing to be taken by the policeman before the magistrates, who have committed them to fourteen days' imprisonment. This sort of thing, I think, is a disgrace to a civilised country. We read in our Bibles, "The foxes have holes, and the birds of the air have nests," &c.

Now, I live twelve miles from a union workhouse, and I have had these, my fellow-creatures, come to me wet through and ask to be allowed to lie down under cover for the night. They have been willing and good minded men for work. I have often given them jobs to do, and I have always found them honest - never at any time having lost any of my tools; and I never put them under lock and key.

I think we ought to have a place in each parish throughout the country, with a piece of land adjoining the building, so that they might cultivate it for the benefit of their country, and also for themselves. We have free access to the air, also to water, and why not to the land? It is man's instinct from his Maker.

Silent Pool.

I have thought, when I have been watching the beautiful stream of water running from the Silent Pool, in the parish of Albury (which stream has been running for a number of years) what a bountiful Providence presides over us! How useful it would be to run into large towns, where I have heard complaining of filthy water. Then there are springs at Abinger, and in other valleys, which would be very useful if properly taken care of for the towns.

But now the sewage is emptied into this beautiful water, and poisons the fish, and also human beings. The sewage ought to be worked into the land for the benefit of mankind. It would be the means of growing all kinds of vegetation. From Wandsworth to Salisbury Plain there is sufficient scope of land to take all the sewage made in and around London for a thousand years, and I think this plan ought to be adopted, as it is a serious loss to our country. Prudent attempts sometimes prove successful beyond all expectations, and I hope it will be the instigation of opening up a new channel of industry. I read, "Wilful waste brings woeful want."

Cost of Fish in London.

Touching the very interesting question as to the cost of fish in London and many other towns, I may mention that hundreds of tons of mackerel, herrings, and other eatable fish are regularly wasted in the Isle of Man, because the ring of buyers or brokers hailing from the nearest English ports will only take a portion of what is caught, the remainder being thrown back into the sea or sold as manure.

I trust that something may be done so that all classes may reap the benefit of the harvest of the sea, and that our legislature will do something to lessen this great and monstrous sin. There are many thousands of people who would like to purchase them for their families, if they were sold cheap.

The collieries, mines, fisheries, and wild animals - all these ought to be reclaimed, and used only in the interest of every individual. Instead of being so used as to benefit all alike, collieries enrich a few private individuals at the expense of all the rest, who often have to pay extravagant prices for coal, beyond all proportion to the cost of getting it; and a large number of the poor, in the most inclement of seasons, are compelled to remain shivering with cold in their miserable hovels, with scarcely a spark of fire to warm themselves. How simple it would be for our legislature to alter this state of things! Those who oppress the poor reproach their Maker.

A Bad Harvest.

There is a great complaining when there is a bad harvest. This is our own making, since we allow monopolization of the land. I have known large farmers, living within four miles of my home, let their wheat ricks stand till the rats and mice have eaten them almost hollow. I have heard of three bushels of rats and mice being killed at one time. One farmer has let his wheat stand in sacks until it has rotted. The sacks were taken away, and the wheat remained upright from the mint getting into it, all because he could not get a certain price for it. I have heard my father say he once knew a farmer who was bid £39 a load for his wheat, and because he could not get £40 he would not sell it. He afterwards sold it for £14 a load.

Now this is what I call a free country. True, it is for those who have their thousands a year coming in. I know one who has £100,000 a year coming in, and he buys up the land, and compels the farmer to lay it down, the result being what I call tumbled down. He could not go to the expense of cleaning it; it lies almost dormant, growing scarcely enough grass to cover a mouse through the summer, with yellow moss coming on it, where it used to grow a load of wheat to the acre, on an average. The staddles that the wheat was on at one time are now tumbling about the rick-yards.

Then this same man has an enormous lot of timber, bringing him a lot of wealth every year. There is no tax upon that. But if the like of myself were to build a pigstye, or a little back washouse, this class of man would come round and put a tax on it. Because I employ labour I have to bear the burden of taxation.

To the reader, whoever he might be: Wake up and send the right men to the House of Commons, so that we may get these unequal laws altered! and don't sell your vote for a meal of victuals, or a pot or two of beer! You must think it is intended for a better purpose than that! Men born to titles and fortunes attend but little to the cultivation of the mind - pleasure is the idol to which they sacrifice.

British Farmers Left Liverpool.

Two hundred and fifty of our British farmers, as well as a great number of labourers, have lately left Liverpool to seek new homes. Now this is a serious matter. I have heard say that there are 66,675 acres in the New Forest, in the county of Hampshire, belonging to the Crown, and a large farmer made a proposition to bring the land into a better state of cultivation, by letting the people have it, and not for them to leave their homes for America, - and do away with the stag and game preserves.

According to an official return, the money taken to the United States last year by emigrants from Europe amounted to £6,000,000. Considerably more than one third of this was taken from the United Kingdom. The sum named does not include passage money or money paid for railway transit after their arrival, but merely available cash.

The Meaning of Agricultural Depression.

What is the meaning of agricultural depression? I look upon the year 1879 as a sort of visitation. As to the seasons, they have worked very true since the years 1814 and 1816: in the one there was a great drought, and in the other a great deal of wet, according to what my father told me. And since that we have had the potato famine as a sort of visitation, and the rinderpest, which was a great loss to the farmers.

As to the foot and mouth disease, I know the public think the remedy is worse than the disease; for where the stock is properly seen to, there is seldom any fatal cases. As for putting a stop to the markets, that throws a great stagnation on trade throughout the country. What the council can be thinking about I cannot understand! The farmers can't have their stock stocked.

I myself had two cows that wanted to be driven, and I had to go three miles to the policeman, and when I got there he was not at home. The result was I couldn't take them, so lost the chance.

Now, there are hundreds served the same way, and we shall feel the effects for a long time. As for stamping it out, that is very unreasonable. There always were plagues, and will be all the time there is so much dilatoriness in our farmyards and rickyards.

I once heard a valuer say that a good cleared-up rickyard, with the ricks well thatched, was worth a hundred pounds a year to a farmer. But I am sorry to say there is scarcely one to be found anywhere. Since they had the machinery they let their kavins lay in a lump and rot, and their strawricks left open to the weather. Then the stock lie down on the wet straw, and the result is they take cold and get fever on them, and then have the foot and mouth disease.

Then, again, the farmers take more land than they can properly cultivate, and a great deal of it is laying dormant; it produces nothing but yellow moss and thistles. The farmer has to pay the same rent, tithe, and taxes as he does for the land that grows more produce; and I am sorry they lose it in that way - that it does no one any good.

The Machines.

Since machinery has been in vogue our land has been going out of cultivation. Sometimes the steam plough is set to work, and at other times, for want of sufficient strength, this cannot be done; the result is, very little good is done, and that at great cost to the farmer. I have been told this by the owners of steam ploughs.

Then they have reaping and mowing machines, and I have seen their work done in a disgraceful way; in fact, if a farm labourer was to do his work in the same way, he would have six months' imprisonment, and serve him right too!

I once saw a machine at work in a park, and the steward observed to me that the grass was cut nice and level. I replied that it was, and, putting my hand down to measure the bottom grass, I found it just the length of my hand. My father used to tell his mowers that one inch from the bottom was worth four from the top.

Now, I have nothing to say against machinery. I think it is a great benefit to mankind, when it can be got into working order. But farmers often have their horses on to their machinery, and the plough lies in the hedge rue and goes rusty; then their land gets foul, and they find fault with the seasons.

The truth is, they have more land than they have capital properly to cultivate. Take our little parish. We have here fields that have not had a load of manure emptied upon them for a hundred years! Then they are called poor fields!

Now, if the landlords were to build cottages on the poor fields, and allow the tenants to keep a pig and a cow, how much more valuable his land would soon become! - as I once told them at a vagrancy meeting, Doctor Stallard and the Hon. A. Herbert being present.

Dr. Stallard and the Honourable A. Herbert.

These gentlemen had been speaking from the platform, and any of those in the body of the hall were invited to speak, as the meeting was about to be brought to a close. There were several clergymen and other gentlemen present. The time was half-past eight, and I, with my old round frock on, was the first called upon to speak; and what little I said I thought was answerable to the cause.

I told the meeting if we could get three or four cottages built upon every hundred acres of land, and two or three acres of land attached to each cottage, so that the labouring class could keep a cow and pigs, then there would be something for the women to do as well as the men, and that this plan would greatly increase the value of the property of the aristocracy, and greatly decrease pauperism; that we should not then need the union workhouse, and that it would almost have the desired effect of abolishing our poor rates.

I then said, "Gentlemen, - Providence guides us in mysterious ways! I was in the village of Ewhurst this morning, and I saw there a child, three years old, which put me in mind of a rabbit after it had been skinned! The woman who has got the child has a large family of her own," - and to make myself understood, I put my hand to my head, and said the woman had shaved the hair from the child's head to destroy the vermin that was on it! The child's mother had had a large family, and a long illness, and had just then died. The poor child had been neglected.

I said I thought some one ought to be placed in each parish throughout the country, as this was not the only similar case I had seen in our little parish. The speaking upon this great and serious question was kept up till half-past nine o'clock.

Now, I saw an old farmer one day, and I said to him, "If you have men capable of driving your team of horses, and fattening your bullocks, sheep, and pigs, surely they ought to have two or three acres of land, if they choose, so that they could provide for old age. As it is, you take every ounce of steel out of them, and the like of myself have to pay for their sustenance in the union workhouse.

This is what I call a great shame, because we have to pay so much more in proportion than the higher classes in the shape of rates and taxes - cottages being so much higher assessed after the rate than larger properties."

The farmer said I talked impossibilities, and that was all he could say. And yet this old farmer could almost talk a dog's hind leg off, as the saying is.

I said I would tell him what agricultural depression was, and how, to a great extent it originated. I asked him if he brought his sons and daughters up in the same way that he and his sisters were.

I said, "No! You used to fat the sheep and bullocks, and hold the plough, and if you went to market you had to walk, or go in an old rickety cart; your sisters used to put on ankle petticoats, which kept them dry and comfortable, and their linsey-woolsey aprons, and perhaps an old round frock. They would go out in the morning and milk the cows and cram the fowls, feed the pigs, and dairy the butter, brew the beer, and shine the good long kitchen table until you could almost see your face reflected in it. They cooked some good pork and souse, and the workmen and all sat down together; you often consulted the men as to the best way to go about different jobs of work, and they studied your welfare; the workmen, from their practical experience, often knew better than yourself how to proceed with the work.

I will now show up the contrast between the farmers' sons and daughters of the present day and the past. Their sons are now sent to college, and they get on their stag-hunting horses, and ride to market in their four-wheeled carriages. Their daughters are sent to boarding schools, to learn to play the piano, and chignon their hair, and draw a great train of clothes behind them up Guildford town, which is almost ready to trip one up!"

Otherwhile the old farmer broke out and said, "You talk of too plain facts for me to converse with you!"

So the next time I went that way he met me again, and he said, "Bad news!"

"Bad news! What's up now then?" I thought he had had a great loss of some description.

He said, "Wheat yields so bad!"

I saw that he was in an excited state of mind. He said the land would go out of cultivation shortly. I said that it would not; all that we wanted was to have the lime kilns put into working condition; it is the lime nutriment that wheat and vegetation requires; it lightens and cleanses and purifies the land. There used to be one hundred lime kilns burning in our little parish, and it took six horses to draw a load of chalk; but now, having good roads, three horses could do the work. Now there is not one kiln burning in the parish.

When farmers used lime they grew twelve sacks and two bushels of wheat to the acre. They used to be very particular as to their seed; they cut wheat with a sickle, and would have it cut high if any rubbish was amongst it, that the rubbish might not be taken into the barn. The men who thrashed it had three-pence a hundred for all the docks they could find, and a pint of good home-brewed ale at night, which revived their spirits after a hard day's work!

The farmer studied his men's good in those days. If he had not got a fat pig in his pound he would sell him one, and find him in peas to fat it with, and had what was called a 'jollification' in killing it. The labourer then had a good large garden, but now he has the greater portion of his garden taken from him, and has to do away with his pigstye, because the proud, haughty people about thought it a nuisance!

I know a farmer who has kept an old stock hog for the last fifty years - and it might be a hundred years old for what I know! - within three feet of his kitchen fireplace, and I never knew but one death in the house in all my time; so that I don't think this to be a nuisance. You see, if a poor farm labourer gets a good fat pig in his stye it is called a nuisance, but I think the greatest nuisance is in his having an empty cupboard.

I once heard of a parson and the inspector of nuisances going to a poor man's cottage, and the poor man took them to the cupboard, and there was only sufficient bread there to bait a few mousetraps, and he said that that was where the greatest nuisance laid; he thought it would be more healthful if he had a good fat pig in his stye.

I once knew a parson's wife who visited a poor man's cottage, and she told his wife that she did not use economy, or she would not be so bad off.

The poor woman said, "Perhaps, ma'am, you would like to take my husband's twelve shillings next Saturday and lay it out for me?"

The parson's wife took the money and laid it out; she got sugar, tea, candles, meat, cheese, butter, and all the things very nice for the week, and brought back one shilling and six pence, which pleased the poor woman to think she had met with such a kind lady to bring her such luxuries; but she said, "If you please ma'am, where are my seven gallons of flour, which come to ten shillings and sixpence?" The lady went and bought and paid for the flour out of her own pocket. The lady never went to lay out the poor woman's money any more; neither did she trouble her head any more about her economy.

All this I know for plain truth. Now this poor woman rolled in luxury the next week after the lady had laid the money out for her; but this is a curious question, not to be laughed at, particularly by those who have an abundance of this world's wealth. We shall all be upon one level in our future destiny.

Contrast in Prices.

I now feel it a duty to show the contrast in the prices of different articles. From 1849 to 1854 everything that a farmer produced was very low in price. I well remember selling 3lbs. of fresh butter for 1s.9d., 3 doz. new laid eggs 1s.9d., 3 rabbits 1s.9d., a bushel of flour 6s., a nice young five-year old horse for 30 guineas, a nice young cow in full profit, £10, fat pigs at 3s. per stone, fat sheep at 4s. per stone, and fat bullocks at 4s. per stone.

But now there is such an outcry about agricultural depression the prices are altered. I have sold 3lbs. of fresh butter for 6s., 3 doz. new laid eggs, 4s. 6d., the average price; 3 rabbits 4s.6d., and I have known five-year-old horses sell for 70 guineas, a nice young cow £30, fat hogs 4s.6d. per stone, fat sheep 7s.6d., fat bullocks 7s.6d., a bushel of flour 9s., average price. All other things are fetching a good price, and therefore it does not look so very bad for the English farmer.

The Annual Eatable Production in this Country.

The annual eatable production in this country is estimated at £250,000,000. In the harvest of 1880 there were 3,000,000 acres of wheat reaped, and, allowing seed for a similar number of acres, there remained only about 10,000,000 quarters of wheat in our country for our own consumption, the estimated quantity we require being 25,000,000 quarters per year; so that we shall now be under the necessity of receiving 15,000,000 quarters from foreign countries in order to supply the hungry with bread.

This reader, is a very serious matter, worthy the consideration of the legislature. If anything were to occur with respect to our food importation, we should be like they were in Paris a short time back; not only that, but our country is now in a sad state.

We have, I repeat, still remaining about 16,000,000 acres of common and waste land. I do not believe that there is one acre but what would pay for cultivating; and if honestly held by the Government in trust for the nation, and let to the labouring classes at a low rental, we should be able to produce 16,000,000 quarters of wheat more than we do now; and that would be the means of keeping our mone at home.

The Income of England.

Our friend the Rev. G. R. P—— recently took an active part in a public meeting held at Newbury upon our poor law reform, the meeting being called by the Liberal club at that place, the mayor presiding.

The rector of Burgclerc, in the course of an effective address, held that our poor law, as at present administered, is economically, morally and politically wrong.

First, economically: the cost is levied on only about one fourth of the property in the country. The income of England is over £900,000,000, while only £250,000,000 are rated for the relief of the poor; so that over £650,000,000 get off altogether. Lands and houses pay; founded property of all kinds pay nothing.

Owing to the enormous extention of trade, the personal property outweighs the other in proportion of over six and a half to two and a half; and yet the two and a half still continues to bear the whole burden of local taxation - not only of the relief of the poor, but of roads, education and sanitary appliances.

This, I think, is economically unjust. Bearing in mind that it is not poverty, but destitution, which is to be relieved, I maintain that this is not a local, but a national question; and if for convenience the government choose to deal with it locally, at any rate the property in the district, from whatever source derived, should bear the burden, and not the property derived from one source - land and houses only.

Second, morally: it is unfair that the spend-thrift should be allowed by law to dip his fingers into his thrifty neighbour's savings, unless every means had been first taken to compel the spendthrift to save. How can we oblige the spendthrift to save for himself, and so lay the burden on the right shoulders?

There is but one way, and that is by the adoption of that excellent plan of national insurance, by which, as you know, every male person would be compelled to invest £10 with the Government by the time he was twenty-one. The daily cost of a pint of beer for three years would more than do this.

Do this class of men ever do any hard laborious work? I say, No! Then why should they envy a poor man a pint of beer? They are drones in the hive, and live in luxury which the poor man has to produce. I think all property ought to be charged with the maintenance of the destitute, and that relief should be administered so as to encourage thrift, and discourage waste. Every parish should manage its own affairs, and, if required assist the neighbouring parishes.

The Letter on Agricultural Depression.

I addressed a communication to the 'West Sussex Gazette', and it appeared in that paper on the 16th September, 1880. The letter was not printed as I wrote it, and therefore I write it again, as it was written for the public good.

A farmer said to me he thought it became every man to trouble his head with his own business, and I quite agreed with him in that idea; but, as I thought there was a little jealousy mixed up in the expression from him, I observed that he was the parent of children, and that was the case with myself; and when we saw land going out of cultivation so fast, I said I thought it only right that we should do all we could to prevent it, for the welfare of our children, as well as ourselves. So this is the letter I wrote:-

"TO THE EDITOR. SIR, - Noticing that a great deal is being said everywhere about agricultural depression, I often think how wrong it is to find fault with the seasons, as that is what I call finding fault with an overruling Providence. There are those who take prizes at Smithfield Show, but I think those persons' land cultivation should be inspected before they are awarded prizes. Take our little parish of Ewhurst, in Surrey. As a rule every farmer who uses one hundred acres of land ought not to have more than twenty-five acres, according to the stock he keeps, and the capital he expends on it.

I know a little farmer who uses twenty-five acres of the poorest land in the county of Surrey. He gave £5 a year rent when he first took it. He started as a farm labourer, and worked very hard himself. His wife has had a family of eighteen children; and she told me this herself. He built a nice little homestead on the land, which is a credit and a model to the little hamlet that he lives in. But after he had done all this they doubled and trebled his rent. He has now taken the property on a lease, and I believe it is paying him a very good profit. He has been enabled to buy a piece of land, on which he has built himself a good compact house.

Then I write to say I one day saw an old farmer, and I said to him I believed his labourer was earning him ten shillings a day. His reply was that he had been a farmer over sixty years, and he never knew before he had a man who earned him ten shillings a day. I continued and said I knew him to be a thinking man, and I asked him to weigh the matter over in his mind, and give me his conclusive opinion the next time we met each other. I knew the work was remunerative.

When I saw him again the old farmer said he had talked to his brother, and also to the workmen, about the amount earned by his man, and they concluded that I was not very wide of the mark. I said I did not at all exaggerate; in three years' time I reckoned he would be getting fifteen shillings a day for his man's work.

Now, in my parish I could find employment for five hundred farm labourers for four months in the year, and each one could earn ten shillings a day for his employer.

Then I write to say that the lime kilns and a great many of the farm buildings are in a terrible delapidated state. And then, again, I think landlords should put guttering round their farm buildings. I inquired in Guildford the cost of guttering, and was told it was ninepence per yard, and that it would stand for many years. As it is, all the soluble salts are washed out of the manure before it is taken on to the land. It has also been proved by chemical process that the wheat, and a good many other grains, consist of lime nutriment; and good manure lightens and clenses the land of vermin. I like to use the little talent I have for the welfare of my fellow-countrymen, for with any disarrangement of our food importation England will be liable to a famine.

I am, yours, &c.,
One who is a Well-wisher to his Fellow-Countrymen.

Ewhurst Green,
Guildford,
Surrey."

Earning Ten to Fifteen Shillings a Day.

Now, I feel it is a duty to explain how these men earn from ten to fifteen shillings a day. In the first place, we have large wide hedge rues, and these are what I call nests of rubbish. Vermin breed in them. The seed of the rubbish is blown out into the field. Now, if the farmer were to set the men to burn the scraps and rotten leaves, and the light mould, into black ashes, I calculate they would be worth threepence a bushel, and the workman would get forty bushels per day.

I have known farmers send their teems four miles for wood ashes, and it would take them all day to collect them, as they had a good many cottages to call at. They paid sixpence per bushel for them. At the same time they could burn the stuff upon the farm, to answer the same purpose, and would do away with a lot of rubbish. But sometimes the landlords are very particular; they will not allow the tenant farmer to do this. It would pay him well to go into his copses for this purpose, there often being a good depth of mould.

If farmers were to set their men to cut heath they would derive a good profit from the work. Heath is good to go on land, particularly for stiff land and wheat crops. It causes the water to penetrate into the surface of the earth; whilst if water is allowed to remain on the surface of the land, it destroys the little fibres of the roots in the ground, causing the wheat to go yellow in the spring, and the farmers to get bad yields at harvest.

Well, take into consideration whatever form of government we might have, it greatly requires looking into. I believe if there were a tax put upon land that did not give its proper produce of vegetation - on timber in the fields, which is a great hindrance to vegetation, and also on shrubs and stag parks, these taxes would do good in bringing the land into a better state of cultivation.

Land held without any regard to whether it is productive or not is surely a national loss, for which its owners are morally responsible. For we are told in the best of all books that the earth was given to the children of men - that is, to obtain from it sustenance for those that dwell thereon; and I feel quite sure that those who are endeavouring to increase its productiveness deserve to be regarded as among the great benefactors of mankind. However they may enjoy the produce, they can't annihilate the land.

I say, thank God that the land remains. If mankind could have had such communications with the inhabitants of the sun or of the moon, or with any other objects visible or invisible, as parting with territory from the face of the earth, to obtain the means of supplying their immediate purposes, long before our time there would not have been a foot of land for an Englishman, and probably not for a man of any other country, to be born upon.

A little tradesman recently told me that he went into the country to bury a relative, and when they got to the churchyard they had to wait there outside for an hour, as Master Reynard had taken the parson in a wrong direction. He knew the time he had to be there, and presently came galloping up with his horse in a lather of sweat.

To the English farmers: so long as March, 1864, a respectable poor man named James Clark, at Broseley, in Staffordshire, had his goods seized for non-payment of a church rate made upon him. He was a labouring man, with a wife and seven children, a bed-ridden mother eighty-three years of age, and an imbecile sister forty-three years of age, the two last receiving parish relief. The amount of the church rate asked of him was 1s.31/2d., and for this the churchwardens seized nearly all the furniture in his cottage, compelling his children to lie on the floor the following night.

In January of the same year, a poor widow of seventy years of age, living at Gresford, had a clock, a mahogany table, four brass candlesticks, three brass pans, a cloth, a pair of scales, and a teapot seized for a church rate of a few pence.

These are the acts of the poor man's church, and this is the way in which the poor enjoy free worship in the Establishment. The rights of the poor mean the right to be imprisoned or distrained upon if they do not pay, whether they go to church or not. Does any other church do this?

If a poor man's child has to be baptized the clergyman exacts his fee; if a poor man gets married, the fee is charged; if he is buried, the fee is charged; and a man can't put a stone over his wife's grave, or the grave of his child, without being compelled to pay more fees.

The clergy of the Established Church, who are paid by tithes granted by the State, are the only ministers of religion who charge the poor man for such services, and yet it is called a "grand old institution." It has stood for over 300 years, true; but it is to draw the last drop of blood out of the poor man and the farmers.

To you English farmers: how long will you let these wicked principles be carried out? The clergy administer the sacrament on Sunday, but I think they put it away in their wardrobes with their surplices on Sunday night, for on Monday morning they are off to their cruel sport, and treading into the earth that which we ought to have for our sustenance. They have spun the web for many years; they have the land, and won't let the working classes have the use of it; the result is, they have sucked the last drop of blood from the wretched fly.

I have seen spades and shovels and furniture sold by auction in the public stock market at Guildford to pay tithes. And then they go round with their plates on Sunday to collect more money. But if a poor man were to ask for a copper, they would give him from fourteen days' to three months' hard labour, on an empty stomach - a heavy load to carry.

I have read in the Liberation papers that one portion was to support the poor, the second portion to support the church, and the other for the support of the parson; but these great spiders have reached over and got it all. Again I ask English farmers, how long will you bear this burden?

I write upon this subject with no ill-feeling towards any man, woman, or child, and hope no jealousy will arise towards me. I feel that I have no superiors, neither have I inferiors. We read in our Master's great Book that we are all one flesh and blood; and it says in that beautiful prayer, "Deliver us from evil," and "Thy will be done;" and I say it heartily too, to the great English nation.

A Letter to the 'English Labourers' Chronicle'.

I wrote the following letter for the 'English Labourers' Chronicle' in 1878. I sent it to Leamington on Good Friday, but it got mislaid, and never went in the press. My little boy had 3d. each from different people for writing copies of it; and got orders for six copies, but he got tired of writing them. So I told him I would write this little book. This is the letter as I wrote it for the press:-

"TO THE EDITOR. Sir, - Noticing one of your correspondents wishes the likes of myself to make a statement as to what I could produce, I beg to say I keep four cows, four weaners, and a horse, by purchasing a few grains. I have only two and a half acres of ground, but I make it a rule to well dress the land every year. Good dressing is what the land requires. Through want of dressing, not one acre in fifty gives its proper produce of vegetation.

Take the poorest waste land in any county, and notice the cottage gardens, and that will show what cultivation and the humble pigstye and other saved manure will do.

I say this is a public question, and must before many years become a foremost question. If a tax were put on the waste land, and also on timber and shrubs and wild hedge-rues, I believe it would be a good tax to bring our land into a better state of cultivation. It would be the means of giving many the chance to have a piece of land who have not got the chance now. There are men who have the land to make a god of their cruel sport.

I thought it was a serious question when I read in one of the London papers that there were seven hundred thousand persons who knew not on the morrow where to obtain a breakfast. Why should these men and women be locked out from the use of the land? To all classes of society this state of things is becoming serious. While, if the land were properly cultivated, and the game laws abolished, there need not be a man, woman, or child without the common necessaries of life.

At present we see one portion of society living in luxury, selfishness, and laziness; others the victims of pinching poverty and the objects of woe. I myself take an interest in helping the poor. I walked twenty-four miles to a vagrancy meeting, where Dr. Stallard, the Hon. A. Herbert and a few magistrates and clergymen were present; and I told them what could be done to prevent so many being unemployed. I hope to be at one of the meetings of the unemployed, and I shall be able to tell them.

Now I believe in an Overruling Providence, and often wonder how those rich people who profess to believe in the gospel of Christ can be so unconcerned as they often are to the necessities and miseries of the poor and afflicted. The magistrates give fourteen days' imprisonment for asking for a crust of bread on an empty stomach! If our Saviour's advice is any good, how will the like of those give an account of their stewardship before their great Master?

Now, as to Joseph Arch and George Mitchell ('One from the Plough'), I think they have done more for the oppressed than any other two men in this or any other generation; therefore, the sooner we get men like these into the House of Commons, the better it will be for the lower and middle classes of society. We want men who will study the welfare of the many, and not the few who have got an abundance.

From your well-wisher,
ELI HAMSHIRE

Ewhurst Green,
Near Guildford, Surrey."

The Franchisement of Property.

I once knew a little tradesman who had purchased for £80 an old cottage and garden. He went to a lawyer to see what it would cost to make it freehold, and the lawyer told him £70. I think there must be something very unjust in this state of things, which should be altered by our legislature. Cottages are much wanted in this part of the country. This little tradesman was anxious to build the cottages, and the lawyer reduced it to £56, and made it freehold.

To the reader: if you purchase any copyhold property, be sure you make it freehold before you build on it, or the lawyers and the lords of manors will take the advantage of your industry, and the money you expend on it.

Then, again, there is primogeniture and entail of property, which requires the consideration of our legislature. I have known property go to ruin through the eldest son coming into it at his father's death. The result is, fathers have an ill-feeling against their sons; and I have known it to be the case where the father would let gentlemen's houses fall to the ground rather than have them repaired. Just the same with the land: he would let that go out of cultivation - the farm buildings dropping to the ground.

Then I once knew a town where they wanted a piece of ground for a bury-ing-place, but, because it was entailed property, the gentleman could neither sell it to the townspeople nor give it to them. This is what I call a very serious question, and I hope all M.P.'s will take it into consideration. Whatever form of government we might have, it greatly requires looking into.

The Guildford Town Council.

I saw in the 'West Surrey Times' - which I take in regularly, being a valuable local paper for information for the welfare of the many - that the Guildford Town Council were getting into a fog about the sewage question, and I wrote this letter to the editor:-

"SIR, - I see the Guildford Town Council have got into a fog as to the sewage question, like many other town councils. I have noticed that there are some fine slopes of fertile plains on the borders of the town; and cisterns might be adopted by which the sewage could be applied to the land. The land would become a great benefit to the town, if let to labouring men, and tradesmen, who keep their horses.

I know there are a great many persons in country villages who would like to have two or three acres of land, if they could get it. There being so much monopoly in the land, those who would are unable to get any. It is well known that there are plenty of large farms in the market, but these are not what the public want. They each want a small piece of land, so that they might grow a little fodder for their horses, cow, &c.

A small farmer once took me into his dairy, where he had just churned 35 lbs. of butter; and this quantity he churned twice a week. I saw a long sewage tank in the little farmyard. He put the sewage on the land, and he found he was well paid by so doing. He had only sixteen acres of land; he could keep nine cows, and grow roots to weigh 14 lbs., and more.

I live in a parish where we have had a piece of allotment land for fifty years. I tell my neighbours in the next parish, Cranleigh, that we are fifty years before them. The Cranleigh people are very much pinched up with small gardens, like many other parishes. If they want a gallon of potatoes they are obliged to get them from America! We find a portion of the allotment very useful. Vegetables are grown there, and in every way the cultivation of the land is helpful in bringing up our families.

I hope to live long enough to see this plan carried out in every village and town throughout the kingdom. In my view this would afford a tremendous impulse to the great weal of industry."

Good Advice to Young Men.

A little piece of good advice to young men that my father gave me when I was young:- he said I was giving my mind to public-house company, that it was more for the sake of the company than for the drink, and bad would become of me if I did not give it up! See how many are brought on to ruin through their black tobacco pipe and public-house company! He seldom ever said much to me and my brothers; but what he said had weight with my conscience.

I remember going to the beershop one night and singing and playing the concertina till ten o'clock. Then I went with my companions to the public-house. There were ten of us in company. A hunting feast was being held in the parlour, and I was called upon to sing, the concertina being the first ever seen in Ewhurst. I could play the lead, and sing seconds.

I began to play gaily "The Troubadour Touched his Guitar." I admit I sang rather loud, for I recollect once singing with a policeman, and set the teatrays on the jar!

The landlady came into the taproom and said, "Hampshire! You ought to know yourself better than to come here and up singing like that, when you knew we had a party on in the other room!"

I said we had a right to be merry, as well as those had in the other room, and that we did not wish to interfere with her company. The gentlemen came out to us, and I felt bound to go on singing! But I told the landlady that she should remember I had brought her a good lot of customers, and that I always paid for what I had. I said I would never enter her house again to spend another evening, and I can set any one at defiance to say that they ever saw me there since!

This is another view of 'The Bull's Head' where Eli had his run-in with the landlady, Mrs Child.

I then went to the beershop as usual for a month; I took this habit into consideration, and I found the expense averaged 9d. each night - three nights a week, amounting to 2s.3d. a week. I thought I could put 3d. to this sum, and save the 2s.6d. every week. I gave up the beershop and did so, until I had accumulated £17.10s.

I do not mean that I would debar any poor man of a pint of beer when he wanted it. We read in our Bible that we should give strong drink to those who are ready to perish; and therefore if a man has been using the heavy irons of toil throughout the day, let him have a pint of good home-brewed beer to revive his spirits, that he might feel thankful to his Maker for the health and strength he has had during the day.

I often pity poor women when I know they have but very little with which to provide for their families, and I think those who take their turtle soup and splendid jellies, and eat their roast beef and venison, &c.; drink their claret and sherries, besides their March and October and Burton ales, ought to reflect upon the circumstances of them. My advice to the wife is that she try and make the home comfortable, and brew her own beer, which is very easy to do.

Now, I should like to see these high class folk teetotallers, as they often bring upon themselves premature death by their free drinking. Then, again, when these people give their mind to that beastly habit, they are apt to hacker and splutter about, and say that which they would not say when they are sober. But I often think it is in their mind when they are sober; they are like the hedgehog, they can't open their minds before they are wet!

Those who have no government over themselves I would advise to be teetotallers; for we often hear of guns, razors, hammers, and many other dangerous instruments being used, besides filling our unions and prisons, and making homes uncomfortable, and poor children feeling so much the effect of it.

Whoever the reader might be, let him go to his Maker, and ask Him to give him the power to keep from this evil habit, instead of going to the pothouse, and standing a pot with one, and a pot with another. These are what I call goodnatured fools! I have often known their friends turn round and fight them - when "the drink was in and the wit out!" It is then that the money goes! So my advice to all young men and women is to learn this poetry, and think of its meaning:-

So, its come, all you frolicsome fellows,
And listen unto my advice,
And while I engage your attention
I will give you a piece of advice:
It's while you are wanton and single,

You are free to do just as you please;
But when you alter your station
It's time to alter your ways.

So always take this as a warning -
You will find as you journey through life,
If you mean to live and be happy,
Be loving and kind to your wife.

There are some men blessed with plenty,
Both gold and silver in store,
Their wives they will slight and neglect,
To sport and to ravish with more.
But, believe me, this sort of behaviour
This bitter reflection will bring -
By harbouring a snake in your bosom,
You will feel the effects of the sting.
So always, &c.

If poverty comes to invade you,
O never deem it as a curse,
But remember the promise you made:
'Twas to marry for better, for worse.
So its join your affections together,
Let strife never enter your head,
You' will find that you're richer than some
Tho' you have but a morsel of bread.
So always, &c.

If you should frequent the ale-house,
I will tell you, as sure as you're born,
When your money is all gone and spent,
They will certainly treat you with scorn.
For the world is got to such a pitch,
It's puffed up with pride and disdain,
And a man for to be without money
Had far better be without brains.
So always, &c.

The tobacco affects the brain and causes dwarfs in our country, it also leads to company, the sin of drunkenness, a devil to the soul, a thief to the pocket, the beggar's companion, expels reason, drowns memory, diminishes strength, distempers the body.

Supposing a man has got thousands,
And he has no government:
His means would waste,
And be a disgrace, And die in discontent.

The evil of the heart defaces beauty, corrupts the blood, inflames the liver, weakens the brain, turn men into walking hospitals, causes internal, external, and incurable wounds, is a witch to the senses.

> *But I'll have you mark the old proverbs*
> *The weakest must go to the wall;*
> *O it grieves my mind, but still I find,*
> *Good government is all.*

A wife's sorrow, and the children's dread, makes man become a sot, and self-murderer, who drinks to others good health, and robs himself of his own.

> *If you will keep good company,*
> *You will never do amiss;*
> *But it grieves your mind,*
> *But still you will find,*
> *Good government is all.*

My Mother's Prayer.

I well remember my mother once telling me that the landlord was going to sell her furniture the next week; and she went down the road and sat down on a stone-lump, and cried to her Maker to protect her in her trouble. The next morning there came a letter to say that she was to go to Guildford, and the Dissenters who preached in her house gave her £5, my mother not having known that she was to receive anything for the use of her house. She said she felt as if she could fly home to my father, who had been ill twelve months. She was never in such distressing difficulties afterwards.

This is what I call 'heart and brain prayer' - a possession, and not a profession. If the reader can get that church in his heart, he will not be far wrong. He will then carry with him a contented disposition, and angry passions will not arise so frequently.

I also remember my mother telling us boys never to make fun of those who are afflicted. I remember a man who used to make fun by imitating her sister, who used to walk with her toes turned in; and when this man had a son born he walked exactly in the same way, and does so at the present time, and always goes by the name of 'Hen-toed Jemmy'.

Then, again, I had an uncle who used to pass remarks and mock and laugh at one poor old woman who had no legs to walk with, and I have heard my mother say that the poor old woman said it would come home to him some day. My uncle had a little boy, about six years old, and some affliction befel him. He lost the use of his legs, and has gone on his hands and feet much the same as the old woman used to go, and does so up to the present day. This visitation happened to occur to a relation of mine. I write this as a warning to the reader.

I think how very wrong it is of any one to make fun of an afflicted one! We have all afflictions of some nature or other to contend with at times.

Then, again, look at poor Tichborne! See what he had to put up with from those Carbineers, and called all kinds of names, because God's mark was on him - different to any other man - not one man in a million like him. But he is as God made him, and that mark no man can take from him. And as those malformation papers are true, who can he be but the true and living Tichborne?

Those people who have not read these papers ought to do so, since I can see no harm in them whatsoever. I think the doctors' evidence ought to have been seen by the public, and then it would not have been such a stumblingblock to so many. The poor mother was a wise woman to keep him in petticoats till he was ten years old. I believe that any mother would know her own suckling child, and more particularly when it has marks on it from its birth - the same as I have myself, and many others whom I know.

Guildford Onslow's Letter.

"THE GROVE, ROPLEY,
Oct. 12, 1881.

My dear Friend, - Pray write what you please about my poor friend Sir Roger Tichborne. A good cause can lose nothing by publicity.

I am confined to my bed with illness. Although nearly three-score years and ten, I thank God I found my Saviour three years ago, and I hope you have Him safe. He is the best of friends. My only regret is I served Him so unfaithfully for so many years. Don't forget: 'Whosoever comes to Me in no wise can be cast out;' and that, 'Now is the day of salvation.'

I return you the slips, with many thanks for the perusal; and I admire your admirable letter. I have an order to see Sir Roger Tichborne on or before next Monday, and if God grants me health enough I shall go and visit him once more - the victim of a papal conspiracy! Wishing you well, with my last words, 'Never forget Him who suffered death for me,' and only ask you to accept His free gift.

Believe me, yours faithfully,
GUILDFORD ONSLOW"

The Tichborne being a great public question - having marks upon him from his birth, and the visitation of Providence befalling a relative of my own, I write this as a caution to the public - never to pass remarks upon those who are in any way afflicted.

I was walking in Guildford on June 30th, 1881, and I saw a poor man playing an harmonium. He was blind, and I went up to him and gave him a penny, and said to him, "How might you have lost your eyesight?"

He said, "I asked God to —— my eyes."

I said, "What!"

He said, "If I tell you the truth, I said, 'God —— my eyes.' "

He did not give me time to get my money out; he stood upon the doorstep of a public-house, and the publican was in a hurry, as there were some races going on at the time. This poor man turned his head, and something seemed to strike his eyes, and he has been blind from that day to this, which is ten years ago. He said to me he thanked God, although he was blind with his natural eyesight in this world, he was not blind to the heavenly paradise.

I said to him, "I wonder you go about playing that instrument."

He said, "I feel happy in singing Sankey's beautiful hymns. I had a hard struggle for twelve months. You read in your Bible that 'Ye must be born again' before you can enter into the kingdom of heaven."

A Terrible Warning.

A short time since a private in the Hampshire Regiment invoked in a profane manner the name of the Deity by making use of the phrase "God strike me blind." He afterwards felt drowsy, and stretched himself on his bed, but when he attempted to open his eyes he found that he could not do so, and he has since been wholly deprived of the use of his eyes. He was conveyed to the Haslar Military Hospital, where he remains.

Ancient Order of Foresters.

I belong to the Ancient Order of Foresters, and there are large mansions in our parish the owners of which would, I believe, if they were kindly invited, patronise our anniversaries and become honourable members. I think the Foresters are, as a rule, a very industrious class of people who try while in health to avoid becoming chargeable on the Poor rates. I think our M.P.s ought to come and assist in this direction.

We have one Esquire in our little parish who does come, and he gave a good lecture at our last anniversary, and put his shoulder to the wheel; he threw down on the table two or three sovereigns on this occasion, to assist the society. This is what I call charity, and setting a good example to his neighbours.

If there were more who would come out like our Esquire it would greatly add to their credit and they would see that our money is put to good interest and that we have good securities for it. How much better it would be for our institutions. We are only getting 2½ per cent. interest at the Post Office Savings Bank. We work hard for our money, and I think we ought to get a better interest for it. We should then be able to have a doctor free for our wives and families, where, as it is now, we find it a heavy burden to pay the doctor's bills.

And I am sorry to say how many there are who can speak from experience as to the burdens of the doctor's bills in this direction; and I think when a man has paid in £35 his contributions ought to be reduced, and when he has paid in £60 he ought to be exempt from paying any more contributions, as he then gets advanced in years and is less able to work; and I think that every man who pays into a society ought to have a share in the land if he choose, as it is man's instinct from his Maker, and the wife and children would have something to do as well as her husband; they would then have a chance to provide for old age. How many young women would like to patronise the matrimonial institution, if they could see a chance of keeping poultry, a pig, and cow, &c.

I believe that this plan would have the desired effect of doing away with our union workhouses and our Poor rates, and I hope these remarks of mine will be read at all anniversaries and have the desired effect of doing a great amount of good.

My subject is short as the time may be taken up at our coming anniversaries in the way of lectures, as this is the only chance the country working classes have to hear them. I am one who is a well-wisher to every industrious man and woman, and more particularly little children.

———————

O money and the land,
Thy praises I will sing:
The fox is my god,
And the stag is my king.
And if the farmers complain,
I take no notice of him but grin;
And we say treading the vegetation is no sin.

To the reader: only fancy forty to sixty horsemen riding over new sown wheat and meadow land in the month of January, breaking down styles, gatebacks and fences; but if a poor old woman was seen taking any home to warm her children's feet, this same class of being would give her from fourteen days to six months' hard labour.

Then again, I pity a few of the English farmers, but not those who patronise it, for I feel afraid I shall have to pay the Poor rates to keep them in the union workhouse. As to Irish farmers, they are waking up in this direction; like other people, they were going to have lynch law on the horsemen, and the farmers would not allow them to hunt.

Now, as to the Irish, they are far in advance of the English, they send Home Rulers and good Liberal members to the House of Commons, and they like myself, don't believe in our Perpetual Pensions List, that they see in the Financial Reform Almanack.

Fox and Stag Hunting, and Perpetual Pensioners, and Civil Service List.

I once knew one of these Perpetual Pensioners who had £11,716.6s.9d. per annum, and he never did anything for the money; he bought a good deal of land and let it go out of cultivation, and he kept a kennel of staghounds.

Mr. Bradlaugh came to Guildford and gave a lecture on this great and serious question. I was invited to be chairman by the secretary of the Reform Club. We want Mr. Bradlaugh or some other Law, to alter this state of things.

The shoemakers of Northampton are a thinking class of men. The Irish are not like us hard-hearted Surrey, and silly Sussex, and simple Essex, and foolish Norfolk, and few others of our little rotten beer and bread and cheese Boroughs. No matter how big a blockhead, if he be a Capitalist, a lawyer, or a parson, or a Perpetual Pensioner, he will do for the above mentioned places.

These as a rule, will support the civil service, and will write out their cheques for £100 and send before they get their goods; but if they run out of a few things such as half a dozen pounds of sugar, or a little salt, &c., they will go to the little tradesman, and get him to give them credit for six months, and when he carries in his bill there is a little deficiency in some way or other; they then keep him waiting for another six months before they will pay his bill.

To the reader: the Liberal members will shortly pass the Franchise Bill. You will then have possession of your vote, and as you have to pay all kinds of taxes to support this Perpetual Pension List, and many other lists besides.

I myself used to pay 1s. as land tax, but now I have to pay 9s.6d.; and I know an aged man who worked hard in his younger days to keep himself from the Poor Rates, and who has no relative whatever, and where he used to pay 2s. as land-tax, he now has to pay 19s.7 1/2d. I consider this tax to be very unjust.

Now these Perpetual Pensioners, bishops and parsons, are staunch Conservatives; they buy and sell their livings, and they make merchandise of their religion; they pay a curate a very small sum to preach; they have got their nests well feathered and all they want is to keep them so; and what they want is to make plenty of gunpowder, and to be able to keep up a strong army to protect their property in every way, and for the English farmer to pay the rent, tithes, and taxes, and to bind the farmer down to grow only what they think proper.

I knew a farmer who wished to grow hops and carrots, but the landlord would not allow him to grow them; they have tied the farmers down so much that they have drawn the last penny from their pockets.

In my own little parish there are farm houses standing empty and where the wheat-ricks used to stand they plant laurels, and evergreen rubbish, and the rick-staddles are kicking about the farm-yards, and the land lying dormant; and the poor old farmer who used this land, and was bred and born in the house that now stands empty, was sent to Hambledon Union; and he said that he should only live a fortnight as he felt so bad at heart; but he lived three weeks and three days, and he was brought back and buried in the Churchyard on January 4th, 1884.

Reforms.

Now, the labourer has to work and toil to uphold those that will not listen to him, but who looks upon his smock frock with high disdain. Reforms will be better for the people; but there is room for great reforms. Give these men the privilege of voting for poor-law guardians, and we shall have things very different from what they are now.

Just fancy a man travelling in search of work - 'hard up,' as the saying is - with a family of children at his heels! A more mortifying picture I cannot conceive. He goes to the workhouse for lodgings, where he is given a bit of bread, for which he has to work the next morning, and is called and entered on the books 'a vagrant,' as the poor distressed half-starved inmates are called 'paupers' - names and words which are a disgrace to the English language.

I remember in 1860 going to the Hambledon Union to see an uncle of mine, who had been a very hard-working man all his days. He was in what they called the hospital, ill, and there were six old people and a young woman with her baby in this little room.

When I went into the room, the young woman's husband was nursing the baby, which was crying, and the general appearance and condition of the place was too bad to be described here. I thought it a deplorable state of things to exist in a so-called Christian country.

One of the old men, who was born in 1800, told me that their usage was very bad. Their vegetables were very badly cooked - the potatoes speared at the beginning of the year, and they did not even rub the spears off, and, as the old man said, they were scarcely fit for swine to eat.

Another poor old man, who had been to prison, said the food he got there was sweeter and better than it was in our unions. The tears ran down his face as he told me he was sent to prison because he could not do his task of work, and insulted one of the officials. He had fourteen days in prison.

I have shown the unkind treatment the poor get, while the great paid officials live in luxury, and are overpaid; and that the money does not go to the poor, who are called vagrants and paupers, but to the officials.

The actual relief of the poor for the year ending Lady Day 1883, amounted to 6s.4d. per week, per head of the population estimated; while the sum levied as Poor Rate during the same period was equal to a rate of 10s.31/2d. per head.

My One Day's Experience of the Salvation Army.

The first thing that caused me to think was the sight of a house of poor shoeless children - a family of eight - in the parish of Cranleigh. The parent conversed with me, and told me he earned 12s. a week, out of which he paid 3s. for rent; upon the remaining 9s. a family of ten had to live! He was then going to Cranleigh churchyard to dig a grave.

I thought to myself, what can he have for dinner? He had got into the churchyard, and I called to him to come to me. He threw his basket down by the road-side. I asked him to bring his basket, as I wanted to see his dinner, and all that he had was from four to five ounces of bread. I then gave him twopence to get a piece of cheese.

There seemed to be a prayer strike me - that the poor man might do better in the future. This was my experience of a poor man's dinner in Cranleigh churchyard. And I thought of our great Master, who once said, 'Suffer the little children to come unto me.'

I once saw a poor old farm labourer, who told me he worked for one family for fifty-three years, and that he was respected by them about as much as though he were a dog! I said that he had worked hard, and done his country good, and now he was respected like a donkey in the wood? He said I was quite right.

I said his naval had got pretty close to his backbone, and I asked if he ever had a brace of pheasants given to him, to keep his naval away from his backbone? He said, no, and he thought a farm labourer never did. I said I thought I could challenge 500 parishes around, and not one farm labourer could come forward and say that he ever had such a thing as a brace of pheasants given him.

He then said they produced their food and everything else for them - it was done with the plough and the spade. I said they boasted of their charities, but I thought they greased the fat hog, and forgot the like of him. He said that was true. He had done his share of hard work here, and hoped he should soon go yonder (pointing to the skies). He wished me well, and bid me good day.

I then went up Sydney Road, and Austen Road (Guildford), where I heard them punching flints into a powder, for the roads round the Union, which is of very little value. I have often thought that it must be a nuisance to the people living around the Union to hear the iron bars chinking, and how much better it would be if these institutions were placed on waste land, so that they might cultivate it, as we have thousands of acres that would pay well for cultivating, and be the means of lessening the Poor Rate, there being so many of the public unable to pay it at the present time. I think that many of our great institutions want working on more self-supporting principles.

These thoughts left me, and I walked to the Town Clock, where I saw nine

This engraving by Walter G. Paul portrays Guildford High Street at the turn of the century.

people leaning and standing on the steps of the corn market. There were two babies. The superintendent of police came and gave them an order for the workhouse.

I then walked into North Street, where I expected to see a grand sight. Hearing much talk of the Salvation Army, I expected to see them dressed up like soldiers; but all that I saw were two little under-sized young women, and about forty persons standing hearing them discourse: 'Ye who are young - come, give your early years to God; multitudes die as young as you - come in tonight for Jesus. Ye who are advancing in years, and ye who are aged - come! Neighbours and friends, you who are accustomed to drinking habits, we invite you in - to try to make your homes comfortable, and stand up for Jesus! My aged friends, you are tottering on the edge of the grave,' &c.

My thoughts were on these young women, speaking to the public. They will be a great hurt to the drinking house. Now, these young women have the nerve to come out boldly. They act differently to the clergy in our district, where some of their livings are £1,000 a year. If a man gets drunk on Saturday night, they might preach about it on Sunday, and on Monday go and grumble at the poor man's wife, just as if she could help it! The poor woman is like the sheep among the wolves - snarled at for her husband's faults!

To the reader: I know one of these clergyman's living is worth £1,700 a year; and a little farmer, whose wife had thirteen children, when he paid his tithe, was not thrown back one penny! - the parson wouldn't do it! The farmer told me this, and he is a very hard-working man.

What a contrast between the clergyman and the two little under-sized women! They have a good nerve to speak in the public streets, as lambs among wolves! And what can two poor unguarded sheep expect amidst a herd of ravenous wolves? Wicked men are like wolves, whose nature it is to destroy; and these young women were advocating good.

They sung -

> *We are bound to the land of the pure and the free,*
> *Where the drunkard might come and the swearer go free;*
> *From sin, fear, and death the Saviour would soon set you free;*
> *Only trust in Him, who suffered so much for we.*

I thought what a great hurt it would be to the publicans. The publicans have all classes of society to contend with, and they have not the Sabbath days on which to rest, and have more to pay the revenue than any other trade.

The Subject of Charity.

The government admitted that something ought to be done, and in a timid, feeble sort of way set forth a scheme which Mr. Gladstone described as 'nibbling' at the question. They propose to charge certain fees for the action of the Charity Commission in particular cases, such, for example, as the issue of orders authorising the sale of charitable estates, granting leases, and so on. It was estimated that the returns under such a scheme of charges would be something over £7,000 a year, about one-third of the amount required.

When it is remembered that the charity property administered in this country amounts to at least four millions a year; and in the City of London alone the charities in existence would suffice to give £33 a year to each of the inhabitants; and that, in spite of all that the Charity Commissioners have done in the way of rectifying abuses, vast sums are unquestionably and grossly perverted from their proper object, it becomes clear how feeble the government proposal is.

No doubt the subject is an unpopular one, and if it were fairly broached, the proposition to impose a tax upon charity property would call forth a great outcry. It has done so before, and Mr. Gladstone himself failed to pass a measure with that object in 1863. This is, perhaps, a sufficient excuse for the government in their dread of unpopularity above all things, declining to do more than touch the matter with the tips of their fingers. Nevertheless, a thorough and frank discussion of the points involved in the whole subject is extremely desirable.

It is idle to talk of unwillingness to exact taxes from charitable funds, while we indolently or helplessly allow those funds to be so largely squandered and misapplied. To secure, if that were possible, an adequate remedy for all abuses of charitable property, and to provide that remedy at the cost of the property itself, would surely be both more satisfactory and more economical than the present system. Timid as the government proposal is, there does not seem very much chance that even it will be brought forward and vigorously carried through.

School Management Committee.

It appeared that in a certain school - typical alas! - many of the scholars came from 487 families, 400 of which had but one room each to live in. In most cases five persons lived in this room, and in some cases as many as nine. Of course the children were half-starved. It is enough to provoke tears of pity and wrath to read of the mistress of a large Board School who dare not put her scholars through the mockery of asking a blessing and saying a grace because they had, as a rule, "nothing whatever to eat in the middle of the day."

I know one poor man in my own parish, who went thrashing oats, and he had a family of six children at home, and nothing but oatmeal to eat, as he was only earning nine shillings per week, out of which he had to pay half-a-crown for rent. The mother told me the children cried, and would not go to school because they had no dinner to take. They owed tenpence for school money, so they were sent back home, and the parents summoned. They appealed to the bench, but these stone-hearted magistrates gave her an order to pay five shillings.

The woman told me she was very weak through having had nothing to eat; and how to get home she did not know. She is a poor, thin skeleton-looking woman, with scarcely any clothes on her back; and yet these flint-hearted magistrates ordered her to pay five shillings. What the magistrates ought to have done was to give her £5 and sent her home, the same as the Dissenters did my poor mother once when she was in distress.

"So God created man in His own image, male and female; and God blessed them. And God said unto them, 'Be fruitful and multiply, and replenish the earth.'"

———————

I hope to live long enough to see that wicked law reformed which separates man and wife, and their dear little children from them. It is not legal to separate man and wife, according to Bible teaching; and poverty is no sin.

I knew a poor old man eighty years of age, who was bred and born in the parish of Ewhurst. His parents and his two wives and some of his children were buried in Ewhurst churchyard. He was removed to another parish with his daughter, but she was ill and could not attend to him, so they took him to the union, where he died in about six weeks. He was buried in Shamley Green churchyard, which is six miles from Ewhurst; so the laws not only separate them whilst living, but even separate them when dead.

I have written a few plain, candid facts for the good of my fellow countrymen, and hope it will prove some good for all classes that are in any way oppressed. My motto is to think for the welfare of myself and family when I get up in the morning, and to ask my Maker to guard me through the day; that my income may be a little bigger than my outlay; and to think for the good of my fellow countrymen throughout the day.

(This was the penultimate paragraph of the 1883 edition – D.A.S.)

CORRESPONDENCE TO THE RIGHT HONOURABLE JOHN BRIGHT.

"To The Right Hon. John Bright, M.P.

Sir, - Being an aged man, and a man of talent, would you kindly read the little book I now send you? I have seen sold in the Guildford Stock Market, by public auction, spades and shovels and furniture - those things, belonging to a sect known as the Quakers, being sold to pay the tithes to the Church of England.

I know a small farmer who is a Dissenter, and whose wife has had a family of thirteen children, and the Church of England minister would not give him back a penny when he paid his tithes. The parson's living is worth £1,700 a year, they say.

I saw the farmer in the field ploughing one day last summer, when it was very hot, and so thirsty was he that he stooped and drank some water from a wheel-rut. My thoughts were, how would the Church of England minister like to be as hard driven as this farmer.

Now, the Church of England belongs to a rich class of people, and why should not every sect support its own denomination? I should like to see civil reforms in this so-called christian country; and, as you are advanced in years, and I myself feel as if I hang on a web, we shall shortly have to give an account of our stewardship.

I had a dream of the Sunderland disaster, which befel the little children. I saw towards the east most splendid scenery, and I went at a terrific speed through the air, the children appearing higher and brighter, till at last I awoke, and it was but a dream. Now, the thought struck me, is that the way the soul goes when the breath leaves the body? If so, we need not dread death.

I am yours, &c.,
One who is a wellwisher as to your future destiny,
ELI HAMSHIRE

P.S. - I was at the Fisheries' Exhibition on Oct. 24, 1883, and there was one great question which struck me, and that was - the waste. As I went to one of the bars to get my dinner, two men went away leaving about half a plate of roast beef and some bread. The waiter came and took the plates, and put the meat and bread into a large basket.

I said to him, "What becomes of the bread, meat, and beautiful piecrust and cake which you clear from the tables?" He told me it was thrown into the pig tubs, and said it grieved him to see the waste, as he should like to carry it home to his wife and family; but if he was caught doing so, he would be liable to a month's imprisonment, and lose his character.

I am sorry to say I see a very great deal of food thrown into the pig tubs at the houses of the upper classes in the different districts through which I travel, the servants not daring to give it away.

Sir, may I ask you to give this letter publicity. If you will kindly do so it will be the means of preventing a great deal of the waste I have mentioned in my book. You have done many great and good deeds for your country.

I should like to live as I would like to die. - E.H."

———————

"To The Right Hon. John Bright, M.P.

Sir, - Will you kindly let me know if you have received the little book, the slip of paper, and the letter, which I sent you?

Your wellwisher,
ELI HAMSHIRE"

———————

(Reply to the foregoing.)

"Sir, - I received your note and also the 'little book'. I read much of what you have written, but I cannot agree with some of your opinions; but this, I am quite sure, will not surprise you.

I am yours, &c.,
JOHN BRIGHT

Mr. Eli Hamshire,
Ewhurst,
Guildford."

———————

"To The Right Hon. John Bright, M.P.

Sir, - I feel thankful to hear you received my letter, &c., and I write upon the principle, 'Be just and fear not.' I read in the best of all books, ' He that oppresseth the poor reproacheth his Maker.' The cry for food in some of our large towns is something fearful, and I should like to see my letter referring to the waste at the Fisheries' Exhibition in print, as it is something beyond all comprehension. How many thousands of children it would supply with food!

Your wellwisher,
ELI HAMSHIRE"

———————

"To The Right Hon. John Bright, M.P.

Sir, - As I am about to have a second edition of my book will you kindly allow me to put the speech delivered by you at Rochdale on November 16, 1881, on your seventieth birthday.

As I am one who would like to forward the liberal cause, and your noble speech would greatly assist me should you kindly allow me to publish it; it is a wise piece of instruction. The last time I was in Mr. Guildford Onslow's company he spoke kindly of your political opinions. As I sat in the room conversing with him he threw up his arms and said, 'I have found my Saviour, and I shall not be in this world much longer,' and he left the room with his wishes that we might meet again in Heaven. I must now conclude with the same wishes to you, and wish you a happy new year.

From your wellwisher,
ELI HAMSHIRE"

(Reply to the foregoing.)

"132, Piccadilly, London,
Feb. 6, 1884.

Dear Sir, - I cannot object to you making any use you please of the speech to which you refer. I do not think you will recover the cost of printing it.

I am yours, &c.,
JOHN BRIGHT

Mr. Eli Hamshire,
Ewhurst, Guildford."

The Right Honourable John Bright's Speech.

The following remarks are from the Speech made by MR. BRIGHT at Rochdale on the 16th November, 1881, acknowledging the address presented by the inhabitants on his Seventieth birthday:-

I think I have once in this town - I am not quite sure - related a little incident that came under my notice in the year 1842 or 1843. I was with a friend of mine in Wiltshire, on Salisbury Plain, among those wonderful remains of ancient and unrecorded times.

There was a man walking about among these ruins with a long, rough coat on. He was evidently acquainted with the neighbourhood, and I entered into conversation with him.

He told me that he was a shepherd, and that, rain or fair, he was on Salisbury Plain tending his sheep. I asked him how many children he had. He said, "Only one, thank God."

"Well," I said, "how is it that you thank God that you have only one child?"

"Well," he said, "would you not do the same if you had to spend seven days a week here tending sheep and your wages were 8s. per week and no more?"

I said, "Well perhaps I might, or I might ask that somehow or other 8s. might be made into 16s.

Mr. Bright then quoted from Mr. John Morley's 'Life of Richard Cobden', the following letter written by Mr. Cobden in the year 1850, that is the year after the duty on corn was reduced to 1s. per quarter:-

He says the only newspapers which enter the parish are two copies of 'Bell's Weekly', a sound old Tory protectionist, much patronised by drowsy farmers. "The wages paid by the farmers are very low, not exceeding 8s. a week. I am employing an old man nearly 70 and his son about 22, and his nephew about 19. I pay the two former 9s. a week and the last 8s., and I am giving 1s. a week more than anybody else is paying."

Then he describes the poverty of the people generally. He says, "They have a quarter of an acre of garden, which the majority rent, and which they work, and get a little help from it after their day's work for the farmer has been completed."

That was the state of the wages then. Now, I once met a man in this town. He was doing some work about our premises under a contractor. I thought he looked ill, and spoke to him. He said he was very ill, and had just come back to work.

I said, "Where do you come from?" and he said he came out of Buckinghamshire, and he had not been in Buckinghamshire for many years. I said, "What wages were they giving in Bucks when you left?" He said his father had 7s. a week when he was a lad, but when he left he had 11s. and he said he had heard since that they were getting 14s. That, according to his statement, was an actual doubling of the wages of the labourers in Lord Beaconsfield's own county of Buckinghamshire.

In a letter published almost immediately after Lord Beaconsfield's death which he wrote to a gentleman who had sent him a book about the condition of the population in the southwestern counties of England, Lord Beaconsfield said he thought he underrated the improvement in the condition of the farm labourers. In his opinion the rise in the wages of farm labourers had been at least 40 per cent. - that is 10s. of wages per week had risen to 14s. per week.

So far about the farm labourers. I believe that in many different parts of the country the wages of farm labourers, taking into account the hours which they work and all particulars, are doubled since free trade was established.

Now, look at another class of men. I walked down from the Reform Club through the park to the House of Commons one day in the past summer, three or four months ago, and an intelligent-looking working man joined me, and addressed me by name. I asked him if he knew me. He said he knew me because, he said, "I have been a good deal in Birmingham and have attended your meetings there, and so I know you very well." I talked to him a little about his business. He said he was then getting 7s.6d. a day as a bricksetter, and he added, "I formerly used to work for 4s. a day." From 4s. to 7s.6d. is a considerable leap.

Now, I should like to tell you something that has happened nearer home, for I suspect there are many persons in this meeting who have not the least idea of the actual increase of wages that has taken place among the factory operatives in this neighbourhood during the last fifty years.

I was looking the other day at one of our wages books in 1840 and 1841. I tell you what I found in it, and what I found in our wages book now. The figures are taken over an average of two months at that time and over an average of two months now, and therefore present a fair statement of what happened then and what happened now.

Many persons here know, of course, all about the interior of a Cotton Factory, and I shall speak as if we were in a mill and looking over the people at work.

I find that in 1839 the throstle piercers - I need not explain who they are - were receiving 8s. a week, and they were working 12 hours a day. I find that now the same class of hands are now receiving 13s. a week at 10 hours a day. If they were paid for that work for 12 hours, and paid at the same rate, it would be 16s. a week, or exactly double what they received in 1839, 1840 and 1841.

The young women who worked at the frames had at that time 7s.6d. a week. They have now 15s., and that is without reckoning the fact that they are working two hours a day less.

The rovers and slubbers got 8s. a week, and they are getting 14s. a week now.

The doffers are considered a class whose wits are a little too sharp, and are sometimes not very manageable. They used to have 5s.6d. a week, and they now have 9s.6d.

The warpers in those days, as far as my recollection serves me, were all women: they earned on the average of the two months 17s.6d. a week. The warpers now are all men, and they have earned in the two months an average of 35s.6d. a week.

Well, at that time we had a very clever man, a blacksmith, whom I used to like to see strike the sparks off. His wages were 22s. a week. Our blacksmiths now have wages of 34s. a week, and they only work factory time, which is 10 hours, whereas the man of 22s. a week worked factory time of 12 hours.

You see the enormous change in the people in these factories; they have two hours leisure, which some had not before, and their wages are nearly double. I know what will be said - that I have more spindles, and their mules have more spindles, and their roving frames or their drawing frames go faster, and a great many other things.

Still, I think it is impossible to account for this extraordinary improvement in the wages of agricultural labourers, of bricksetters, of gardeners, and all your factory operatives, and all your mechanics upon any other theory than this - that the new policy with regard to trade, which has made our trade fourfold, has been the cause which has made this stupendous and unimagined improvement in the condition of the people.

The Right Honourable John Bright, Mr. Gladstone, &c.

I am thankful that we have such men as John Bright, Mr. Gladstone, Labouchere, Chamberlain, Sir Charles Dilke, Firth, H.Y. Fawcett, and Sir W. Lawson. And could we have a man like Bradlaugh in the House; he would keep the team moving: and as well he would make a first-rate Carter for the House of Commons.

This was a commemorative plate which Eli bought to demonstrate his support of his favourite politician, Mr. Gladstone.

It is not the oath that so puts the members out, it is because he is for reducing the high salaries, and perpetual pension lists, and bishops lists and a good many other lists, that are oppressive to the working classes of this country. As to the oath, go into any law court and hear the public take their oaths, and then hear them contradict each other, and if you want to hear

141

anything of the sort go into the county courts and there you will hear nearly all false oaths contradicting each other.

When Mr. Gladstone went into office a few years back he discharged a lot of dockyard workmen, and these men were doing work that was not needed; as for instance, I purchased a horse collar for 4s. when the contract was for the government 12s. each collar; all surplus stock is sold for mere nothing to what it costs the government. We, as tax payers, have to pay to support all this state of things.

Mr. Gladstone is a good hand at cutting down trees, but he wants to get at the roots better; the greatest evil is the perpetual pensioners, and bishops, and lawyers. I hope he will soon be able to discharge a few of them.

If a middle class man purchases a little piece of property the lawyers get out the writings and then charge from £10 to £50 for about one to four hours work; why should we not buy property the same as we buy a horse or such like, and get a receipt for our money, and that would be sufficient; sometimes simple proposals prove useful, to which I hope it will to the above.

Mr. Gladstone took the duty off the tea and the sugar. I have paid 5s. per lb. for tea, and 10d. per lb. for sugar, and now I can buy the same tea for 2s.6d. per lb., and the same class of sugar for 2d. per lb. Mr. Gladstone took the duty off the malt, and he has given us cheap postage, and cheap newspapers, and a good many other useful reforms, such as a cheap loaf; but the Conservative government want to stop the meat being imported into this country, if they could, perhaps to keep the price up; surely good fat bullocks, and fat sheep, and fat hogs, would not bring any disease with them; I never knew any of the dumb creation get fat if it was unhealthy.

I cannot understand how a working class man or a middle class man, can be a Conservative. I can understand a perpetual pensioner, and the bishops and Church of England parsons, and lawyers, and the great owners of the land being Conservatives, but then it is wicked to own the land, whether it is productive or not. "He that oppresseth the poor reproacheth his Maker."

––––––––––

Monopolization must be done away with in trades as well as in the land. It would be the instigation of doing away with strikes; and see how many thousands of poor children there are in want of bread, through the strikes. Only fancy our new law courts being let to one man to build; it seems all out of reason, there ought to have been at the very least one hundred contractors; and I think all great colleges want making into smaller ones; only fancy fifty or sixty boys sleeping in one room, if there happens to be any epidemic you see how it will spread. We sometimes feel the effect of this in Surrey.

In the large towns no one man ought to have more than one front shop, and in great manufacturing districts if the manufacturies were built on smaller principles how many industrious classes of society it would employ; there would then be more owners; and we have beautiful regular running streams of water in this part of Surrey: and how much labour could be done by this water, if there were manufacturies built in these districts, where there are regular running streams of water; and then we should be able to manufacture for exports, and cause to make a great deal of industry; and the bowels of the earth ought to belong to the nation, and also the waste land.

If there could be any intermixture of the different soils nature would yield a far deal greater produce of vegetation of every description; surely we should not have shoeless children; surely we should not have children with hungry stomachs, if my propositions could be carried out, which could be simply done, if we one and all turned our attention to it England could be made like a little paradise.

Conservatism must be stamped out
Before my propositions can go in the right route.

The Surrey Farmer.

Just one word for the Surrey farmers. - I saw a little farmer who told me he had ninety young sheep eleven months old, and they were fat, and he wanted over £300 for them; and I saw he had nine good large milking cowes, and I was told that there was not a gallon of couch on the farm, which was seventy acres. This man is bound to do well if the landlords don't raise his rent.

If the Surrey farmers were to turn their attention to rearing more sheep, and not to take in the Kent sheep to keep through the winter; if they had a few of their own it would pay them much better. Surely if they could winter the sheep, they could keep them through the summer; if the farmer were to study rearing the stock, and using lime on the land, he would find it profitable, and be satisfied with one farm.

And I think farm labourers ought not to be a tenant under a farmer, as they often take the advantage of his industry; he has a right to make the best price of labour, the same as the farmer who takes his fat bullock into the market.

I know a farm labourer who receives eighteen shillings a week; because he was a tenant and paid half-a-crown a week for his cottage, the farmer would not allow him to work for the other man, or he would have to leave his cottage. But the farmer would not pay but thirteen shillings a week. I know a great deal of oppression is carried on in this sort of way by all kinds of tradesmen.

The Vaccination Act.

We read of the visiting of the iniquity of the Fathers upon the children, and to the third and fourth generation. To those who read their Bibles, don't you think the venal blood is running in your veins, such as the kings-evil and the erysiplas; and a great many other eruptions running in our blood. I read of sixty French soldiers who were revaccinated and were all attacked with syphilis; and how many little children I have seen with sores breaking out on them after the vaccination. The remedy for the cure is worse than the disease.

The Burnley Co-operative Society, sketched the life of Doctor Jenner, the founder of the system of vaccination, who received £30,000 for a discovery which he stated was a preventative against smallpox, but which the essayist contended was no preventative at all, and gave numerous statistics to show that smallpox had increased up to the last great epidemic in 1871 and 1872. Since that time sanitary measures have been better attended to, thereby causing the mortality from smallpox to be lighter.

'Twelfth Annual Report of the Local Government Board': -

The total expended under this head since the year 1840, had been £2,220,798. In 1882, bonuses or awards paid to public vaccinators had amounted to £14,264; and since 1868, when they were first granted under section 5 of the Vaccination Act, £159,808; which in my opinion, is a scandalous waste of public money. If we could have had one or two midwives in each country parish, how much suffering in confinement this enormous amount of money would prevent.

I often see advertisements like this, 'those who have incumbrances need not apply', this means little children; now the persons who put these advertisements in, ought to think of their great Master who said, "Suffer the little children to come unto me and forbid them not, for of such is the kingdom of heaven."

To My Patrons.

I feel thankful to the public for their patronage for 20 years as a carrier to Guildford and Horsham, and also for the last 20 years in the fresh Butter and Poultry line, &c. and I see no reason why I should not enjoy my political and religious opinions, which, I hope, will be interesting and instructive to all who read them; and I am very particular never to sell anything to any of my customers that I could not eat myself.

I hope that my patrons will not lay this book aside as they would a newspaper, but think over the meaning of it, for our lives are like being among brambles; no sooner do we get one hook out than we get another hook in.

My prayer is that I might do good for the oppressed, and the weaker vessels, and the little children of all nations; and to every reader I desire health, happiness, and prosperity, and pray that we may meet again in heaven, where the wicked cease from troubling, and the weary are at rest.

This is a copy of the letter I wrote on my birthday, the 25th of December, 1888, to the Right Honourable W.E. Gladstone; and I also wrote to the Right Honourable John Bright; and also to the Right Honourable Randolph Churchill:

"Taking Guildford as the capital of Surrey; in the circumference, the exact measurement of this circle is 1,256 sq. miles, 407 sq. acres, 0 roods, 6 2/5 poles, or

stated simply in square miles, would be 1,256 63/100 square miles. There are 640 acres to each square mile; and there are only 40 acres in every 600 that gives its proper produce of vegetation for the benefit of mankind. We are paying one hundred and twenty millions annually to foreigners for eatable provisions when we ought to produce it in Great Britain. We are paying fifteen millions for dairy produce alone.

(To the reader:- only fancy, fifteen to twenty millions paid as taxes on coal annually to lords, dukes, and earls, causing misery, woe, and lamentation! And I maintain and say that the minerals, and all the uncultivated land ought to belong to the nation. We can now speak two hundred and forty different languages; and surely we ought to settle all disputes by arbitration.)

And if kings and princes and presidents will assert their rights,
Then, I say, put them in the front of the battle
And let them be the first for to fight;
And if John Bull and the Bear are for over-reaching everywhere,
Then, I say, let other powers be in unity,
And settle all disputes in tranquillity;

And, I say, may God defend the rights of all, that we may all enjoy good health, happiness, and prosperity, is the hearty wish of

ELI HAMSHIRE

Ewhurst, near Guildford."

"10, Downing Street, Whitehall.

Sir, - Mr. Gladstone desires me to thank you for the book you have kindly sent him.

I am, Sir,
Your obedient servant,
G.W. SPENCER LYTTELTON

Mr. E. Hamshire."

FROM THE RIGHT HON. JOHN BRIGHT, M.P.

"One Ash, Rochdale,
December 30, 1886.

Dear Sir, - I thank you for your letter, and for your good wishes and the kind present you have sent me. I will not write at length on the matters referred to in your rather long letter, and have not time to reply, except with extreme brevity.

Yours very truly,
JOHN BRIGHT

Mr. Eli Hamshire,
Ewhurst, near Guildford."

FROM LORD RANDOLPH CHURCHILL.

"Chancellor of the Exchequer,
Treasury Chambers,
Whitehall, S.W.,
December 28, 1886.

Dear Sir, - Lord Randolph Churchill desires me to acknowledge, with many thanks, the receipt of your kind present and the accompanying letter.

I am, yours faithfully,
CECIL DRUMMOND-WOLFF

Mr. E. Hamshire."

December 28ᵗʰ 1886

Dear Sir

Lord Randolph Churchill desires me to acknowledge, with very many thanks, the receipt of your third present and the accompanying letter.

I am
Yours faithfully
Cecil Drummond Wolff

Mr E. Hampshire

This letter from the Chancellor of the Exchequer is one of several which Eli's family still possess.

John Bull and the Vaccination Question.

I must have a few words on the bull, and the subject of vaccination.
I think that old John Bull ought to turn his attention more to growing corn,
And not to have so much in the Divorce Courts to reform.
Moderation should be our guide,
And a good cultivation of mind should be our pride;
And no poor man's voice never spurn,
And that is the way to live and learn.

And he who will his wild oats sow,
Will burn down his barn, and come to poverty, grief and woe;
And he who will to the brothel-house go,
Will sow his own destruction;
And his body and soul will waste,
And he will die with blood in his veins full of corruption.
Never a truer passage in Scripture spoke about
Than "Be sure your sins will find you out;"
And never touch of the forbidden fruit,
For your constitution it will not suit;
The aristocratic government compels vaccination from all such blood,
And causes more destruction to little children than Noah's flood.

Extracts from the 'Financial Reform Almanack', 1885.

"My opinion is that Religious Equality is a phrase which requires further development, and I will develop it further by saying, that in Religious Equality I include in its fullest extent - Disestablishment." - Right Hon. W.E. Gladstone.

"The property of the Church belongs to the State, and the Legislature has the power and right to deal with that property according to the circumstances at the times." - Lord Palmerston.

"The Church of England has continued for more than 150 years to be the steady enemy of public liberty." - Lord Macaulay.

I am a Dissenter because the Bible gives no authority for the enforcement of money for the service of God.

The union of Church and State is a serious injury to the Church, because the union of Church and State hinders the spread of the Gospel. State churches are persecuting churches, and all persecution is wrong. The union of Church and State is oppressive and unjust.

148

For God in His wisdom created man and woman, and ordained the matrimonial laws at the time of the flood, saying, 'Go out and multiply and replenish the earth;' and our Saviour said, 'Whom God hath joined together let no man put asunder.'

The Church of England ministers are the first to separate. There they sit as chairmen at the Board of Guardians, and have splendid mansions and large salaries themselves, but pay a curate a small sum to preach for them.

They are making the Church look like a theatre, dressing up in their white gowns. They go round with their bags to collect money two or three times on a Sunday. I would sooner be a tanner's dog and gnaw horns than do such a thing, for if a poor human being were to ask for a crust of bread on an empty stomach - which is a heavy load to carry - he would be called a cadger and a vagabond.

The Church of England is what many would call an unlimited company, full of priestcraft, pride, and oppression. And surely what is sauce for the goose is sauce for the gander; and they are an unlimited lot of what the majority of the public would call carpet-paupers, living on the fat of the land. Covetous idolators.

> *From the first step on earth,*
> *To the brink of the grave,*
> *They will not put their hands*
> *To the plough nor the spade.*

And when the plough and the spade is not used it puts a stop to all kinds of trade. We have our Bibles and the different commentaries, and can't we think for ourselves as religion is a personal matter? In that little prayer it says 'Deliver us from evil,' and 'Thy will be done;' if this little prayer could be in our conscience, morning, noon, and night, there would not be that evil carried on with poor little girls that we have read of in the London papers. Such inhuman and monstrous great sin.

ELIZABETH WHEELER,

AGED 28 YEARS,

'Who was done to Death by English Justice for the Crimes of Homelessness, Sickness, and Destitution.'

Let the Poor have ovens to bake their own bread, and let them have a little copper to brew their own beer. As they work hard, and they have heart and brains that need a little cheer. And, I say more fat hogs, and not so many carpet-paupers.

And monopolization must be done away with in trades, as well as in land. Only fancy a brewer purchasing eighty to one hundred public houses, or a miller eighty to one hundred bakers' shops, and they have shares and influence in other trades. Now the bakers and publicans are in bondage. They are not allowed to purchase in the best and cheapest markets, whereas if they were allowed to, how much better it would be for the country at large.

I maintain that every man ought to be a free man that pays rent for a building of any description, but as the law now stands he is in bondage. The Liberal members have given us the Franchise, and we now have the privilege to send men to alter these unjust laws; and I have known public houses and beer shops to be what they call free houses, but as soon as the brewer purchase them they will charge six shillings more for a barrel of beer.

All kinds of trades are working on the same system; and the labourers feel this bondage very much; for instance, I have a boy that worked for a farmer and he had eight shillings per week, and my neighbour had a boy exactly the same age, and worked at the same work, and he had only five shillings per week. Now, this boy was in bondage because his father rented a cottage under the farmer.

Monopolization is becoming a serious question. The loss of sewage and waste of manure is estimated at £100,000,000, whereas if this were utilized on the land it would be beneficial to every branch of trade, as we all have our existence from the plough and the spade. All would feel the good effects, and the value of it would be worth £160,000,000 per annum. It is nonsense to say the land will not pay for cultivation!

My opinion is that the welfare of those that venture their lives on the water and in the mines, ought to be studied as well as those who work upon the land. And the collieries, mines, fisheries, and wild animals, all these ought to be reclaimed, and used only in the interest of every individual, instead of being so used as not to benefit all alike.

Collieries enrich a few private individuals at the expense of all the rest, who often have to pay extravagant prices for coal, beyond all proportion to the cost of getting it. A large number of the poor, in the most inclement of seasons, are compelled to remain shivering with cold in their miserable hovels, with scarcely a spark of fire to warm themselves.

How simple it would be for our legislature to alter this state of things.

Those who oppress the poor, reproach their Maker. Where will the merchants' conscience be when they are in the hands of the undertaker?

At Denby, in Yorkshire, no less than 10,000 tons of coal are disembowelled weekly. Of the miners who night and day send forth this black stream to our manufacturers and homes, over 200 of the heads of families have been served with an ejectment writ. The village looks as if it suffered with a violent plague. The most terrible scenes occurred at the evictions; it is said the police even could not help crying over this cruel work, and they helped out of their own pockets the sufferers whom they had to turn out of their homes. On one bed lies a sick man in pain, and a pale mother sits near the fire, nursing a poor baby, whose breathings plainly show that it has bronchitis.

They were turned out on Easter Tuesday, 1885; the memory of it makes one's throat feel queer. Only fancy what a wretched life to live in. Is such a state of things possible?

Thirty-six Reasons why I am a Liberal.

The following are thirty-six reasons why I am a Liberal.

1). Because they established freedom of speech, the right of public meeting, and the freedom of the press.

2). Because they passed great Reform Acts.

3). Because they abolished negro slavery in British possessions.

4). Because they abolished hanging for forgery, sacrilege, embezzlement, stealing to the value of forty shillings, and other minor offences.

5). Because they abolished the press gang.

6). Because they abolished public execution.

7). Because they repealed the Corn Laws, and restricted navigation laws.

8). Because they removed the disabilities of the Nonconformists.

9). Because they removed the disabilities of the Jews.

10). Because they abolished university tests.

11). Because they abolished Church-rates.

12). Because they passed the Burials Act.

13). Because they abolished purchase in the army, and flogging in the army and navy.

14). Because they passed the Factory Act of 1833, and many subsequent Acts of the same character.

15). Because they abolished imprisonment for breach of contract.

16). Because they passed the Employers' Liability Act.

17). Because they passed the Municipal Reform Act, and established local self-government in towns.

18). Because they repealed the tax on paper and the newspaper stamp duty.

19). Because they repealed the tax on fire insurance.

20). Because they repealed the taxes on windows, glass, soap, candles, butter, cheese, eggs, rice, hops, malt, corn, and very many other articles.

21). Because they largely reduced the taxes on tea and coffee.

22). Because they largely reduced the tax on sugar, and left the surplus which secured its repeal.

23). Because they passed the National Education Act.

24). Because they did justice to Ireland by passing the Irish Church and Land Acts.

25). Because they passed the Ballot Act, and secured freedom of voting.

26). Because they introduced the penny postage, the halfpenny post card, the halfpenny book and newspaper post, the parcel post, and sixpenny telegrams.

27). Because they introduced Post Office Savings' Banks, Government insurances and annuities, and penny savings cards.

28). Because they repealed the malt tax, and thus enabled the farmer to use pure untaxed malt for feeding cattle.

29). Because they passed the Act to prevent the farmer suffering from the ravages of ground game.

30). Because they passed the Act to secure to the farmers compensation for their unexhausted improvements.

31). Because they passed the Married Women's Property Act.

32). Because they passed the Act for the extension of allotments.

33). Because they passed the Corrupt and Illegal Practices Act.

34). Because they passed the Bankruptcy Act, to protect creditors from dishonest debtors and trustees.

35). Because they passed the Patents Act, to secure the rights of inventors.

36). Because they have shown their determination to secure the passing of much needed and long-delayed measures of reform by improving the procedure of the House of Commons, and establishing Grand Committees.

Questions for Voters to Ask.

The following are a few questions which the author would like each Voter to ask his Representative in Parliament, at the next coming election.

1). Do you not think that the Charity property in this country, and which amounts to at least four millions a year, is taken from the poor in an ungodly and cruel manner?

2). Will you assist in the restoration of all lands that have been taken from the poor?

3). Will you stand up for the immediate alteration in our Land Laws, so that land may be bought and sold as easy as having an infant registered? - and not have a lot of old musty parchments that are puzzling for a lawyer to understand, and for so doing he will milk the cow, whilst the vendor and the purchaser hold the horns and the tail.

4). That the country should have the power to compel complete cultivation of the land, and to tax all land that is lying dormant. This law would give a poor man a chance to have an acre of ground to cultivate, as it was intended by his Maker he should have.

5). Would you vote for the entire abolition of the Game Laws and all other break-neck cruel and idle sports?

6). Will you advocate freedom in all religions, and that every denomination should stand upon its own basis; and that all the tithes and glebe lands be restored for the full benefit of the distressed poor?

7). Will you vote an immediate abolition of the House of Lords, as they are obstructions in the way of all good and useful reforms?

8). Will you vote that there be a searching inquiry made into the matter of Perpetual Pensions, and all other things that are not only oppressive to the poorer classes, but also to the middle classes of this country?

9). Should the House of Commons have the power to exclude a duly elected member? If they do exclude a member, ought not the constituency be freed from taxation?

10). And, I think, there will be a race in the House of Commons, in less than ten years hence, to see who is to be the first President of the British Dominions Republic.

11). Why could we not have some kind of Building or Alms Houses on all the waste lands; that would restore to its proper channel all tithes and produce for the benefit of mankind, and the poor would not then be called paupers, but parishioners; that they may retain their freedom?

12). Will you strive to lessen rent, abolish tithes, lessen taxes, and support every measure which may be brought forward that is calculated to bless everything and everybody?

The meaning of the word 'Conservative' in politics is one who desires to preserve the institution of his country.

The meaning of the word 'Liberal': generous, noble-minded, candid, free from restraint. One who advocates greater freedom in political institutions and free doing.

The meaning of the word 'Radical': one who strikes at the roots of evil. One who advocates Radical reforms.

I think the public will conclude I belong to the Radicals.

As to my book, 'The Source of England's Greatness,' it has been read by a large number of people, and the price of it is one shilling; and one man, seventy-four years of age, told me, "It ought to have a leather cover and a steel hasp to preserve its leaves," as he had never heard or read anything like it before. One gentleman gave me a sovereign for one of my books.

I have been the means of saving little children's lives when they have been on the brink of starvation; and also young women's lives, when they have been disappointed with their false-hearted lovers.

I have also written on the Land question, giving the experience of old practical farmers and farm labourers, and experienced market gardeners.

Just a word for the domestic servants. Now I think they ought to have half a day once a week to themselves; as it is they are shut up in the underground kitchens, and they often have to work from 6 o'clock in the morning till 10 and 12 o'clock at night, from one six-months' end to another; and I have actually seen them crying when they have been overworked, running up and down stairs for the most frivolous affairs; their masters and mistresses ring their bells, and have no thought or care for them that answer it.

Will you try to abolish wars, not to carry the sword in one hand and the Bible in the other? The Bible is translated and printed in 240 different languages; surely our ruling powers ought to be able to settle differences by arbitration. Our Great Master never intended there should be any bloodshed according to His Book, and we ought to turn our guns into spades and our bayonets into ploughshares, and our swords into reaping hooks, and I say -

When the wars and the dangers are drawing nigh,
God and the soldiers are all the cry;
But when the wars are over and the dangers are righted,
God and the soldiers are ofttimes slighted.

The Cost of War.

From 1875 to 1884, the cost of war was £286,057,310. To the reader: only fancy what a million is. My little girl, ten years old, reduced one million farthings to pounds, and the answer was £1,041.13s.4d. She did it in two minutes and a half; and my little boy, thirteen years old, gave the answer in two minutes; this shows the good of education.

Could we not choose a number of men by the Government of all nations, and all countries to be in unity; those who are for going to war, put them in the front of the battle.

And if John Bull and the bear
Are for over-reaching everywhere,
Let all powers be in unity,
And settle all barbarity in tranquility;
And where the barbarous governments are carried on
Try and settle all disputes by civil reform.
That we may live in the land
Of the pure and the free,
And I trust that Mr. Gladstone
And her Majesty both may be free
From dynamite and massacre.

Letter to Jesse Collings, M.P. on the Three Acres and a Cow.

"TO JESSE COLLINGS, Esq., M.P.

May 8th, 1891.

To your Honour, - I think you hold the most responsible position on the Commission, as we all have our existence from the land.

> *We have our bishops and parsons and they can preach for our*
> *poverty and pray for our grief;*
> *But that won't produce our temporal bread, neither will it old*
> *England's roast beef;*
> *Then, I will tell you the men who do - the men who use the*
> *plough, the spade, and the peck;*
> *These are the men who produce our temporal bread, and also old*
> *England's roast beef.*
> *Then I say the men who use the plough, the peck, and the*
> *spade,*
> *These are the classes of men that cause everything to flourish*
> *in all kinds of trade.*
> *Then, the men who use the peck, the spade, and the plough,*
> *These are the classes of men that ought to have the privilege*
> *of having three acres and a cow.*
> *Then there is the glebe land, and I think Hodge is entitled to*
> *it now;*
> *For neither the lord, the bishop, the duke, nor the Queen,*
> *Can do without Hodge and his machine;*
> *Then why should Hodge be locked out from the use of the soil;*
> *While the great overpaid sweats out of him the great profits*
> *that they get out of his toil?*
> *Then, I say, abolish the game-law, and the stag-hunting,*
> *where they ride and gallop over it for many a mile;*
> *Doing any amount of damage and cruelty; breaking down*
> *gate-backs, fences, and stiles.*
> *This class of men never do any laborious work, and therefore*
> *their hands they never soil;*
> *Neither will they let the working classes have the three acres*
> *and a cow,*
> *Or we should have had England like a little paradise long*
> *before now:*
> *We should have the fruit blossom in the Spring, and vegetation*
> *in every grade,*
> *If they would only allow the working classes the use of the*
> *peck, the plough, and the spade;*

And I trust that our conscience may be clear with an overruling
Providence when we are placed in the grave.

ELI HAMSHIRE

Ewhurst,
Guildford, Surrey."

Letter to Thomas Burt, M.P. on Railway Servants.

"To Thomas Burt, Esq., M.P.

I read in the 'English Labourers' Chronicle', May 2, 1891: The Amalgamated Society of Railway Servants. - The credit balance had risen on the year from £73,773 to £81,763. During last year 125 additional children were left fatherless; and there are now 551 children deserving benefit from the orphans' fund, the total annual expenditure on this amount last year being £21,557.

There are nearly 400,000 men employed by the railway companies, but there were only 200,000 members of the society. It is believed the total capital of the railway companies is something like one thousand millions. The railways of England cover an area of 20,000 miles.

Now, I have travelled a great number of miles myself, and I have always found the railway servants obliging, and always use civility and honesty, and I never remember seeing one of them intoxicated, and I don't believe I have ever lost one pennyworth yet of anything at any time; and I think that the ten hours' question to be in bondage would be quite sufficient, and when the servants step on the companies' premises their day's work would begin; and as they are a civil, intelligent lot of men, I think it is a pity but what they should belong to the society, as unity is strength.

They would then be able to provide for necessities that befall them through life; they would then be able to stand up for their own rights, and not to have an old union workhouse staring them in the face in their old age; and I think that every class of human beings ought to be exempt from labour of every description on a Sunday, except feeding and attending the animal creation.

Written for the welfare of the railway servants.

ELI HAMSHIRE

Ewhurst,
Guildford."

Letter to Sir William Harcourt on Taxation.

"To The Right Hon. Sir William Harcourt, M.P.

April 24th, 1890.

May I ask you a favour, as you are about to attend a meeting in Guildford? Will you kindly review the little books of which I am the author, and of which Professor Rogers said, in reviewing them, that our legislature was ignorant of the common sense and principles upon which I had written?

As the late John Bright suggested a free breakfast-table, I wish to point out how it could be done. I know it takes money to keep up the revenue, therefore I would suggest to you to bring a Bill into the House to put a tax on the land.

I can afford to pay half-a-crown per acre per annum for my three acres; and every man who owns over one hundred acres should pay three shillings and six-pence, and he who owns a thousand, and can afford to form rings, squares, and triangles and plant laurels and evergreen rubbish, I think should pay five shillings per acre. There is in the United Kingdom 77,513,600 acres.

I would also suggest a tax upon timber in our agricultural districts, as it causes a blight upon the crops a great distance around out in the fields.

If this wouldn't raise sufficient money, put a ten pound tax on all underground kitchens, so that domestic servants might enjoy the light of the sun and fresh air for the benefit of their well-being; and there are many other classes who have to work in underground cellars that ought not to be allowed by law.

From one who studies all classes of society, your obedient servant,
ELI HAMSHIRE

Ewhurst,
Near Guildford."

Letter to Right Hon. W.E. Gladstone on Compensation.

"To The Right Hon. W.E. Gladstone.
To your Honour, - May I ask you a favour to read my opinions on the compensation. About eighty years ago there was a company formed and dug the river Arun, and then about forty years after the railways came and took away their trade, and the shareholders had to lose their money, and the coaches had to lose their money, and we poor carriers had to lose our money. Neither of these three ever got any compensation.

I think it would be very unfair to give compensation to the brewers and publicans. The brewers have kept the publicans in bondage for a very long time by selling their adulterated waters, and the brewer ought to pay the publican the compensation. The publican has all classes of society to contend with, and he has been a tool for the brewers, and has been in bondage through renting his bricks and mortar. Will you read pages 12 and 13 of 'England's Greatness;' and also read the 'Three Great Locusts', pages 60 to 64, the two books which I am the author of.

Dear Sir, - I was in a park one day where they had got a great lump of faggots; and the squire was going to burn your effigy because he thought you were an unwise man; but since that he must have thought it a waste of faggots to do so, as he has come out a good staunch Home Ruler. Every Englishman wants a home, and not to be in bondage. Please read pages 46 to 48 in 'Three Great Locusts.'

To your honour, - Professor Thorold Rogers told me he gave my works a good perusal, and he gave me credit for putting it so plain; and that our legislature was perfectly ignorant as to the common sense and principles what I had written upon. And now I must conclude, wishing you long health and happiness; and I look upon you as a monument of God's sparing mercy; wishing prosperity in your future destiny.

ELI HAMSHIRE

Ewhurst,
Guildford, Surrey."

Letter Received from the Late J.E. Thorold Rogers.

"My Dear Sir, - I have read your little volume, which is curious and instructive for its experience. It would be well if you could give them at greater length, and deal with those only which treat on the life of agricultural labourers. I am persuaded that the world does not know enough about them, and what they could and would do if they had the chance. I hope I may have some opportunity of giving them the chance in the next Parliament, for the legislature is so fully ignorant about their condition. -

Yours faithfully,
JAMES E. THOROLD ROGERS

Oxford, Sept. 18, 1885."

My Interview with the Right Hon. W.E. GLADSTONE, M.P.

Meeting Mr. Gladstone on the Eldermore Road, leading from Felday Church, the Hon. Leveson-Gower introduced me to him, and Mr. Gladstone, taking off his glove, shook hands with me. I told him that I took a great interest in the Liberal cause, and was pleased to see him regain his strength again, and hoped that we should again see him at the helm, guiding our great national affairs, as there was not another man capable of doing it like him.

I told him that I had been the means of saving little children's lives when they were on the brink of starvation, and therefore I could not help being plain in my speaking and also in my writing.

I then told him what a serious thing it was for the present Conservative Government to do away with all out-door relief, and that it would be the means of the Liberals winning more seats in the House of Commons than anything else. He then put his hand to his head, and seemed to think, and then asked Mr. Leveson-Gower if it was not left for the guardians to decide. Mr. Leveson-Gower replied that he thought it was so. True, I said, it may be so; but the guardians, as a rule, are neglectful. They are oftentimes Conservatives, and keep the poor from their rights.

The homes of agricultural labourers are being broken up, little farm home-steads pulled down, and the land is growing dormant, and a very serious state of things is caused by the game laws. I have the list of the names of those who voted to do away with all out-door relief, and I will let you have it in the morning.

He then thanked me, and wished me good day.

Letter to Mr. Gladstone.

The next morning I sent him the following letter:-

"To the Right Hon. W.E. Gladstone.

To your Honour, - I have sent you the division list of out-door relief, which the Conservative Government passed in July, 1888, which was one of the worst measures that could be passed, and one that would give the Liberals more seats in the House of Commons if the public only knew.

There is nothing the English people have such a dread and horror of as the union workhouse; and this is not without occasion, for I read that in the Steyning Union a poor sick patient had his flesh eaten into by lice and bugs, and that the filth and stench were horrible.

Dear sir, may I ask you the favour to review the little book, on page 24 of which is where I spoke of it in the Guildford Public Hall, and will you kindly give me your opinions.

From one who is a well-wisher to you in your great talented cause. -
Your obedient servant,
ELI HAMSHIRE

Ewhurst,
Guildford."

This picture, representing Mr Gladstone at various stages of his political career, was sent to Rebecca in 1908 by the Hon. Leveson-Gower, in acknowledgement of Eli's and Rebecca's support of the great man.

Letter Received from Mrs. Gladstone.

"My husband asks me to thank you for sending the list of out-door relief, which he will read, but is too busy to write.

I thank you for the present of beautiful butter.

Yours faithfully,
CLARA GLADSTONE

Holmbury, Dorking,
June 8th, 1891."

This is the original letter from Mrs Gladstone. Her handwriting is rather difficult to read and could be the reason why Eli copies her name as Clara, instead of Cath, in his book.

The following is from the 'Pall Mall Gazette':-

Mr. Gladstone and a Rustic Admirer.

Even when on his quiet visit to Dorking, as the guest of the Hon. Mr. Leveson-Gower, Mr. Gladstone could not escape the attentions of his admirers. The service at Holmbury Church - one of the prettiest in all Surrey - was attended last Sunday by the ex-Premier, Mr. Gladstone, Mr. John Morley, Mr. Stuart Rendel, and Mr. Leveson-Gower.

As Mr. Gladstone was walking away from the church, he was accosted by a villager named Eli Hamshire, a 'character', who not only claims the authorship of the 'three acres and a cow' policy, but who manifests a keen delight in publishing in pamphlet form his own thoughts and opinions upon political and social subjects of the day. He is remarkable for his appearance - always, Sundays and week-days, is his burly form seen encased in a quaint smock frock.

The enthusiastic rustic shook hands with Mr. Gladstone, congratulated him on the state of his health, threw out a few airy suggestions upon the poor-law relief question, and promised to supply the ex-Premier with some information thereon.

He was as good as his word, for the next morning he rose with the lark, indited a letter to Mr. Gladstone, and delivered it personally to Mr. Leveson-Gower's residence, together with a small present of butter of his own make for Mrs. Gladstone.

Yesterday he received a short note from Mrs. Gladstone, expressing her thanks for the present of 'beautiful butter', and informing him that her husband would give the matter his attention.

Letter to H. Chaplin, M.P., on the Game Laws.

"To H.Chaplin, Esq., M.P.

To your Honour, - As you are possessed with great talented opinions, may I ask you a favour to review the little book which I have sent you. It is a little history of my experiences through life. I gave my mind to study for the welfare of the masses of the people.

The Conservative Government passed a bill on the 3rd of July, 1888, to do away with outdoor relief; and they are building our unions larger throughout the country. This will cause them to lose a number of seats in the House of Commons, as the English people have such a horror against the union workhouse. I read of it in 'The English Labourer's Chronicle', a paper which is printed with more common-sense than any other newspaper I ever read.

Joseph Arch, during the time he was a Member of Parliament, passed a measure so that we might brew our homebrewed-beer free of taxation. Whatever form of government we may get, I think that Great Britain ought to have a free breakfast-table.

A great number of the democracy have only the clothing they wear; but they produce all the great profits for the merchants, who then purchase the land, and make stag-parks, and game preserves, and pull down the little farm homesteads, and the workmen's cottages, and the lime kilns. They are doing away with labour all they can, causing great influx into the towns. God intended His vineyard for the use of mankind.

Now, a small farmer in an adjoining parish to the above merchant's, grew fifteen sacks of wheat to the acre in 1891. There are not many farms that get so good a yield, for why? Because the farmers, as a rule, take so much more land than they have capital to cultivate, and they cannot take advantage of the season.

It was never intended by our Maker that one man should have so much. God looks down upon us as children, and, therefore, there is no distinction in His sight; and I think we ought to act like men, one towards another, so that we might carry out the principles of peace and goodwill towards mankind.

Wishing you health and prosperity, from your well-wisher,
ELI HAMSHIRE

Ewhurst,
Guildford,
Surrey.

P.S.- The rate collector told me that the above merchant wanted his assessment lowered now he had pulled down the workmen's cottages and the farm-houses. Instead of lowering his assessment it ought to be raised double or treble as the land is getting like a wilderness.

Surely we shall be able to bring the candle out from under the bushel so that it may give light that the masses of the people may see that which is right; for the class of the people who use the peck, the spade, and the plough ought to have the privilege of having three acres and a cow."

Letter from Mr. Chaplin.

(Reply to the foregoing)

"Board of Agriculture, S.W.
March 8th, 1892.

Dear Sir, - I am directed by Mr. Chaplin to acknowledge the receipt of your letter of last week and the pamphlet you have been good enough to send him, thanking you for the same. I am to inform you that there was no Bill passed by the Conservative Government on July 3rd, 1888, to do away with outdoor relief.

The proposal made on that day in the House of Commons by Sir U. Kay Shuttleworth in the debate on the Local Government Bill, to base the amount of probate duty granted to the counties on population, and not on indoor pauperism, was not carried, but the Government finally decided upon a distribution in proportion to the amount of the discontinued grant.

I am, yours faithfully,
P.H. BAGENAL

To Mr. Hamshire."

A Discourse with a Farm Labourer.

"Just making a new hedge, then?"

"Yes, trying to a little."

"Election time is over. How did you get on then?"

"We chaps was out in the field swede pulling, and we got a fussy old maid, and she came to us and wanted us to vote for the Conservatives. She said these we should find our best friends; she then said, 'Your master is going to vote for the Conservatives.'"

We said, 'Yes, if you think they are our best friends.'

She said, 'Yes, you will find them so.'

"Nobody never said nothing to we chaps about the voting, you know; we chaps didn't understand, so we voted conservatry and after we voted we saw an old man, and he said, 'Which way have you chaps voted, for God Almighty, or for the Devil?'

So we said we did not know; we have been and voted conservatry 'and you will know you voted for the Devil before another election'."

The Carrier's Boy quite endorsed the views of the old man; for the Conservatives had the privilege to take the duty off from the tea, which is sixpence in the pound; then they voted to do away with all out-door relief; and now they are building unions bigger. And these Conservatives spend a lot of the rate-payers' money.

I saw one contract of £60,000 for one union being enlarged. The Carrier's Boy suggests refuges and almshouses in each parish, so that they might use more industry - so that the inmates could grow their own vegetation, and plant nice fruit trees; now at the unions the poor inmates receive very bad treatment.

Steyning Workhouse Scandals.

Then, again, on March 6th, 1891. 'The West Sussex Gazette' gave the Steyning Workhouse scandals, and shameful mismanagement.

Charge number one, general dirty state of infirmaries; the beds having bugs in them, and lice in patients' heads.

Number two, no provision for brushes.

Number three, no provision for washing; only one piece of flannel.

Number four, dirty state of patients.

Number five, no meat inspection.

Number six, individual patient named Clark, suffering from paralysis, on water bed, covered with lice eating into the flesh; now Clark had only been taken out of bed once in nine months, and his body was covered with lice and bugs.

B. Jones, a vagrant, admitted into the infirmary suffering from carbuncle, shirt sticking to the carbuncle, and saturated with matter. Jones had been altogether neglected, and the nurse found the shirt sticking to the wound and the discharge running off his body on to the bedclothes; the paralysed man's body was not clean, his feet being the most dirty, his armpits were almost raw, the lice had completely eaten into him, and there was the most fearful stench imaginable; his back was in a fearsome state, quite raw. The nurse did not consider it a bedsore.

To the reader, - You can imagine what sores they were, when you look at the crevices that harbour lice, bugs, and cockroaches, and they spread their tails. One of the guardians said a homely bug is not unknown in Shoreham.

Then, again, a poor woman attended Greenwich Police-court for advice; she wanted a little out-door assistance for herself and children, until her husband came out of the hospital, in three weeks' time. The Greenwich Guardians met this reasonable request by telling her she could not be relieved unless she went into the Union Workhouse.

She said, "Then I must break up my little home and be called a pauper all my life; and to be separated from my dear little children, and be a burden upon the ratepayers, when a few shillings would tide me over, and help me never to trouble you Guardians any more."

To the reader, - This was a Conservative law that was made on July 3rd, 1888. Surely this would prevent your being Conservative in the future.

Look at the three enormous rich places - Canterbury Cathedral, and St. Paul's, and Westminster Abbey - and see the poverty around, within sound of their bells; then look at the enormous amount of wealth around them. Why don't the speakers suggest new channels of industry? Joseph Arch, General Booth, the Rev. Ben Waugh, Dr. Barnardo, and the late C.H. Spurgeon have done a great work in assisting the poor little children; but the above-mentioned places do but very little good for the temporal wants of the people.

Life in the Westminster Workhouse.

Look at the following from 'The Daily Telegraph' of April 8th, 1892:-

Mary Callagham, 42, who was assisted into the dock, causing her much pain, was charged with attempting to commit suicide at the workhouse institution. Mr. C.W. Wright, the master of the workhouse, said the prisoner was ordinarily a good worker.

On Wednesday afternoon, the witness, hearing screams from the dormitory, found that the prisoner had jumped out of a window. Owing to its peculiar construction, her dress caught the casement, and she was hanging head downwards over an iron grating, thirty feet below. With difficulty she was rescued.

The prisoner said, "I suffered such violent pain your worship, and the doctor who saw me said it was a pack of rubbish, and that there was nothing the matter with me, and that I was to get about and pick the oakum; I felt so hurt that I thought I would put myself out of misery."

She had complained of great pain in her left side. She was blistered, and the blisters were put on at half-past ten at night, and left till half-past seven the next morning before it was dressed. The master said until three months ago, when she had first complained of pain and illness, she was an excellent working woman in the laundry.

Now this poor woman had to go back to the workhouse, and the blister mark was then upon her. She was assisted out of the dock by two policemen, who supported her whilst she walked with difficulty.

To the reader, - I think the doctor ought to have been placed in the dock, for he deserved punishment for using such hard-hearted language to such poor, helpless creatures as this woman. I think it wants putting a stop to, for they often get ill-treatment by the officials throughout the United Kingdom.

Angmering Primrose League.

'The West Sussex Gazette', April 2nd, 1891. The Angmering Habitation of the Primrose League, the Conservatives having smoking concerts, and singing concerts, and they want to stifle the brain in some sort of way; they say they uphold the Empire - grand institution - cause of religion - but where is their Christianity?

Look at Wringmore, a distressed Sussex parish; look at the auctioneers being pelted with addled-eggs. Then there are the canons and arbitrary parsons in Wales.

Now the Church of England is nothing but priest-craft, hypocrisy and idolatry, it's nothing more and nothing less. If I have a rogue I want to stop him; now I think the priest-craft has been a rogue long enough, or why should I have to support a religion that I don't believe in? Then I say, let every creed of religion stand on its own merits, and not be in Pharaoh's bondage any longer.

Now, as to the farmers, you look to the landlord and priest-craft as your best friends; but if you get into difficulty the landowner and priest-craft are the first to set the lawyers to work and sell you out. You can read from Genesis to Revelation, and you will never read of such arbitrary wicked power there. As to the publicans, they are in bondage, and are taken advantage of in a great many ways; they have all classes of society to contend with.

Then I say to the farmer and to the publicans, come out of these ruts of Conservatism and the Unionist party, and get some of these cruel institutions altered.

The Grand Old Man gave us the privilege of the vote and also the secret ballot - the two greatest gifts that ever were given to man; therefore I say to the democracy, do everything to benefit yourselves as much as you possibly can, and do away with monopoly in the land; the game law is the greatest evil, therefore abolish it as soon as possible.

Horsham Workhouse.

'The West Sussex Gazette' of June 19th, 1890, gives an account of an inquest at Horsham upon a man named Robert Steel. He was found dead, having placed his head upon the metal in front of the train. He was an army pensioner and kept the Alexander beer-house; through failure in trade and a bad leg he went to the workhouse infirmary. About eight days before his death he complained of the food he received; he was determined never to go back any more. The jury brought him in temporary insane.

Now, the Carrier's Boy thinks this man had the use of his talent in every way, but he could not put up with the food he received at the Horsham Union Infirmary, and with a determination of mind he put an end to his existence; and I think that the officials, one and all, wanted censuring for allowing such a state of things to go on, when the ratepayers pay sufficient money to keep the poor on roast beef and plum-pudding every day.

Horsham Magistrates.

Just a word on the little-minded magistrates at Horsham. Signs of 1892. J.T. Naldrett, of the King's Head Hotel, and five other landlords, made application for the extension of one hour on New Year's Eve; but these little, one-eyed, sitting magistrates could only allow them half an hour. Mr. Cotching said it was innocent recreation to a large number of people, many of whom came in from the country.

Now, I must ask these proprietors if it does not make them look like serfs to have to appeal to these little-minded magistrates to grant them an hour. Why should this trade be in bondage any more than other trades?

Surely you proprietors will come out of this rut of Conservatism! You have had one knocked to pieces by a railway engine through the dread of the union workhouse. Your Sir Walter Bartelott voted to do away with out-door relief on July 3rd, 1888, and they are building our unions larger, the treatment in which is horrible in Sussex, as the foregoing extract shows.

Look at the unequal laws. See 'The West Sussex Gazette', April 16th, 1891. Case of Cruelty. Ellen Strudwick was summoned before the Guildford County Bench of Magistrates. The Society for the Prevention of Cruelty to Animals summoned her for keeping her stock with a short supply of food. Being a poor and afflicted woman, she could not see to them properly, and the magistrates sentenced her to one month's hard labour; and the poor woman fainted whilst having her hearing. I think the magistrates at Guildford are very hard-hearted towards the weaker sex.

I once read of a lord who starved one hundred sheep and lambs and got clear, and yet it was proved that he starved them. Now, this lord had plenty of £.s.d., so he could find a way for to get free.

Now, why did not the police and the inspector of the society report the case of the poor woman before? We had a very severe winter, and the stock wanted a great deal of attention. The poor woman being afflicted, they had no right to give her a month's hard labour; or what does that class of people deserve who allow human beings to be eaten with lice in our union workhouse at Steyning? Why should these officials go free and only get a mere discharge? What is our government thinking about to allow this state of things to go on in the open daylight?

———————

I once knew a young woman who had three months' hard labour for being homeless and destitute, and the policeman told me that he took her to the Guildford station, that she was in such a fainting condition that she could not walk to the station, and that he was forced to borrow a wheelbarrow to wheel her there, and she only lived three days after committal.

———————

Game Laws.

Then, again, there are the stag-hunters, who often consist of magistrates, lords, squires, counter-jumpers, &c.

In February, 1891, the stag-hunters came galloping over my three acres and frightened the cow, and the poor stag stopped in the front of my house with its tongue hanging out of its mouth, and the dogs came up, and it bleated out. It was exhausted, but it ran on about five hundred yards into a pond of water; then these hardhearted hounds on their horses came up and kept the dogs back, and they whipped the poor stag out of the water; then it ran another three or four miles in this exhausted state, and I saw one of the poor horses' mouths all in a lather of blood. These hounds will ride over any poor man's garden.

A little boy told me the next morning that they galloped over his father's cabbage plants and trod them into the ground, and broke his mother's clothes-line, and broke down her flower border fence.

———————

April 13th, 1892, I have just read of four men losing their lives over a pheasant. The game laws are causing England to get into a wilderness state.

I have been conversing with a farmer's wife, and she told me her husband had to get up from his tea to frighten the pheasants off his new-sown corn, as there were thirty-six of them working it out of the drills. Another little farmer told me that there were eighty-six out in his field. Now, this is ruination to the little farmers, for the great merchants do not feed their pheasants at this time of the year.

Whatever form of government we may get, surely they will abolish these laws and stag-hunting. If they are going to bring this Small Holdings Act into operation, the small holders must have the sole control of the game.

While waiting for the train at a railway station I had a conversation with an agricultural labourer's wife. I asked her how her husband was paid for his work.

She said, "Oh, he don't get much of pay considering the dirty work he has to do. His master is a brewer, but he takes care never to give him any beer. He has a lot of old London dung down, and my old man has to load it. My old man said there is a lot of old stinking fish, and dead cats; one day he found a slimy calf in it. Any one would think the brewer would give him some beer.

These men have their great parties which cost a lot of money. But we live under the hill, and they live at the top! The brewer's wife is terribly mean; she told me if there's any tramps to tell them there is no houses on the top of the hill; they can't bear to see a poor wretch about. You said ladies were pinching in their waists.

My daughter Jennie is out in service, and she is a bit of a lady's maid; she gets hold of one end of the stay-lace and the young lady gets hold of the other, and then the young lady says, 'Pull Jennie, pull Jennie.' "

The old woman said pride never feels pain; but I said it is first vanity and then destruction.

As I passed by Bramley Station on April 14th, 1891, I saw a few trucks of London manure; the wind was blowing north-east, and the steam blew off the manure, and the windows stood open at the young ladies' school. I thought what a pity that the school should stand so close to the railway station, where there was so much of all kinds of filth unloaded. I am one who would wish every one's health improved.

Tobacco.

'A Boy Killed by Cigarettes'. - A boy named Samuel Kimball, sixteen years of age, a chorister in St. Mary's Church, Brooklyn, died recently at St. John's Hospital. Almost his last words were: "Let any boy who smokes cigarettes look at me now and know how I have suffered, and he will never put another into his mouth."

To the nurse he confessed that his trouble had originated from cigarette smoking. The appetite grew upon him with such force that he could not shake it off, and it began to affect his constitution.

During all his sufferings he never forgot what had brought him to this terrible condition. He kept asking her to warn other boys against their use. A few days before he died, he called her to his bedside and said that he thought he had not lived in vain if only those boys who are still alive would profit by his suffering and death.

There is no other form of tobacco so dangerous as cigarettes, because the nicotine in the smoke is not absorbed in the loose tobacco, smoked clean up to the end, but is taken unfiltered and undiluted, into the lungs. It was not the poison in the paper, but the poison of the tobacco, which killed Samuel Kimball, and is ruining the health of thousands of other pale-faced boys. May I ask every parent to warn their children out of this poisonous, deadly habit.

The average work performed by the heart in a healthy adult man was traced as follows: presuming that the blood was thrown out of the heart at each pulsation in the proportion of 69 strokes per minute, and at the assumed force of nine feet, the mileage of the blood through the body might be taken at 207 yards per minute, seven miles per hour, 168 miles per day, 61,320 miles per year, 5,150,880 miles in a lifetime of eighty-four years.

To the reader, - I have worked these figures to show how necessary it is to keep our blood pure and clean, and it is a very dangerous practice to use the nicotine. It causes the blood to be out of order; and I ask you that are the subject of smoking to smoke three pipes of tobacco on going to bed, and then put your finger on your pulse in the morning, and then go without three days and three nights; you will then be able to see how it acts on your blood. It affects the heart and also the brain, causes cancers in the throat and tongue, and also on the lip, and so many evils that I cannot enumerate them.

There are many young men and lads who lose their lives through nicotine, which causes rapid digestion and pale, thin faces, heart disease, and cancers on the lip, in the throat, and on the tongue. I have known a great number of men and boys starved to death through nicotine. And there is about as many young women lose their lives through pinching their waists in, which stops the passage, and causes inflammation, and after a confinement it will often be death's sting.

In 1841 the consumption of tobacco in the United Kingdom, with a population of 26,000,000, was 23,000,000 lbs. Today with a population of nearly 40,000,000, it exceeds 55,000,000 lbs.

In 1891 the amount of money spent on tobacco, at the rate of 3s.6d. per lb., was £12,833,333.6s.8d.

The Millions Spent on Drink.

The Archbishop of York, presiding at a great meeting in the Drill Hall, Sheffield, under the auspices of the Church of England Temperance Society, spoke of the enormous amount spent upon drink in this country, and gave a fact which he said was astonishing. The drink traffic reached £136,000,000 per annum.

And I say, if the wives in the United Kingdom were to brew their beer, and all kinds of licensed houses were to have off licenses, and Sundays exempt, and to sell free from license, it would not cost this country more than £10,000,000 per annum; and how comfortable it would be for wives and their families if these suggestions could be carried out, which could simply be done, but not if we have lawyers, brewers, and merchants for members of Parliament. The democracy have got it in their hands to do away with great monopoly.

Letter to the 'English Labourers' Chronicle'.

"To the Editor of the 'English Labourers' Chronicle'.

Dear Sir, - As I am the founder and originator of the Three Acres and a Cow, I think that some of your readers might like to know my history.

I remember, in 1849, when I went to take the meadow, the big farmer said that the landlord saw the fool coming, as I agreed to pay too much rent for it. I agreed to pay £4 a year for it. The farmer was right in what he said, for I had nothing but horse-mint and moss the first year. I cut the horse-mint, and raked the moss off and put it into the pig-stye. I then got some mould together, and put the pig-stye manure on it; and by this means I got the meadow into good heart, and it produced over two tons of hay to the acre in eight weeks' growth.

After I had had it about twenty years, the landlord came to see me, and said that I had improved it, and must pay more rent for it.

173

'What,' said I, 'after using my industry on it! The farmer said you saw the fool coming when I took it.'

He said, 'Yes; I am about to sell it, and must have more rent.'

'How much do you expect?'

'Fifteen pounds a year.'

I said, 'What! From £4 to £15?'

He said, 'Yes.'

I then said, 'If you are about to sell it what is your lowest selling price?'

I there and then bought it, as I knew that I had some friends who would like to get it away from me. I then built a little lodge with six rooms to it, and also some out-buildings. I also planted some nice young fruit trees.

Now, sir, a great number of people will ask, 'Can a man live on three acres and a cow?' I am the author of the lines of poetry:-

I say the Bishops and Parsons can preach for our poverty, and pray for our grief;
But that won't produce our temporal bread, neither will it old England's roast beef;
But I will tell you the men who do:
The men who use the plough, the spade, and the peck;
These are the men who produce our temporal bread, and also old England's roast beef.
Then, I say, the men who use the plough, the peck, and the spade,
These are the men that cause everything to flourish in all kinds of trade;
Then the men who use the peck, the spade, and the plough,
These are the men who ought to have the privilege of having three acres and a cow.
Then there is the glebe land, and I think that Hodge is entitled to it now.

And now I must tell your readers how I first got my cow. I purchased it when a calf, about a fortnight old, for 14s. By the time she was three years and three months old she had had three calves, and I made 11 3/4 lbs. of butter a week. I then sold her for £25.

(To the reader, you see how simple it is to get a cow, but it is a very hard matter for an industrious man to get three acres of land.)

For a fuller account of my views, I would refer your readers to the two little books I have written, price 1s. each: the title of one is 'England's Poverty', and the other, a copy of which I sent you to review, is the 'Three Great Locusts'. You will see, in reviewing it, that I have written on four great standing evils that are very detrimental to the health of mankind - the vaccine, the nicotine, young women pinching their waists in, and intermarrying.

Now, I must say, thank God there is such a man as Joseph Arch, to stand by the men in union. Surely he is a man close to the steps of our Great Master, who said, 'Suffer little children to come unto Me!'

And now I must conclude, wishing you every success. I have been a constant reader of your paper ever since it has been issued, and I am very pleased to see a revival in your union. I have written about Mr. Joseph Arch and the 'English Labourers' Chronicle' on pages 55 and 56 of the 'Three Great Locusts'.

From your well-wishing friend,
ELI HAMSHIRE

Ewhurst,
Near Guildford."

The Allotment Bill.

Read page 68, how the miners were ejected on Easter Tuesday, 1885. As the Allotment Bill is about to take place, surely something can be done so that the working classes shall not be so much in bondage with their employers, so that they cannot eject them from their cottages, for if there is anything gets the least wrong it is, "Get out of your house!"

Why cannot they have the allotments on a permanency, so that the labourer might build a shed of any kind upon it, or purchase it if he chose, and this by getting it registered, and not to have to pay the lawyers a lot of his hard-earned money.

I think the law wants altering so that the farm labourer shall not be so much in bondage, for if he has an allotment now and happens to kick over a rabbit as big as a rat, or if he doesn't grow just what the parson or squire wants him to, they will give him six months' notice to quit.

These are my own home personal experiences within the last twelve months, and I think the working men of the United Kingdom will have more intelligence than to vote for any form of government that will not alter these unjust laws. We shall never get them altered by the Conservatives or Unionists, but there is every chance of getting these reforms by a civil Radical government. The meaning of the last three words is getting at the roots of evil.

A Caution to Stepmothers.

I think I should instance the following case as a caution to step-mothers. When I was a lad of thirteen years old, I went with my mother to the next door neighbour's, and saw the step-mother lying in bed very ill, and the little step-daughter lying in what we call a chip-basket, and eating a dry gingerbread cake. The little girl was four years old, and was a complete skeleton - nothing but skin and bones. I told my mother I would take her in an egg, and she ate it.

My mother looked after the little girl from that time, and the step-mother died in a week, after which the father had a housekeeper, who took pride in looking after the little girl, who grew up strong, and is now the mother of a family of grown-up children. I give myself and my mother credit in saving this little girl's life - being so near being starved to death.

To the reader, - I was too late to save the little girl I spoke of in 1869 at the Guildford Public Hall (see page 24), as she lived only three days after. I would caution step-mothers to see to the little children well, as we never know which is going first; the above step-mother was taken ill and was dead in less than a week.

I one day had a tradesman come to my house to clean a clock. I asked him which was the best watch and clock manufacturer in England, and he told me that Sir John Bennett's were the best and most permanent goods.

"I know him personally, and am glad to hear such news of him from such an intelligent tradesman as yourself. Mr. Older, you watch and clock makers seem to have a good deal of intelligence. There is Mr. Salsbury, of Guildford, Mr. Marsh of Dorking, and Mr. Baker, of Horsham, all five intelligent men for the temporal wants of the masses of the people; and I think you can supply the masses with good timepieces, and timepieces as time are valuable.

I saw Sir John Bennett at Mr. Bradlaugh's funeral, and he came up and shook hands with me, and said, 'I know you very well; you are one of our land reformers.'

I said, 'Yes, Sir John, I am, and there are four great laws that wants reforming - heredity in the land law, the game law, the church and tithe law, and the lawyers law, so that we can purchase land and property by getting it registered.'

Sir John gave me a paper called, 'The Butter King of London', and in reading it I found how much need there was that more people should have the privilege of three acres and a cow."

"Yes;" Mr. Older said, "I knew a man who started with one acre and a cow and he lost her; he then got out a brief and bought two cows, and now his widow has got twelve."

'Happy Cranleigh'.

"At Cranleigh we have got a great pavilion built for the cricketers - we Cranleigh people only think about sports. And we have got what a good many people would call a vanity church, where they go to see and be seen, and to see the fashions and so forth - like a silver pin, bright outside and foul within."

"You speak rather plain facts," said I.

"Yes; but they are facts like your own."

"Yes; I think they ought to turn our churches into almshouses, for there is not proper respect shown to the poor. Why don't they put up an almshouse on Cranleigh Common, and not send the aged poor to Hambledon Union?

There is a space leading from the Onslow Arms to the pavilion which the poor could cultivate, and it would look beautiful if planted with fruit trees and vegetation, and would be almost self-supporting. I think we ought to do something of the same kind in every parish throughout the United Kingdom. It would reduce our poor laws, and more especially so if they could get allotments.

What we want is, that the working classes can purchase their allotments, put buildings on them, and not have a burden of rent all their lives, and not to have them on lease for another family to come in and claim what they have been getting together all their lives.

Only look at these Lords and Dukes coming in for the leasehold properties. As they have never had to lay out one shilling on it themselves, surely they ought to pay more towards keeping up the revenue. They have had the great ship in their own hands, and have steered it for their own interest, but Mr. Gladstone has reversed this, and put it into the hands of the democracy. It will take two decades before it will get into its right motion. Mr. Gladstone is about to move one of these great useless blocks.

I find that the amount of personalty sworn to upon the deaths of the various bishops, who belonged to the state church in England, during the last 30 years was £2,105,000. The personalty of one clergyman, whose will was proved in January last, was upwards of £342,000! Only fancy an archbishop having £15,000 a year, and a poor clergyman, who is paralysed, only £60 a year to maintain himself and a family of seven young children.

I say it is time to abolish this popery, for we have got so much of the High Church party that they keep us in bondage, and the Lord knows that we cannot understand them at all; for they say, 'Lay not up for yourselves treasures upon earth, where moth and rust doth corrupt, and where thieves break through and steal.' And, 'Whoso hath this world's goods and seeth his brother hath need, and shutteth up his bowels of compassion from him, how dwelleth the love of God in him?'

And they say, never turn thy face from any poor man, but act according to these principles, so that the above bishops are wicked to the extreme in the sight of God."

So I say:
Praise God from whom all blessing flow,
For none of us poor helpless people can cause a blade of grass to grow.
We may dig, we may plough, and we may sow,
But it is the over-ruling Providence that gives the increase before we can reap or mow.
Seedtime and harvest God said shall never cease,
And you know that He will give the increase.
If we dig, dress, plough, and sow,
We never need dread a famine if we trust in Providence in doing so.
Man is full of deceit and sin,
And £.s.d. is what they want to win.

Vaccination.

Old John Bull and Science are causing the deaths of thousands through vaccination, which is a bond and plague and a fearful corruption to mankind. It is a seat and a root of all kinds of diseases, a brand of infamy, devolution and a dilusion. Now, I trust my readers will come to a conclusion that this filthy habit ought to be abolished, so that there would not be such a terrible confusion. Surely our Great Master did not set this example when He said peace and goodwill towards mankind.

Now if a certain class were to intermarry, and carry out Dr. Jenner's vaccination scheme - to be vaccinated once in seven years - they would soon know what it was to have the death sting. If they were to use the four great standing evils - the vaccine, nicotine, young women pinching their waists in, and intermarrying, the females at the age of twenty-one, and the males at the age of twenty-eight, would meet with death, and go home to the New Jerusalem, and, I believe, this class would soon be extinct.

Then I say, think of our Great Master, who said, 'Deliver us from evil,' and, 'Thy will be done,' and always use temperance in your language and in all things, and bad company always shun. - With the author's hearty good wishes to every reader, and to use thought and read it over again.

———————

When I was in the 'Welcome' Coffee Tavern eating my midday meal, in Guildford, one of the councilmen came in and sat down beside me. He said, "As you are an author, I should like you to give me your views on vaccination."

I then said, "Well, sir, you know what a greasy-heeled and mangy horse is? You also know what a foot-and-mouth diseased murrain-heeled cow is? You also know what a scourey and scurvy ringworm calf is? You know what these three animals are?"

He then said, "Yes Mr. Hamshire, I do, as well as any man."

I then said, "If we must have animal blood mixed up in human being's blood, I think we ought to get it from the ass, as I have never seen a dead donkey yet."

He then said, "A very good answer to my question."

I then walked up the town and went into a tradesman's shop, where I saw the tradesman's wife. I told her the suggestion that I had made to their town councilman.

She said, "I don't believe in having asses' blood, or any other filthy blood mixed up in human beings' blood. I once had an old jenny myself and a nasty stubborn tempered old thing she was; and there are plenty of old stubborn jennies in the country now, and I'm sure there are a lot of old donkeys, or they would never use that filthy blood which you have written upon in your little book."

The vaccination is the seat of diseases, a brand of infamy and devolution, and a delusion, and a monopoly for the medical practitioners. Take away the £.s.d., and we should soon be free from vaccination, for the physician and philosophy cannot gainsay what the Carrier's Boy says. Surely conscience will tell them not to poison our blood in any sort of way, or after generations will say how very unwise we were in the 19th century.

I then said, "Is it reasonable, or is it feasible that our Great Master should say, 'Feed My lambs, and suffer the little children to come unto Me.' " Surely the presence of His mind never thought that they would use this humoury blood in these Christian times; and surely voluntary principles ought to be carried out in our minds.

179

Old John Bull and Science might as well try to stifle the rays of the sun on a Midsummer's Day as to stifle these facts what the Carrier's Boy says on the intermixture of bloods. If Old John Bull and Science don't believe in what I say about this filthy and humoury blood, let them come to the author of 'Three Acres and a Cow', and he will point out to them these evil effects.

Letter to the Editor of 'The Star'.

"To the Editor of 'The Star'.

Dear Sir, - As your paper is largely circulated in the southern part of England, and particularly in Guildford, the capital of Surrey, may I ask you a favour to insert this letter, and to review the little book called the 'Three Great Locusts' in your valuable paper.

One of the Guildford town councilmen asked me my opinions on vaccination, and I said, "You know what foot and mouth and lung diseased cows are, and you also know what scurvy and scoury and ringworm calves are, and they are also liable to warts and tumours, the same as a human being.

I once heard of a butcher who cut his hand whilst killing an unhealthy bullock, and the blood got into the cut and poisoned his blood, and he only lived fourteen days. Therefore, I think, if we must have animal matter mixed up in our blood, they ought to get it from the ass, for I have never seen a dead donkey in all my life."

Science and Old John Bull ought to point out how to keep our blood pure and clean. They cannot do it by intermixture of blood, nor yet by vaccine. It is the blood we want to keep pure and clean. If we use animal matter and human beings' humoury blood, it will cause more destruction and pain than Noah's Flood!

The Commissioners might like to see this letter, by the author of the 'Three Great Locusts', and 'England's Poverty', by the Carrier's Boy, the originator of the Three Acres and a Cow.

ELI HAMSHIRE

Ewhurst,
Guildford, Surrey."

Let me instance four young people - Jones and Smith, Miss Mote and Miss Neat. Between the age of fifteen and thirty years, Jones gets a disease that he ought not to get. He marries Miss Neat, and she has an increase. Smith marries Miss Mote. Smith and Miss Mote are free from all disease, but we read in our Bibles of visiting the sins of the fathers upon the children unto the third and fourth generation.

Now Smith and his wife have steered clear of the disease, but have got to have their child vaccinated from Jones's child, the consequence being that the child gets the same disease. This disease may not show itself until a twelvemonth after its birth, and then break out into a fearful mass of sores.

I advise young people to refrain from marrying if they once get the disease on them, for the cleverest physicians in the whole world cannot tell what will be the results when they use the vaccine.

There are a great number of diseases running in our blood, and there are thousands vaccinated daily, and not a single doctor can tell what will be the results when the infant is vaccinated.

(The engraving above, and on page 87, is taken from the 1892 edition of Eli's book.)

Acrostical and Impromptu Lines Addressed to-

E njoyment, with instruction, your little book contains.

L abourers, and farmers, too, are bound in Tory chains.

I n less than two decades from now these fetters shall be broke;

H eaven knows your grievance, and will remove the yoke.

A ll that our Great Creator doth - it may be slow, but sure -

M an cannot always understand; the way seem dark, obscure.

S teadfastly live out each day - your pilot, Providence!

H eed the voice of conscience, hate sham and false pretence;

I mpress your fellow-tillers of old England's soil!

R eligion of the Gospel kind is best for all who toil,

E ither at the plough, or forge, at desk, or at the loom;

G od is ever near those who'll give His Spirit 'room'.

O n Him, then, cast your burden, He hath borne the Cross,

D ied upon it, brother, to redeem our loss.

B elieve on Him and follow Him wherever He commands;

R ejoice in that He bursted for us Death's mystic bans.

I n all we think, or say, or do, let's give to Him the praise,

D are to live like Christians true throughout our length of days.

G reatly to be loved is the Founder of our peace.

E ngland this may know when greed and war shall cease.

L abourers, arouse! Awaken from your slumber!

O n God and selves rely - millions strong in number.

D etermine through your future ne'er to mourn the past,

G ladness, like an oil of love, can soothe the poor downcast.

E nvy not the wealthy ones, they on your strength depend;

E v'rywhere 'tis proven you are the classes' friend.

W ealth can never be produced by grandees 'at their sports'.

H orny hands are seldom seen at palaces or courts,

U nless it's at the police courts, where one-eyed justice sits,

R ebuking honest labour 'for getting in a fix'.

S oon cruel laws shall be repealed, our leaders see the way!

T ake courage, oh, my brethren, the dawn proclaims the day.

THE THREE GREAT LOCUSTS.

BY THE

UNADULTERATED RADICAL,

"THE CARRIER'S BOY."

WITH HIS NEW IDEAS ON

VACCINATION,

PRESENT-DAY FASHIONS, &c., &c.

WITH

MRS. HAMSHIRE'S

VIEWS ON FARMING.

BY THE AUTHOR OF

"THE SOURCE OF ENGLAND'S GREATNESS."

WITH PORTRAIT.

Published by

ELI HAMSHIRE, GODBRIDGE LODGE, EWHURST,

GUILDFORD, SURREY.

1889.

This photograph of Eli was used as the frontispiece for both 'The Source of England's Greatness' and for ' The Three Great Locusts.'

INTRODUCTION.

Twenty years ago I walked twenty miles to a vagrancy meeting to speak on the subject of the three acres and the cow. It was a hearty wish to better the working classes in those days that compelled me to walk twenty-four miles, as I was not getting one penny by so doing. When I suggested the same to Mr. Chamberlain in my letter it was made known throughout the United Kingdom.

Now I can always lay my head down upon my pillow and say, "Thank God, my three acres pay me a very good profit." It enables me to kill a couple of nice fat pigs, weighing from sixty to seventy stone, and always to have a supply of dairy produce, besides giving employment to the family.

Therefore I wish to improve the working classes' condition in every sort of way,

If I have to be a martyr for the facts in what I say.
I trust I shall not be a martyr in my future destiny,
For, as the Great Potter formed us out of the clay,
So we keep returning to it every day.
I want to get the cobwebs out of the crevices of my own heart and brain,
And no individual character I ever wish to stain,
But to tell them of their errors, I wish to make it plain.
To reform our lives and have a happy destiny, that is all I aim.
And let these be the ruling principles running uppermost in our mind;
And always think of our Great Master, who said, "Peace and goodwill towards mankind."

(The engraving at the top of this page is taken from 'The Three Great Locusts'.)

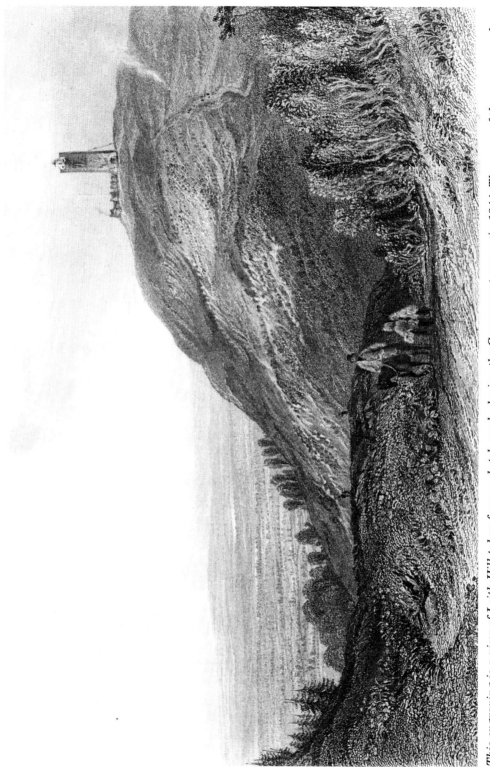

This engraving is a view of Leith Hill taken from a sketch made during the Government survey in 1844. The camp of the sappers and miners who were undertaking the survey can be seen near the base of the tower which was built in 1766. Evelyn, in his 'Diary', stated that 'twelve or thirteen counties can be seen from it.' On St. Swithin's Day 1844, the air was so clear that the spires of 41 churches in London were visible, as well as the scaffolding around the new Houses of Parliament at Westminster. Rebecca's family farmed on the slopes of Leith Hill between 1821 and 1838.

MRS. E. HAMSHIRE'S VIEWS ON FARMING IN HER SINGLE LIFE.

Written when confined to her Room with a long illness in 1884.

My father (William Gibbs) and my mother (née Mary Allen) natives of Ashbourne, Derbyshire, were married in the year 1818. They had a small farm in Derbyshire for the first few years, but having heard that Surrey stones were made of gold, my father came to that well-known place called Leith Hill, and took a farm called High Ashes.

But finding that it did not pay, he spoke to his landlord, and he agreed to take off some of his rent, which he did, but having no written agreement, it did not stand good, and when my father was about to leave, the landlord made him pay all the back rent, which almost broke my father up.

But having a friend who lent him a little money to go into his fresh farm with, which was near Guildford, under Lord Onslow, which my father found more prosperous, he soon saved the money he had borrowed, and paid the man off; where my father still farmed up to the time of his death, 1864. My brothers still use the same farm, and they have been there forty-six years last Michaelmas.

Now some people have an idea that farming don't pay. Now my father and mother had a family of fourteen children, and brought up nine of them. Now, I write this to show that why farming don't pay is because the farmers don't go the right way to work to make it pay.

Now, instead of bringing their children up to play the piano, we were brought up to work. Now, I can well remember being left to mind the house when I was seven years old, and had to keep the pot boiling while my mother and sisters were fagging wheat in the field. And when we went to school we only went in the winter, as we had to pick the stones in the fields and scraps in the meadows, and cut the thistles in the wheat, and pull the kedlock, which makes the fields look yellow nowadays.

Now, I think one great evil in farming is the machinery - the threshing-machine in particular is a great loss to the farmer. You see when the corn is threshed by hand the straw is kept tied every day or given to the stock, which is sweet when threshed by hand, but when threshed by steam it often lays about the rickyard to rot; in particular the cavings, and all the best of the straw you may see laying rotting most every day if you drive out a few miles.

Now, there is the mowing-machine, which I consider is a great loss to the farmer. Now, in the first place, the mowing-machine leaves behind it all the bottom grass, which, of course is all the best; as you well know all the herbage grows at the bottom; and when the men mow by hand if they have some homebrewed beer they will cut down close to the sward. Then, again, there is a great loss of time with the horses; when they ought to be busy with cleaning their fallows, they are tiring their horses with their mowing-machines.

Then, again, I can see one great evil in these parts - the farmers sow their corn broadcast instead of drilling it, and then it all gets choked up with rubbish, and then that causes the corn to yield bad. Now, you see, if they would drill it what a nice pastime it would be for the farmer in the spring, when the birds are singing, to take the hoe and take his part with the men; but instead of that, as soon as they take a farm nowadays, they think they are gentlemen, give up work, if ever they have done any, and go off hunting and shooting.

Then, again, some might think I am so much against machinery, but that depends on the kind of machinery, as I think the swede-cutting machinery and oilcake-crusher are of great help to the farmer in fatting the beast, as I can remember mother and one of my sisters, when I was a child, cutting swedes for six fatting beast at one time with a table-knife.

I can well remember my brothers being so busy with their fallows, that they never came to carry hay until four o'clock, and we had it all ready for them to take up, and we always had lunch at four o'clock; and I know we often carried as much hay after lunch as some farmers would carry in a day.

Then, again, see what the farmers lose by the Kent sheep; if they had but a lambing flock of fifty ewes, see what they would gain by that with taking care of them. I have two brothers that keep fifty ewes, and one always sits up one half and the other the other half of the night for three months while the ewes are lambing. And that used to pay in my father's time. And if that paid in his time, of course it would do so now.

Just look at the price of mutton! Now, when I was a girl, I can remember father buying the breast of mutton at fourpence per pound and shoulders at sevenpence per pound; and then some say farming don't pay.

Just look at the price of everything! I can remember my mother selling fat turkeys at ninepence a pound; now the farmers are making one shilling a pound of them. Now, when I was at home with my father, after the death of mother, as she died when I was eleven years of age, I kept an account of what we made of our fowls for three years running, and we sold fowls enough to average £1.5s. a week all the year round without geese or turkeys.

But we never got time to dress twice a day as the farmer's daughters do nowadays; if we had a wash and put a clean apron on, we thought it enough, for we could not spare time for more, as we had the little chicken to feed five times a day, and fowls to cram night and morning, and the calves to hob, and the dairy to attend to. We generally weaned ten or twelve calves a year, and we had ten or twelve cows to sell every year.

I maintain and say it is no matter what the man does if the woman don't try; they must do something besides play the piano and go to balls and parties, as that is what the farmers' daughters do nowadays. I often say I was one generation too soon, for I am sure the farmers are better off now than the farmers were sixty years ago, from what I have heard my father say.

This row of tombstones, in the graveyard of Worplesdon Parish Church, is the final resting place of Rebecca's brothers and sisters.

DOMESTIC SERVANTS.

by 'The Carrier's Boy'

I once knew a young woman who held a situation for two years and six months; and she left and went to another situation, and she only stayed her month. And then she got another situation, and they wrote for her character; and the lady would not give her a character; and she then went and saw a lawyer, and the lawyer told her to go and demand the two years and a half character that she carried with her. The lady objected to her having it. She then told the lady she had been to see a lawyer, and the lawyer told her that she could demand her character.

"Well," the lady said, "I will go and see Jack," which was her husband; and Jack told his wife to give her her character. Now this young woman lost a situation where she was going to have £26 a year through their keeping her character; she then got another situation, and only got £16 a year.

To the reader: you see what a detriment to this young woman through their keeping her character; and had she not been an intelligent young woman to go and see the lawyer, she would have lost her character.

To the reader: And what would become of her? Why she would have had to walk the streets or go to the brothel-house, and, perhaps, for Jack's purposes - and then to be called 'a bad woman!'

To the reader: I appeal to your conscience - Which of the two is the bad woman? Why, the woman who lives in luxury, laziness, and idleness, and, perhaps, carrying out a profession with a prayer night and morning - what a good many would call a lot of written-out tongue prayer, not heart and brain prayer.

True passage in the Holy Writ, where it says the first shall be last, and the last first. It will be easier for the camel to go through the eye of a needle, than for Jack and his wife to enter into the kingdom of heaven. Inhumanity is what I call a monstrous great sin, and my hearty wish is to try and reform our lives, that we all might be at the gate of heaven and be prepared to enter in.

To the reader: I think it will want a big eye to the needle for Jack and his female camel to get through with her pinched-in waist and her Vanity Hump on her behind.

Those who oppress their servants, it is a great sin. Then I say to Jack and his female camel - reform your conscience, you might then find the straight

Here is vanity on the brain.
! ! ! ! !
( ) ( )
o o o o
o o
o o
0
o o
o o
o o
o o

o This o
is the
s h a p e
of a woman's
waist on which a
corset tight is laced.
The ribs, deformed by
being squeezed, press
on the lungs till
they're diseased.
The heart is
jammed and
c a n n o t
p u m p
(and
here is
the great
vanity hump),
the liver is a
torpid lump, the
s t o m a c h, crushed,
cannot digest, and in a
mess are all compressed.
Therefore this silly woman
grows to be a fearful mass
of woes, but thinks she
has a lovely shape, though
hideous as a crippled ape;
and it is the death of
thousands in their confinement
through their vanity shape.

Here is wisdom on the brain.
! ! ! ! !
⌣ ⌣
o o
o o
o o
0
o o
o o
o o
o o

o This o
is a woman's
natural waist,
which corset never
yet disgraced. Inside
it is a mine of health. Outside of charms it has a
wealth. It is a thing
of beauty true, and
a sweet joy for
ever new. It
needs no art-
ful p a d d i n g
vile, or bustle
big to g i v e it
"style." It's strong and
solid, plump, and sound,
and hard to get one
arm around. Alas!
if women only knew
the mischief that
these corsets do, they'd
let Dame Nature have
her way, and never try
her " waste " to " stay."
And never to remain an old maid
to go grey.

gate to enter in. Some people will laugh at me, and some people will almost cry. But they are critical passages, and conscience tells me I must not pass them by, for there is a great many of these evils that are carried on by the sly. The poor servant-girls are shut up in the underground kitchens and they never scarcely see the sky.

I once knew a father, and he went to London to see his daughter, and it took him by such a surprise, he told me that his daughter was got such a skeleton that he could scarcely recognise her with his own eyes. And I would caution parents when they read the advertisements, and when they go to London to inquire into the character of the place, to use a little judgment.

The Three Great Locusts Cause the Blight of England.

"To Herbert Gardner, Esq., M.P.

October 30th, 1888.

To Your Honour.

Dear Sir, - I have made inquiries of old practical farmers in Surrey and Sussex, valuers, and farm labourers, in answer to your two questions. As to growing one acre of wheat fifty years ago, the cost would be from six to seven pounds to the acre, and at the present time it would be from four to six pounds per acre. We have rivers, railways, and roads for conveyance now different to what there was fifty years ago, and if the owners of the soil were to study their own interests, how much better it would be for all kinds of trades, and for those who labour and toil.

One of the old practical farmers said they had got the school boards, and the poor law boards, and the burial board, and the highway board; and it is the paid officials that get the money, and not the poor. And we poor farmers shall not be able to get the nails to keep these boards together much longer.

Then they talk about protection in our little parish! We pay ninety pounds a year as police-rates. Then the farmer said, "Do away with public-houses, and the game laws, and the priestcraft tithes; the Church is nothing else but harbouring pride and vanity, dressing up in their white gowns and their surplices, and wearing their crucifixes, and they are nothing else but a lot of Popes, and they don't want you to dictate to them. And we poor farmers have been foolish enough to scrape and bow to them for this last two or three hundred years."

I said, "I suppose you are speaking plain facts"; for I knew a little farmer who had about a hundred acres of land of his own, and he farmed it first-class; but Mr. Conservative M.P. got a big farm close by, so Mr. Priest he wanted some of the farmer's land, so he let his tithe run on. Mr. Conservative let his rent run on, and then they set Mr. Lawyer to work.

The Conservative perpetual pensioner got hold of the front door, and Mr. Priest got hold of the back door, and Mr. Lawyer got hold of the w.c., and the poor little farmer went off his head, and he had scarcely anywhere to be.

And the farm labourer who held the plough, and took the prizes at the ploughing-match, for rick-building, and thatching etc., and he is a very clever, industrious man, and his wife has had a family of twelve children, and he kept one of his eldest children at home to go to work with him, and for so doing he was summoned before the Guildford Bench of Magistrates; and the tears ran down his face when he told me he had to cut a red herring into joints, with potatoes for his children's breakfast; and he could not get the money to pay for the school fees.

To your Honour: is it just and right that the farmer and the farm labourer should be oppressed in this sort of way? The perpetual pensioner, the lawyer, nor the Conservative M.P., did not trouble about the farmer after they had got his property all right and free; these three great locusts cause the blight of England.

I want the masses of people of England to see I am the originator of the 'three acres and a cow'. I can always lay my head down on my pillow and say, "Thank God, she pays me a very good profit now." And the man who ought to have the use of the land is he who uses the pick, the spade, and the plough.

The old farm labourer said, "They talk about the cost fifty years ago; the farmers used to plough their land a good depth, and they used to lime it, and dress it; but now there is no encouragement for a farmer to farm well. The gentry bring up a lot of pheasants like barndoor fowls, and turns them down, eating and treading down everything; then the stag-hunters come two or three times a week, and the counterjumpers' sons, and the land-mudlers' sons, and the squires' sons, and the rectors' sons, and the perpetual pensioners' sons, treading into the earth, and there is no chance for the farmers nowadays.

Then the squires, and the parsons, and their daughters, and the primrose dames will come around and ask for our votes at the election times. So election day I got home and went to bed, and our Conservative farmer sent his son, and horse and cart, to take me to vote for them; but I did not go; I then said Mr. Gladstone has given me a free conscience, and it's perfectly secret as to who you vote for, and I believe Mr. Gladstone to be the best friend for the masses of the people."

I must now conclude, with my best wishes to you, and I trust you will give the letter publicity, and I trust you will be an M.P. for many years to come, as I think you study for the welfare of the masses of the people; and I trust good health and prosperity may attend you in every way.

ELI HAMSHIRE

Ewhurst, by Guildford,
Surrey."

———————

"46, Dover Street,
Nov. 3rd., 1888.

My Dear Sir, - I am very much obliged for your letter you were good enough to forward to me. You are quite right in thinking that I take the deepest interest in all that affects the agricultural labourer and the struggling sections of our rural districts. The subject has long had my attention, but is especially brought near to me in my political life by the number of these classes who form my constituents, and with whom in many cases I am personally acquainted. It would give me much pleasure to hear, at any time, from one who, like yourself, has so practical a knowledge of the subject.

Believe me,
yours faithfully,
HERBERT GARDNER

Mr. Eli Hamshire,
Ewhurst, by Guildford,
Surrey."

Three Acres of Land to Keep a Cow.

"To the Right Hon. Joseph Chamberlain.

Dear Sir, - As you are what I call a working-class representative, and likely to become the Prime Minister, and as I see you take an interest in the agricultural labour, I feel it a duty to point you out the evils in the parish where I live.

One man has bought a charity farm that formerly produced twelve to thirteen sacks of wheat to the acre, or any other kind of vegetation that was beneficial to mankind; but now a man has bought it that is a great merchant, and don't ought to have a rod of ground, for he is having it planted with yew trees, holly, laurels, and evergreen rubbish, which will be no earthly use for the sustenance of mankind.

Then there is another man that is called a lord. He is having acorns planted, which will be no earthly use for generations to come.

Then there is another man, and his father was a great pensioner, and he bought the land which used to be little productive farms, and he turned them into stag-parks. Surely there ought to be a heavy tax put upon land that is held in this sort of way. And where I used to pasture my cows by the roadside, this man has enclosed it, and added it to his stag-park, where before it was a great help to me and to many others in bringing up their families.

These great landowners have got so much of the land it is got in a wilderness state, and what they plough and sow they often-times cannot neither reap nor mow. It is the game laws, and that is the great evil of this state of things.

Surely thirty millions of people cannot live as though living in a desert.

Then, I say, let any industrious man have two or three acres of land to keep a cow, and it is the straight road to prosperity and happiness; be wise, and always have free trade in all kinds of industry, and tax everything that is not making its proper produce for the benefit of mankind.

And I say thank God we have a man like yourself who studies the welfare of those who spend their lives for our comforts on the great wide ocean; and as you have accepted an invitation to be present at a dinner to be given in your honour on January 5th, by the working-men of Birmingham, perhaps you will kindly read the letter, and a few pages out of my little book that I sent you, to the working-men, which you think is most instructive.

I have a great respect at my heart for the working classes. The late George Oger and Shipton came to Godalming, Peasmarsh, and gave a lecture on the labour question. How many thousands of chickens and eggs could be produced if the working-classes had a share in the land?

I have great respect for the working-men, who use the heavy irons of toil, which you can see by reading the little book. I have sent you a copy of Mr. Spurgeon's letter, and may I ask you a favour to give me your opinion?

I must now conclude, wishing you a happy New Year, and many of them.

From the Author,
ELI HAMSHIRE

Ewhurst, near Guildford."

(Reply to foregoing.)

"Highbury Moor Green, Birmingham.

Dear Sir, I thank you for your kind letter and for the book you have sent me. I am very busy at present, but as soon as I have leisure I will read it, as I am interested in everything which will help to explain the wishes and the wants of the working-classes.

J. CHAMBERLAIN"

Highbury,
Moor Green,
Birmingham.

Jan. 14. 1885

Dear Sir,

Mr Chamberlain directs me to thank you for your letter & for the woodcock, which he has only received. I am, yours obediently

Wm. Woodings

As a dealer in poultry, it seems appropriate that Eli should send Mr. Chamberlain a woodcock in order to elicit a reply from him.

Thinly Clad and Empty Stomached Little Children.

"To the Right Hon. Henry Fawcett, M.P.

Sir, - As I live in an adjoining parish to Major Garrett, I was in his company, and he kindly advised me to send you a copy of the little book that I have written, which I hope you will find instructive and amusing.

And I heard say that the birth-rate is 1,200 more than the death-rate every week in the great metropolis. Surely there will have to be some great thinking class of men in this country; surely the great monopoly will have to be done away with, or we shall have shoeless and thinly-clad and empty-stomached little children, which would heighten the passions of parental feelings in all sorts of ways, such as the dynamite, &c.

And I pray that these wicked principles will be routed out, and that each parent, one and all, and more especially our great ruling powers, would think of the Great Master, who had the plat of thorns put upon His head, and who said, "Suffer little children to come unto Me." Surely the little children did not have empty-stomachs in those days, as they have now.

Neither did the parents have the briars and thistles and taxation hooked into them as we have now, and in my little book I have shown how to open up a new channel of industry, and will you kindly hear it read."

The Evils of Ockley and Ewhurst.

"To H. Labouchere, M.P.

To your Honour, - As you study the wishes and the wants of the working-classes, and being a native of Cold Harbour, I wish to point you out the evils of Ockley and Ewhurst.

One man, who owns thousands of acres, has, I think, encroached upon his neighbours' rights - he has enclosed a piece of Ockley Green.

And at Ewhurst they are planting laurels, yew trees, hollies, and evergreen rubbish; and a man that is called a lord is planting acorns; and one of these men, whose father was a perpetual pensioner, has added the land by the roadside to his stag-park, where I used to pasture my cows, and it was a great help to me in bringing up my family, and many others in the same way. And on the land where they are planting this rubbish there used to be little productive farms.

And all the lime-kilns are done away with; and I have read that we are paying away one hundred and sixty millions for food that we ought to produce at home. How long will thirty million people allow England's soil to go into a wilderness and desert state through the monopolization of the few.

I have sent you one of my books. Please to read page 12, as I see you are about to be at a meeting on Thursday at St. James's Hall.

From your obedient servant,
ELI HAMSHIRE

Ewhurst,
near Guildford, Surrey."

Mr. Labouchere, editor of 'Truth', says:- *"The book seems to me as likely to be useful to bring home to the agricultural population the injustices with which they are treated."*

Mr. Bradlaugh and the Guildford Wolves.

"To Mr. Bradlaugh, M.P.

March 3, 1884.

I saw you when at Guildford, and spoke to you on the Perpetual list. I hear so much backbiting as to your creed of religion. I often think you have more religion in your little finger than those backbiters have in their whole bodies. I wish they had to come on the platform. I think you could tell them of their hypocrisy. They want to make me believe that you don't believe in a Creator at all, and I don't believe it.

And being a talented man as you are, surely the Northampton people will be exempt from paying taxes, as the Government will not allow you to represent them.

P.S. - Would you kindly give me your opinion after you have read the little book. Your leaders ought to lead you in the right path when you went to the House of Commons. I think they are afraid of you shaking their sinecures, like the Guildford wolves. When you put your hand up it was like the lion's paw, and the Guildford wolves were very quiet, if you remember.

And had I known that they were going to invite me as chairman that night, you would not have gone back to Northampton without three cheers for yourself, and three cheers for the Northampton people for choosing such an out-speaking man as yourself as a representative.

From your obedient servant,
ELI HAMSHIRE"

(Reply to foregoing.)

"20, Circus Road,
St, John's Wood,
London, N.W.

March 10, 1884.

Dear Sir, - Mr. Bradlaugh desires me to thank you for your little book, which he has read with much pleasure.

Yours truly,
TRIGARDE HUMPHREY"

Mr. Spurgeon and the Church of England Minister's Wife.

"Godbridge Lodge,
September, 1884.

To Mr. C.H. Spurgeon.

Sir, - You being a minister of the Gospel, and being so near like St. Paul, I hope you will read my little book, and kindly give me your opinion.

Surely the rich don't study their own interest or they would study the waste, as the waste is something like £78,000,000 a year. The sewage confuse all the Town Council. I have not got my intelligence from lords, dukes, and squires, nor engineers, but from practical farm labourers, and old farmers, and market gardeners, with my own experiences. And don't you think we ought to get our lamps filled with the oil of charity?

When you look around the great metropolis and see the great amount of poverty, don't you think, according to the reading of the slips of newspaper, that the Charity Commissioners are men who are taking the charities, or the oil, from the poor to give it to the rich.

As I was driving home from Guildford with my horse and cart, I gave a poor woman a lift on the road, and she told me she had got a large family, and she had to walk a mile night and morning to the laundry to her work. And the Church of England minister's wife, on the 23rd of August, 1884, said, 'I did not see you at church last Sunday. I was there last Sunday afternoon, but I did not see you there. You must come to church regular, or we shall stop your subscriptions at Christmas.'

The system of the poor is to pay 1s. a month, and the subscriptions is 3s., so they get 15s. out at Christmas if they go to church regular; and I have known the poor have four miles to walk to pay the shilling once a month. And is this the way you get your hearers together in your Tabernacle? I say now I see you assist the orphans, for I think there will be a fine lot of them in their spiritual prosperity.

I now conclude, wishing you well in surety, and in your spiritual prosperity, and that you will be for ever with the little orphans.

ELI HAMSHIRE"

———————

Westwood
Beulah Hill
Upper Norwood
1887 June 7

Dear Sir,

I sent you two of my books by Parcel Post. You are exceedingly generous to send me so handsome a present. Thank you very heartily.

If I ever get near the windmill, I shall want to see yr three acres & cow, & you also. Long may you live & prosper.

Our housekeeping friends rejoice over yr gift. I cannot eat flesh meat myself, but I am glad others do so do. I pray our Lord richly to recompense you for yr kindness to his servant.

Yours very heartily

C. H. Spurgeon

This letter from Mr Spurgeon again illustrates Eli's ability to obtain a response from the rich and famous by bombarding them with presents.

(Reply to foregoing.)

"Westwood,
Beulah Hill,
Upper Norwood.

September 10, 1884.

Dear Sir, - I thank you for sending me your book, which is certainly amusing, but much more painful to the heart. I trust the day will come when the agricultural labourer will be heard. He has suffered much because he has been, as a rule, too ignorant to know his own rights. But education is already awakening him, and he will be able to speak for himself.

I do not think we can lay the blame on any one class, or prescribe any one infallible remedy; but if the whole class be raised, the men will take care of themselves, and, in the natural order of providence, burdens will be divided, and profits be shared. Go on expressing your views in your own way, with hearty good-will to everybody.

Yours truly,
C.H.SPURGEON"

Depression Which We All Regret.

"To Mr. Broadhurst, M.P.

1887.

I propose to you if you will kindly bring a bill into the House, that the working-men might have 100 acres out of every 640, and that would leave 540 acres for the aristocracy.

There is a large amount of charity that belongs to the poor, and the charity money could be used for building cottages and refuges for the poor wayfaring men to lie down in, and for poor old people to have a home, and I trust that I might live to see the scheme brought into working order. It would cause to reduce our poor-rates by many thousands of pounds, and do away with a great many of our poverty institutions and breeding dens of all sorts of diseases.

And, I say, the soil of this country is in too few hands, and this is the real and the true permanent cause of that depression which we all regret. One-fifth of England and Wales is held at the present by 523 persons; in Scotland 24 persons hold one quarter of the land, and 1,700 persons own between them nine-tenths of the whole of Scotland.

Now what is the case abroad? In France there is something like six millions of proprietors, of whom more than five millions are small owners, owning, on an average, less than ten acres a-piece. In Belgium there is one million people who are absolute owners of small estates.

There is not a civilized country in the world in which so small a number of the population are directly connected with the soil as there is in England. And, for no other reason than that, I would ask you to support with all your might and all your heart the Liberal cause, and Liberal members everywhere will do their best to bring about a change.

I am the originator of the three acres and a cow. I spoke on the subject eighteen years ago in the Guildford Public Town Hall, which you can read in page 24 in the "Carrier's Boy's", the book of which I am the Author. And I also wrote to Joseph Chamberlain in 1884.

We have many schemes and plans devised to celebrate the Queen's Jubilee. If the 'Carrier's Boy's' plans could be carried out the masses of the people would be set free, and there would not be so much vanity over the Jubilee to have great fires burning. It will be a great waste, and I can see nothing in the glee.

Then, I say, carry out my propositions; it would be remembered down to doomsday if it took place in the year of Her Majesty's Jubilee.

And now I must conclude, with hearty good wishes to every reader, and to read the twenty-fifth chapter of Leviticus.

Wishing permanent prosperity to all.
ELI HAMSHIRE

Ewhurst, near Guildford."

(Reply to the foregoing.)

"With regard to the suggestion contained in your letter there is a great deal of value in it. I shall send it on to Mr. Cobb, who has charge of the Parish Allotment Bill; he is a good man, and I am helping him all I can in his movement.

Yours very truly,
H. BROADHURST"

To the Right Honourable W.H. Smith, M.P. - The Butchers' Shops in Guildford on December 24th, 1887.

"To the Right Hon. W.H. Smith, M.P.

I was in Guildford on December 24th, 1887, on Christmas Eve; and Guildford is called the capital of Surrey. At seven o'clock in the evening I walked down the main street which is called High Street, and I looked into all the butchers' shops, and all the customers there were in them was five, and there was some of the most splendid show meat that could be found in England. I also looked in a street called Friary Street, and there they were rather busy selling the Billingsgate two-eyed steaks, the sprats, and herrings, &c. This is a rather curious state of things in the year of the Jubilee.

I am the originator of writing to Joseph Chamberlain on the three acres and the cow; I also spoke on the subject eighteen years ago in the Guildford Public Town Hall, which you can read in page 24 in the book which I have sent you. And I can always thank God the three acres and the cow are paying me a very good profit.

P.S.- I forwarded one of my books to your firm, and they wrote back to say they had not room for it on the bookstalls. Perhaps you will kindly read it, and favour me with your great talented opinions."

(Reply to the foregoing.)

"10, Downing Street,
Whitehall.

Dear Sir, - Mr. W.H.Smith has now returned, and he desires me to thank you for your letter and the suggestions you have made.

I am, dear Sir,
Yours faithfully,
J.D.PATTISON

Mr. E. Hamshire."

To Mr. O'Brien - Home Rule in England as well as Ireland.

"To Mr. O'Brien, M.P.

To the Editor, - As I am a reader of your valuable paper called 'United Ireland', will you kindly review the little work which I am the author of. The price is one shilling.

Now, sir, I think we very much need Home Rule in England as well as in Ireland. The land has got into the hands of the few. They are making a god of their cruel sport, such as the game laws.

I know a little farmer who is assessed over two pounds ten shillings per acre and about six feet over the hedgerow. The man who owns thousands of acres is only assessed at five shillings per acre because the land is lying dormant only as rubbish grow to seed. The other man's land growing over it, he is using all kinds of industry striving to get a living.

You see the game laws and the merchandise in the people's souls and the perpetual pensioners' list is what the masses of the people will see is the greatest evil we have to contend with.

I am the originator of the three acres and the cow - in writing to Mr. Joseph Chamberlain in 1884, and I also spoke of it eighteen years ago in the Guildford Public Town Hall. And I can lay my head down on my pillow and say, Thank

God, my three acres and a cow pay me a very good profit; and the farmers could do the same if they were to come out and not to have their eyes so much bigger than their pockets and to have such a burden of rent, tithes, and taxes, and be independent Radicals and get some of the unjust laws reformed, and come out of the rut of Conservatism.

I must now conclude, wishing the Irish good health and happiness, as I am glad to say I have relieved some when they have been in great poverty in England.

Your obedient servant,
ELI HAMSHIRE

Ewhurst, by Guildford."

Aug., 1886.

Dear Sir,

     I am instructed by Mr. Parnell to write and thank you for your letter of the 13th. July, and also for the kind present which you sent to him.

     I am,

     Yours Very Truly,

     H. Campbell

     Secty.

Mr. E. Hamshire,

     Ewhurst,

     Near Guilford.

This letter from Mr Parnell was subtly altered in Eli's book to indicate that he had sent him a copy of his book.

Mr. Parnell, M.P. - Irish in Bondage.

"To Mr. Parnell, M.P.

Dear Sir, - I feel it a duty to forward you one of my books. Will you kindly read the few first pages in the book? Please read page 11 and page 45 on monopoly and bondage. I know your time is very much taken up.

And I say man is man, and I have just relieved one of your fellow-countrymen, and the tears were running down his face. He had slept out of doors all night, and he thought he must criminate himself as he felt so ill; I do trust you will study to benefit this class of beings, and I believe it would be a great benefit as to your future destiny.

And as to your Home Rule, I think Surrey and Sussex and Kent of it, and I think it is a pity we cannot have two or three Irishmen to give us lectures on the subject. It appears to me there is a lot of aristocracy; it appears that they want to keep the Irish in bondage, and we have to keep 30,000 soldiers and police to keep them in subjection to our English laws.

From one who is a well-wisher to you and to your fellow-countrymen.
ELI HAMSHIRE

Godbridge Lodge,
Ewhurst, near Guildford.

(Reply to foregoing.)

"August, 1886.

Dear Sir, I am instructed by Mr. Parnell to write and thank you for your letter and also the book you sent to him on the 13th of July.

Yours very truly,

H.CAMPBELL (Secretary)

Mr. E. Hamshire,
Ewhurst, near Guildford."

Letters from Lawrence T. Baker, J.E. Thorold Rogers, and W.E. Stone.

From Lawrence T. Baker, Esq.

"28, Queen's Gate,
South Kensington.

March 4, 1884.

Sir, - I am much obliged for your letter and the pamphlet, with which I have been both interested and amused. The desire to improve the position of the labouring classes is one which should constantly press on all thoughtful people.

I am, yours faithfully,
LAWRENCE T. BAKER"

Extract from a letter I received on April 1st from Professor J.E. Thorold Rogers.

"I am quite certain that the Agricultural difficulty is best met by aiding the agricultural labourer in getting again on the land."

From W.H. Stone, Esq.

"Lea Park,
Godalming,

November 13, 1886.

Dear Sir, - I am very sorry that I have kept your paper so long, but I have been away from home, and it was overlooked before leaving. I have read it, as well as the pamphlet, with a great deal of interest, and many of your ideas are good ones.

No doubt it is very important that the land should be well cultivated, and give healthy and useful employment to as many as possible. The time has gone by, however, when England could produce all the food required for her population; and we must now keep open communication with abroad, by living on good terms with other nations, and having our navy so strong that they will not care to attack us.

We require nothing, and need never fight, except to take our fair share in maintaining the police of the world. By developing the resources of India, we can obtain all the corn we can possibly require.

I remain, yours truly,
W.H. STONE"

Chats with a Farm Labourer.

"Sunday, June 6th, 1886.

Parson's Daughter Asking for Vote for the Conservatives.

"You're just going to eat your earnings again, then, John?"

"Yes, just going to get my dinner once more, Master Hamshire."

"I hope you have got a good one, John."

"Well, I think it is a sheep's steering-point."

"I daresay the sheep's head is mostly what you get with your large family?"

"Yes; but I sometimes get the waist-coat piece - what some people call the breast of mutton; I can't get enough of that for a pudding; my dame is obliged to put the tea-cup in to keep the lid from falling in."

"Do you ever get a taste of the leg of a sheep?"

"Yes, Mas' Hamshire; otherwhile gets a piece at our club-feast once a year."

"I suppose you sometimes allows to have piece of beef otherwhile?"

"Yes; but that most times comes off pretty close to the horns, and sometimes has to buy a piece of bullock's liver. I had half a bullock's head eating for my dinner, and I had the queed choer lying on my plate." (John means the lower jaw-bone of a bullock's head.)

And John said, "The parson's daughter came in when I was having my dinner, and asked me to vote for the Conservative. I said, 'I am now come in from holding the plough; now you see this jaw bone lying on my plate, and the meat is rather stringy.'

John said, opening his mouth - 'Just look in here, and see how it do hang in my teeth, and I have not got time to sit down and puck it out; I think it is very near time there should be a change. I think we farm labourers ought to have the rump-stak, and you and your father ought to have the sheep's head and the bullock's head, then you and your father would have time to pick the stringy meat out of your teeth, instead of coming round to see we poor farm labourers, and asking us for our vote.'

They take us down on a polling-day in their carriages, and get us to vote for them, and we are so foolish, some of us, that we goes and votes for them the same as they bags for us to do. They have now just done away with all practical out-door relief, and they are building our unions bigger, and if illness befall me I should have to go. The Conservative Government passed this Act in 1888."

Well, John, after reading this, I should think everybody would be Radicals, like you and me!

———————

Parson's Wife Breeding Lunatics.

"Now my missus went to see the parson's wife about the confinement bundle. And the parson's wife said, 'Are you come again already? You ought to know better than to come so often; you think of nothing else but breeding paupers.'

'I can't help it, ma'am; you must talk to John about it; we always brings our children up to work, ma'am, and John and I always works hard, and our children's talents seems all right, and I did not marry my first cousin like you did; you are breeding lunatics to fill lunatic asylums.'

'And do you really think that is the occasion of it?'

'I can see no other reason for it, ma'am.'"

To the reader. I know deaf and dumb and poor blind children, who have continually the discharge from the nose, and sometimes not sufficient skins for their bodies. It is something wonderful why it is that nature does not do its work in a systematic way. And therefore I would solemnly warn every reader never to intermarry with their own relations.

———————

Liberals are all Rebels.

"Good morning, John. How is it you're not going to church? The bells are chiming."

"O, I had to goe another road this morning, Master Hamshire."

"But you won't get any blankets if you don't go to church."

"I don't care about their blankets now I've lost my dame."

"Yes, but they will come around for your vote again before long; how shall you get on then?"

"I don't know. They squires' and parsons' daughters says the Liberals are all rebels, and it don't make much odds to me which way I wotes. Our Squire was good enough to send us down his waggon, so I woted the same way as he wanted me to wote."

"Well, you remember when the sugar was tenpence a pound, and the tea five shillings and sixpence a pound, and flour twelve shillings a bushel?"

"Yes, I remember. Aunt Sall come to see mother wonce, and I went to old Dame Longherst's, at the Jurry, up Cheapside, and got half a pound of sugar, and an ounce of tea, and it was ninepence-halfpenny. We din't have tea and sugar in they days, only when anybody come to see us; we others wille had a bit of burnt bread put in the teapot. To get a little bit of tea and sugar was quite a rarity in they days.

I remember going home one night, and mother was crying, and I said, 'What you crying about, mother?'

'I han't got nare a morsel of bread for supper, boy.'

'Well, I am dused hongerd, you know, mother. What shall I do?'

'I don't no, boy. Your father only has nine shillings a week, and flour is twelve shillings a bushel, and we have not got a mouthful of bread left for your supper.'

'Well, I will go down in the parson's wim (the name of the field) and get sum sweeds.'

So I got a bundle of wood, and carried them home, and cooked some, and had some for supper and brakfast next morning, and carried some for my dinner next day. And then I tould the cook about it wair I worked, and she gave me a great hunch of beef for my dinner, and then I chucked the sweeds over to the pigs.

I was a big hungry boy, and I could only get three shillings a week then, so I thought I would board myself; so I don all I could for the cook, and she very often ust to give me some odd pieces."

"I suppose you otherwhile stole a kiss?"

"No, we chaps wan't so fast in those days; we wan't edakated same as they be now, you know."

"No, you was brought up to the school of Difficulty in those days, and the Conservatives would like to have it so again if they could have their way, but the Librels have given you the vote. And you have a creed of religion belongs to your conscience, and no man has a right to ask you for your vote, nor what creed of religion you are."

"Well, as to religion, I don't understand it much. In your 'Carrier's Boy' - I heard it read - you know you says that the Almighty didn't see it fit for man to live alone, but created woman for a helpmate. Now the parsons marries the people at the church, and they most times gets a smartish lot of money. They gets into office, sometimes chairman at the Board of Gardens, they marries people together, and are the first to separate them."

"Yes, that's why the bishops and rectors are so wicked to uphold that state of things; their religion is all vanity. They may go to church three or four times a day, but if they don't think about the poor their religion is no good then, I say.

Now, John, what we free-traders want is to have a little more free use of the land, to build refuges in every parish throughout the United Kingdom, and we think the glebe land belongs to the poor. You have now got your vote, and, I say, send free-traders as your representatives to the House of Commons.

Stag-hunters comes two or three times in a week, and the counterjumpers' sons, and the land-muddlers' sons, and the squires' sons, and the rectors' sons, and the perpetual pensioners' sons, treading into the earth, and there is no chance for the farmers nowadays. Then the squires and the parsons and their daughters and the primrose dames will come around and ask for our votes at election times.

So election day I got home and went to bed, and the Conservative farmer sent his son and horse & cart to take me to vote for them; but I did not go; I then said, 'Mr Gladstone has given you a free conscience, and it's perfectly secret as to who you vote for, and I believe Mr Gladstone to be the best friend for the masses of people.' "

"Well, Master Hamshire, I shall wote for the man that will do most good for the masses of the people."

"That's right. John, and you won't vote wrong. Good morning, John."

Conservative Meeting at Ewhurst.

A Conservative meeting was held on September 25, 1885, at Ewhurst. Mr. Webb was Chairman, and Sir George Bonham and Mr. Brodrick were the principal speakers. I presented the Chairman with 'Monopolization and Bondage', and Mr. Brodrick criticised it and called me on to the platform to speak.

And the subject I spoke on was the Land Question. I told them it was a great and serious question, and I thought charity ought to begin at home, as they were turning the little farms into parks, and pulling down the barns and little farm homesteads; and I said to the Chairman, "I must be candid - it is my creed of religion to tell the truth.

We will start from Cheapside, and there you have enclosed the church towpath, where there was a curkel in the roadside, and I in my younger days have sometimes taken on my arm a young woman, and stolen a kiss (Laughter).

And then I go to another gentleman's property, and he has enclosed the land by the roadside and added it to his stag-park, where I used to pasture my cows, and pigs, and poultry used to run; and it was a great help to me and to many others in bringing up our families. And this class of men will write their cheques for £100 for the Civil Service instead of patronizing the little tradesman.

I know a poor old man, who worked on the estate for 22 years, and took all the steel out of him, and he got disabled for work; and he cried, and said he did not know what to do, and I then went to the Relieving Officer, and they allowed him two shillings a week. The poor old man told me that, having a large family in his younger days, he could not get sufficient mutton off the breast of a sheep to make a pudding, so they put the tea-cup in the dish to keep the crust from falling in.

Now if this industrious man could have had three or four acres of land to keep a cow, &c., in his younger days, he would now have had a nest-egg of three or four hundred pounds; he could then have enjoyed himself under his own fig-tree."

I then spoke to a large landowner, and I told him if they were all such farmers as he and his neighbour, England would be liable to a famine in less than a week, for he pinched the farm labourer up with only two roods of ground for a garden, buried in with timber; and yet the land did not produce 5s. per acre per annum.

The Conservative working-man spoke in opposition to my views; he said, "If Mr. Hamshire's views could be carried out, one man would say he had got gravelly soil, and another would say he had sandy soil, and another would say he had got loamy soil, and another would say he had got clay soil; and they would fall out over their row of potatoes."

(To the reader. Don't you think this is ignorant bosh? This is Conservatism in its brightest colour!)

And then he went on to condemn a good-hearted man like Mr. Chamberlain, who acts so honourable towards the working-classes of this country; Mr. Chamberlain does not only preach charity, but he acts up to it. I can speak from my own experience, as he sent me a very nice family present, and he sent the man Field a five-pound note, who had to go to prison for not paying for the support of his father in the Union Workhouse, which I think is a black spot on so-called Christian England.

Mr. Brodrick then said the Conservative working-man made the best speech; and he said, "I have got a pamphlet the man Hamshire put into the Chairman's hand, and here is a piece I will read to you. It says, 'I have been the instigation of saving little children's lives when on the brink of starvation, and a young woman's life, when disappointed with her falsehearted lover.' "

He then said, "I can't compare this falsehearted lover now better than to Mr. Gladstone; he has promised the people of this country a good many things, and he has never performed them. So Mr. Gladstone is like one of these false hearted lovers."

He said the Conservatives passed the Artizans Dwellings Act, and it was the occasion of saving a great many lives; he named the different streets. But these Conservatives forget that where these artizans used to pay 3s. per week they now have to pay 6s. or 7s. per week; they have raised the rents because the landlords had to put the houses into sanitary condition; and for so doing he would have to lay out from £10 to £40, perhaps.

(To the reader. The landlords always get great interest for their money; this is Conservatism.)

Then, I say, be an independent Radical, and come out of these fever and smallpox and poverty-stricken dens. The land is your birthright, and why not have the use of it, and brew your own beer and bake your own bread? And I trust that England with her greatness will pluck out poverty of every kind; Mr. Gladstone is the great axis of the revolving wheel of industry.

Mr. Brodrick said Mr. Gladstone promises, but he don't perform, like the falsehearted lover; but I say Mr. Brodrick is one of the cogs that throws the great wheel out of gear. Then, I say, it is the Conservatives and the House of Commons and the House of Lords that throw the great wheel of industry out of its motion.

To the middle and working-classes: How long will you remain in this darkness? We don't bring one pound of earth into this world with us, neither can we take one pound out when we leave it. Then there is the sun that we revolve around; and our great Maker said, "From the sweat of thy brow thou shalt till the ground."

Mr. Brodrick then said, "The man Hamshire has caused some merriment here to-night, as much as at any meeting I have attended, and I think he is a terrible man for the land and the ladies too."

I said, "Yes; I study the land, and also the welfare of the weaker sex, and I am the originator of the three acres and the cow." (This subject I spoke about at a public meeting, held in the Town Hall, at Guildford, 20 years ago; a report of my speech will be found on page 24 of my 'Source of England's Greatness'.)

I want to put everything right in a plain sort of way,
And not to use a lot of highty-flighty words and know not what I mean or say;
It is the blood that we want to keep pure that is running in our veins.
They might as well try to stifle the rays of the sun on a midsummer's day
As to stifle these facts in what the Carrier's Boy say.

I like to put plain truths for Mr. Brodrick, as I wish to do good for the benefit of the public. Mr. Brodrick said I was a terrible man for the land and for the ladies too. And I want to direct old John Bull which way to go. The three acres and the cow went throughout the United Kingdom, and I want the Bull to go throughout Europe, Africa, Asia, and America.

The New and Great Scheme on Vaccination in Poetry and Prose.

Blood is the life of man, I say,
Then keep it pure and clean in every kind of way,
And always keep from houses of ill-fame in every sort of way;
From the highest to the lowest you want to keep from going astray.
And, I say, ring old John Bull and muzzle the Russian Bear,
And I think other nations would live in peace and quietness everywhere.
Science ought to point out how to keep our blood pure and clean,
She cannot do it by intermixture of bloods nor yet by vaccine.
Blood should be a pure red, but it's all sorts of colours, sometimes yellow and
sometimes green.
When the blood is intermixed through the vaccine.
Old John Bull ought to give Science six months' imprisonment and a little bit of
cat,
For using bad blood for vaccinating, for if a man is poor he is a man for all that;
But Science seems to treat him worse than I should like to treat a dog or a cat.
I have oftentimes seen poor people with neither house, home, nor habitation,
But they have been compelled to have this humoury blood for vaccination.

Do away with prostitution or the filthy blood will be as pregnant to us all, causing dangerous sores and discharging matter, and the fluid causing us to be in an unhealthy state.

I attended a meeting at the Ewhurst Schoolroom. Mr. Brodrick, the member for West Surrey was present, and he said, "This has been one of the most enjoyable meetings that I have attended, and carried on in a good friendly spirit; and as to that man Hamshire, he has caused a good deal of merriment here to-night, and I believe him to be a terrible man for the land and for the ladies too." This is the character that Mr. Brodrick gives to me.

In answer as to my character, I write these few lines, with my best wishes to Mr. Brodrick, and also for the welfare and the benefit of the masses of the people. We hear much complaining of the masses of the people upon the subject of vaccination, and therefore I wish to bring out a new scheme and a new plan for the benefit of the nation, and he who needs no physician can pass a few of these lines by, as I feel it a duty to treat upon subjects that are carried on by the sly. I am the originator of the three acres and the cow, and I don't see why I shouldn't have a word about old John Bull and sciences and the bachelor of arts.

I think that old John Bull ought to turn his attention more to growing corn
And not to have so much in the Divorce Courts to reform,
For if he will his wild oats sow
He will damage his seed, burn down his barn in doing so.
And if he will to the brothel-house go
He will sow his own destruction in doing so,
And as sure as the sun shines at the noonday
He will die with his blood full of corruption.
A great many people will say that smallpox is prevented by vaccination,
But I say it is more prevented by good sanitation.
I think old John Bull would say it would do a good deal of good if a few of these
drunken, adulterous wife-beaters were put through castration.
Old John Bull and science and the bachelor of arts they might as well try to stifle
the rays of the sun on a midsummer's day
As to stifle these facts in what the Carrier's Boy say,
And if they don't believe in what the Carrier's Boy say,
Let them come to the three acres and the cow, and he will point them out these
evil effects any day.

The Canterbury Subject.

I wrote a letter to Mr. Broadhurst on this great and serious question, so that the aged, and the poor, and the afflicted, and the unfortunate, might have permanent homes, and I will also give the Press of all descriptions permission to put it into print.

And, I say, try and abolish our poor-law system altogether, as the Guardians act so hard-hearted towards the poor, and also the tithes of the Church of England, and let every creed support its own denomination. There will be a day when every soul will have to stand by its own merits.

We have the Queen at the head of our realm, and a good, kind-hearted, motherly woman she is in the districts where she remains; and why don't the bishops, the lords, dukes, and squires, and the canons, and the rectors, act the Samaritan's parts more.

No! They are often riding in their carriages at ease, with their hot-water bottles, and have their splendid carpeted rooms at sixty degrees, whilst their unfortunate neighbours have neither house, home, nor habitation, and their poor little children dragging about the country with empty stomachs and almost to freeze. God hath given us eternal life; then we must try and do good to one another throughout this temporal life.

Are the Guardians and the above-mentioned titles trying to do good? I am afraid the Great Judge will say, 'No; your case is human destruction to your own souls.' Only fancy a rich place like Canterbury, and a poor woman applying for relief, and to be told to work for her husband, and not to trouble the Guardians again!

Copied from Reynold's Outspoken Newspaper, May 19th, 1889:-

*The **Mock Court-Martial**. - The Canterbury coroner has continued the inquiry into the circumstances attending the death of Private Alfred Byford of the 3rd Battalion East Kent Regiment (Buffs), who is alleged to have died from injuries received by being tossed up in a blanket by his comrades during a mock court-martial. The coroner having summed up, the jury returned a verdict of "Death by misadventure".*

---

*A **Distressing Case**. - An Inquiry held by the coroner for Canterbury (Mr. S. Johnson) on Saturday into the circumstances attending the death of a labourer named Stephen Beer revealed a melancholy state of things. Deceased, who was 62 years of age, had for many years past resided at Nonington with his wife.*

Of late years he was incapacitated for work owing to acute rheumatism. Parochial relief being refused, the life of the couple has been a hard and penurious one, and a day or two since deceased was found to have cut his throat as he lay in bed. He was removed to the Kent and Canterbury Hospital, but the wound was a very severe one, the windpipe having been severed, and he succumbed.

Replying to the coroner, deceased's wife, who appeared greatly overcome, stated that when she applied for relief some time since she was told to go home and work for her husband, and not to trouble the Guardians again.

The coroner commented severely upon the facts elicited, observing that it was the worst case he had had to inquire into of late. It seemed a sad thing that with the poor-law organisation in the country, deceased, suffering as he did, should have been refused relief during the last part of his life. Had some small allowance been made Beer might not have been led into committing such a lamentable act.

Moreover, was it right that his aged wife, who had not always been in her present poor condition of life, should have been treated as she stated she was? Doubtless this and his other troubles preyed upon the poor man's mind. A verdict of suicide whilst of unsound mind was recorded.

A Man named Jewis died from Epilepsy, caused by Lashes from the 'Cat'.

The Coroner for East Kent, Mr. R. M. Mercer, last night investigated the circumstances attending the death of a prisoner in St. Augustine Gaol, named Jewis, about thirty years of age.

He enlisted two or three years since in the Buffs. His military record was a bad one, and in September, while stationed at Dover, he committed an offence, for which he was sentenced to six months' imprisonment and to be dismissed from the regiment.

On arriving at Canterbury Prison he feigned madness; he destroyed everything breakable of which he could get possession, and had on several occasions to be removed to different cells. He systematically disobeyed orders, refused to do any work, set alight to the oakum given him to pick, and stabbed one warder and assaulted others.

In November he was brought before the Visiting Justices, and ordered to be placed on bread and water diet (three days on and a similar time off) for fifteen days. Later in the same month, for destroying public property, he was sentenced to 36 lashes with the cat.

When, however, the medical officer of the prison examined Jewis, preparatory to the punishment, he found that the man had with his finger-nails lacerated the skin of his back so severely as to form a large wound on the place where the punishment would fall. It also transpired that the prisoner was in the habit of drinking large quantities of salt and water, thus getting himself into a low state of health and unfitting him for work.

In the circumstances Jewis was removed to the infirmary, and his injury treated, but a carbuncle formed, and he did not recover until the 28th December. It was then resolved to inflict the punishment on the lower part of his back, but hearing of the decision the man repeated his former tactics. He was, however, discovered before his self-inflicted injuries were serious, and twelve strokes of the cat were administered.

Jewis, on promising to discontinue shamming, and to behave himself properly, was then excused. On Friday he was seized with epilepsy, and died on Sunday. A verdict in accordance with the medical evidence was returned.

Only fancy a poor man lying in bed with rheumatic pains cutting his own throat because they would not allow him common necessaries of life!

———————

Then, near the same date, ('The Standard', January 22, 1889), another, sentenced to six months' imprisonment at Canterbury Prison, being stubborn-minded, received a severe punishment (36 lashes with the cat). He also inflicted injuries upon himself. Do they ever use their thoughts about their great Master, who said peace and goodwill towards mankind?

Then, I think, they ought to try kindness upon these poor unfortunate people, who are possessed with a rather stubborn mind - a discharge from the army I should have thought would have been sufficient for the crime. This is a little bit of their hardships in Canterbury in 1889.

———————

Thomas a' Becket was murdered in 1170, but before his death he had got great power, and he very much studied the welfare of the poor, and did not do as the King wished. He also gave up his rich and costly manner of living and all his long train of vanities; he also gave up some of his dainty dishes, because he might supply the necessaries and wants of the poor. It is also said that he washed the feet of thirteen beggars daily.

The Bible says, "The poor ye shall always have with you" - fine text for the rich. It was never intended by our great Master that there should be any in want of temporal bread, as he is a most bountiful benefactor. I look upon Thomas a' Becket as one of these poor. It is the man that stands enriched with this world's wealth is the meaning of the word poor, because he does not distribute it as he ought for the benefit of the temporal wants of the poor.

And the King's conscience troubled him because he was the instigation of the murder of poor Thomas a' Becket. He saw that the poor needed something for their temporal wants.

And surely it stands worse with us in these days than what it did then; surely the bishops in these days are hypocrites, and Pharisees, and misers, as we often read of their dying worth their thousands of pounds, and with their splendid mansions to live in, surely it would be more becoming to them if they were to act more of the Samaritan's part; surely they ought to turn their great mansions into almshouses, and also their great parks into vineyards; or surely the working-classes who use the heavy irons of toil are

The gist of the message on Eli's loving cup is similar to much of his own poetry, although it scans more easily.

fallen among the thieves as in olden times.

It is the working-man who uses his ingenuity that have to support the lords, the dukes, and the Queen. It is the pick, the spade, and the plough, that causes everything to flourish now. Then I say to the bishops, do away with vanity and pride, that feasting ourselves and our friends, and at the same time forgetting the distress of the poor and afflicted.

Surely was not he very poor when the poor man cut his own throat for want of the common necessaries of life, and the poor soldier who was lashed with the cat? Surely this will be very provoking to God and damning to the soul.

Only fancy a great gulf being fixed, and the poor man and his wife and the soldier on one side, and the bishop, and the magistrates, and the guardians, on the other, and, because of their hard-heartedness, judgment without mercy; the bridge is drawn and the door of the pit is locked up; our conscience will terrify us and will be for ever in misery through living in luxuries, and sensuality, and unmercifulness to the poor temporal.

Poetry for the Present Time.

The bishops and the parsons might preach to our poverty, and pray for our grief;
But that won't produce our temporal bread, neither will it produce old England's
roast beef.
The man who uses the spade, the plough, and the pick;
Then why should the poor man be tied down to scarcely twelve shilling a week,
When it is the plough, the pick, and the spade
That causes everything to flourish in all kinds of trade?
The man who uses the pick, the spade, and the plough,
These are the men that ought to have the privilege to have the three acres and the
cow.
Naked we came into the world, empty we go out;
We brought no money into the world, and we take no money out.

Suggestions for Cottage Property.

A church is built on a hill, north side of Surrey sand-hills, called St. Martha's Chapel. Just at the foot of the hill is a regular running stream of water, and there is the great Government Gunpowder Works, and also Messrs. Unwin Brothers' Gresham Printing Works carried on, and these manufactures employ a large number of hands, and these men and boys have to walk three and four miles night and morning. Then we have, on the north side, Albury Downs and St. Martha's Hill, and on the south side there is Blackheath and the Surrey sand-hills.

Now could there not be some invention so that each working-man could have about thirty to forty rod, so that he might build himself a cottage, so as to have a permanent home, and not to have a burden of rent to pay, and a Union workhouse staring him in his face at last. I trust that my suggestions may be carried out at last.

I understand that Mr. Samuel Barrow has purchased Lord Grantley's rights as lord of the manor. Lord Grantley some years ago gave permission to the working-classes to take in some small plots the same as I now propose.

Mr. Barrow, knowing him to be a good, liberal-minded man, I have not the least doubt whatever but what my suggestions will be carried out by calling a court of the copyholders, and these men would not object to paying a reasonable price for the land, but I am afraid some of these Conservative lords would greatly object to it. They would sooner see them herd into the towns, and have pestilence and famine; and I trust that our towns may diminish in the way of cottage property, so that we might have more cottages placed upon the waste land; and I trust that my suggestions might be carried out throughout the United Kingdom, and I hope to see it begin at Blackheath, as I know Mr. Barrow personally to be a good, open, broad-minded man.

He is a Dissenting gentleman, and has provided an unsectarian mission-room in happy Cranleigh. The villagers flocked to the room. The local Church folk felt it necessary to make a desperate effort to stem the tide of heresy; but they did not do as they did in my grandfather's time - about a hundred years ago - they threw addled eggs and all sorts of filth.

My father told me that the first of Dissenters' preaching was in my grandfather's barn at Cranleigh. Then they came to Ewhurst, and preached in my father's house, and then they built a nice little chapel, and they still carry on preaching up to the present day, and it is amusing to hear the working-men offer a prayer when the preaching is ended. They never were such bigots at Ewhurst as what they were at Cranleigh.

'The Christian World' on Happy Cranleigh.

Not long ago Mr. Samuel Barrow, a Dissenting magistrate, provided an unsectarian mission-room in the little Surrey village of Cranleigh. The villagers flocked to the room with such eagerness that the local Church folk felt it necessary to make a desperate effort to stem the tide of heresy.

Ineffectual thunders have pealed harmlessly from the pulpit of the parish church against the wickedness of attending an unconsecrated place and listening to an unordained preacher. The children at the National school have been solemnly warned against the danger, and the curate, in his eagerness to save the souls of the parishioners from travelling to perdition, has called upon the wives, and used every art of persuasion.

But the mission-room still keeps open, and the people still throng to it. No wonder the clergy are expecting a flood or an earthquake as a judgment on such disrespect to the spiritual pastors and masters of Cranleigh. 'The Christian World'.

And I say thank God we have such an enlightened paper as 'The Christian World', as it shows up the bigotry in many of the country villages. I think it is a pity that the paper is not more known in the dark places of Cranleigh, and also in Conservative Sussex.

I think Mr. Barrow will be the means of opening our eyes in sleepy Surrey, as I hear he is opening up several chapels and mission-rooms. He is a very persevering man, and I give credit to those to whom credit is due.

Interview with Mr. Samuel Barrow.

I had an interview with Mr. Samuel Barrow, and he gave me permission to enlighten the working classes on the subject. He told me, at the present, that no common lands could be enclosed, as they passed an Act in 1887. But that Act was passed to prevent the great landowners enclosing so much; and it is a pity they did not pass that Act before to the working classes.

My suggestions could very simply be carried out, that I made to Mr. Broadhurst and Mr. Barrow, if they were to put my suggestions before the Members of Parliament, and not allow any one man to enclose more than one acre of land.

The waste land is free of taxation; and, as it is scarcely any benefit to mankind, it ought to be free of taxation when they build on it, and get it registered - the same as you would get your infant registered - and therefore I see no necessity of any law expenses. The democracy have got the privilege of the vote, and therefore I trust that you will see that my suggestions are carried out, as it lies entirely in your hands to do so.

I think that Mr. Barrow, if he were chosen as M.P., would be one of the first to carry out my proposal, for I know him to be a good disposed gentleman.

Land Facts.

143 great landlords own 21,167 square miles of land. One square mile equals 640 square acres; 21,167 square miles equal 13,500,000 acres, or equal to 10 acres each for 1,350,000 men, or one acre each for 13,500,000 men. 143 men own land equal to more than one-third of England and Wales.

1 Man owns	2,125 square miles
6 Men own	4,838 square miles
12 Men own	6,615 square miles
26 Men own	9,954 square miles
41 Men own	5,659 square miles
76 Men own	5,554 square miles
143 Men own	21,167 square miles

Since 1861, 600,000 agriculturists have left the soil.

The number of acres of the United Kingdom are 77,513,600.

Vote for Liberals and Land Law Reform.

The democracy have got the power in their hands
To do away with monopoly and cultivate the land.
Then why should this great band of locusts be allowed to go on?
It's the landlords, the lawyers, and the bishops, that cause this great blight;
And why should the working classes be always in a fright?
Mr. Gladstone has given them the privilege of the ballot;
Then, I say, vote, vote, according to your conscience, and be a man for that;
And vote against these great locusts as much as you can;
And then you will have the privilege of having the use of the land.

Unequal Taxation.

One of the tax-collectors told me that he knew a little farmer in Sussex, and he paid £2.15s. per acre, because he got all of the produce off the farm he possibly could; and on the other side of the hedgerow it was only taxed at 5s. per acre. This belonged to a perpetual pensioner, and he let it grow dormant for the sake of the game. Now I think they ought to reverse the taxation - they ought to charge £2.15s. for land held for sport, and the man who uses all means of industry, he only to be taxed 5s. per acre.

In my own parish I knew a great merchant that bought a good many acres of land, and the steam plough was set to work breaking it up in great clods. Now England's soil is getting into the hands of the few.

Now this great merchant is letting his land lie dormant, and grows nothing but moss, thistles, docks, rushes, &c., and the little farmer the other side of the hedgerow uses all kinds of industry, and the seed of the merchant's rubbish is blown over the farmer's land, which makes so much extra labour; and he is obliged to get his little boys up at five o'clock in the morning at the spring of the year to go into the fields to beat the old tea-trays to keep the merchant's pheasants from eating the trifolium grass.

The Cost of Every Pheasant Shot Down.

I calculate that every pheasant that is shot down costs this country £10. On an average it costs the owner 25s.; therefore it would leave £8.15s. for the people to pay, causing our land to grow dormant, and filling our Unions and our prisons, and causing so many sudden deaths, one of the greatest evils under the sun.

Enormous Mistakes by our Legislature.

I contend that a nation is responsible for its actions, and I contend that the agriculture of this country is suffering to an enormous extent through the violation of God's laws by emptying our sewage into the rivers instead of restoring it to the earth. The land of this country was incapable of producing the food required by the population, because we disobeyed the law, and, unless we attend to it, the most serious consequences must ensue. Were we to get into trouble with nations abroad, and hungry people could not be kept in control, and England's sun would be set.

That enormous mistake, which the sanitary authority of London were about to make of letting all the sewage of that great city go down into the Thames, would have the inevitable result, sooner or later, of destroying the Thames as a way for ships, and it would be dealing out death and destruction to all those living in the vicinity of it.

It behoves, us therefore, as a nation to prevent that mischief by returning this material to the land. The soil is crying out for it in all directions. And what are the consequences for want of this natural manure? Deficiency of crops and deficiency of food for the people, and that was when England's back was broken; when £6,000,000 of our money was taken from the United Kingdom, which you can read in pages 20 and 22 in 'The Carrier's Boy'.

And I look to our unfortunate sister Ireland. We have there a nation becoming less numerous year after year, which is diminishing by thousands every year, and they were under the government of this country, and we as a nation are responsible for its deeds in the eyes of God. We are responsible for the slaughter which has taken place in our sister Ireland; and, depend upon it the blood of those slaughtered in various ways was calling aloud to our great Master, who can right the wrongs.

There has been a great neglect of this country in the management of their laws, and did they not hear in all directions the cry of vengeance and coercion? And they were kept in bondage, and the worm had been trodden upon and turned, and England would have to recognise the squeeze. Here is the great evil, and our rulers were responsible for it.

The landlords of former times had not done their duty towards those who lived on their estates, and to-day their successors were reaping the harvest, result of their own neglect. Surely the Irish people have a right to their Home Rule!

The Three Acres and the Cow, the Little Swallows, and the Conservative Cock Sparrow.

I live at the little cottage, and I have the three acres and a cow, and the little swallow comes every summer and builds her nest and hatches her young, and the old cock sparrows comes and destroys her young and robs her of her feathers which she had lined her nest with.

Now I think that the old cock sparrow resembles England. The great landgrabbers goes over to Ireland and tears down the swallows' mud huts, and these old Conservative sparrows has made bad coercion laws to keep the swallows in bondage and to tear and burn down their huts, and turned them out on the roadside, there to die.

The Population of 1881.

The population in 1881 was near upon 35,000,000, which, by the time of the next census, in 1891, will probably increase to 39,500,000. If there are 35,000,000 people, and each one consumes one sack of flour per annum, then it will want 35,000,000 sacks to supply the demand. It would take 52,500,000 sacks of wheat to produce the flour. Then, if each acre produced ten sacks of wheat, it would take 5,250,000 acres to grow the wheat.

What Mr. Bright said at the Covent Garden Theatre.

December 19, 1845.

The landowners have had unlimited sway in Parliament and in the provinces. Abroad, the history of our country is the history of war and rapine; at home, of debt, taxes, and rapine, too. In all the great contests in which we have been engaged we have found that this ruling class have taken all the honour, while the people have taken all the scars.

No sooner was the country freed from the horrible contest which was so long carried on with the Powers of Europe, than this law, by their partial legislation, was enacted - far more hostile to British interests than any combination of foreign powers has ever proved.

We find them legislating corruptly; they pray daily that in their legislation they may discard all private ends and partial affections, and after prayers they sit down to make a law for the purpose of extorting from all the consumers of food a higher price than it is worth, that the price may find its way into the pockets of the proprietors of land, these being the very men by whom this infamous law is sustained.

HAPPY CRANLEIGH.

At the last election the Cranleigh people, when I went to give my vote, they called me the Ewhurst Liberal roundhead, and I in return called them (the Cranleigh people) the Conservative diamond-top.

Now at Ewhurst we Liberals have got the allotment-ground, and we have had it near upon sixty years; but Conservative Cranleigh have not got it yet and they don't seem likely to get it, and yet the great merchants take parts of the gardens away from the agricultural labourer and plant it with ash, and allow the stock to run in the garden where the poor man planted his fruit-trees in former days.

One poor man told me he worked for a farmer in Cranleigh, who asked him to sit down to have his dinner, and he had bread that was made from crammings and bullock's liver for his dinner, so he did not like to go in to sit down to eat it.

And then another man who took prizes for holding the plough and building ricks, &c., and his wife has had a family of twelve children, and for keeping his eldest boy at home he was summoned before the Guildford bench of magistrates and they fined him 2s.6d.; but the magistrates could not draw blood out of a flint, the poor man could not pay the fine. He had to cut a red-herring up into joints with potatoes for his children's breakfast before he started for Guildford, and the tears ran down his face when he told me.

So these two men know better than to vote for the Primrose Dames and the parsons and the perpetual pensioners and squires; they will vote for the Liberals, for they don't want the rising generation to live on bullock's liver and crammings and potatoes and the Billingsgate two-eyed steaks as they have had to in the past.

Now, in the dark, heathen countries, the rich have more thought for the poor; they fix troughs up to the back doors and put the waste food in the trough, and the poor have access to it. If this simple plan was carried out throughout the United Kingdom there would not be the waste of food.

I wrote a letter to John Bright on this great and extravagant waste in so-called Christian England.

And He who was born and in a manger laid,
What does He think of the poor woman who had three months of hard labour
who had nowhere to lay her head?
And she was so ill when committed that she only lived three days before she was dead.
She could not walk to the station she was in such a fainting way,
The policeman had to borrow a wheelbarrow to wheel her the other half way.

Coming into contact with a woodcutter going the same road as I was, I said, "Don't you think it is a serious thing to separate old people like poor old Tickner and his wife, in the month of February, 1887, and the poor old man paid into Cranleigh Old Club when it first opened? And his poor old woman only left a fortnight when she was brought back and buried in Cranleigh Churchyard. And the poor old man is over eighty years old, and they had a large family."

"Yes, but Cranleigh is such a terrible Conservative place, and for any one to get into poverty it is such a disgrace."

"But they say poverty is no sin. It causes a good deal of inconvenience when the wolves enter in."

"Now, who are these wolves, then?"

"Why, the parsons, and the lawyers, and the landlords, and the perpetual pensioners, to be sure."

"Yes, there are a good many other paid officials the farmers and the working-classes have to pay."

"Yes, but the parson and the landlord is where the biggest burden lays. I know a farmer that was the best farmer in the parish when he used his own land; but there was what I call a trap set for him. The big landlord saw he had got his own land, and he was not contented with his own land, so he took some more, and the landlord agreed to put him up some convenient buildings, and charged him 5 per cent., and it was not done properly, and it was not worth twopence to him.

So the landlord got hold of the front door, and the parson got hold of the back door, and the lawyer hold of the w.c., and the poor farmer was near upon being sold out, and nowhere to be."

"Do you mean to say this is true?"

"Yes; and the farmer planted a parcel of laurels and evergreen rubbish; then they rose his assessment."

"Yes, some people are planting it out in the fields in round rings."

"All such rubbish ought to be heavily taxed. It is a harbour for rubbish of all sorts. And a great merchant planted a lot of ash in a poor labourer's garden. He has a large family. These Conservatives want people to do their labour and live on the air."

The Poor Man who Sprained his Ankle.

I knew a man who sprained his ankle at mudding a pond, and he was laid up for eighteen weeks; and he made an application for parish relief. The officials told him he could go to the Union.

He said, "No; mother is ill, and I cannot go there." His mother was an aged woman, and had been a midwife, and a very clean, respectable woman she was; and her son paid into the parish benefit society, but that became exhausted, so the poor mother and her son had nothing to exist on. So they put a brief paper upon the mantlepiece in a beerhouse; one gave a sixpence and another a sixpence.

So I said to the woman at the beerhouse, "You have got a raffle on, then?"

"No, it is a brief for a man that sprained his ankle."

I said, "Oh, well, here is a shilling for him."

Then she said, "Shall I put your name down on the paper?"

I said, "No." Then I went down the next week, and she said the poor mother was very ill, and had scarcely anything to eat. I then gave her another shilling.

Then I went down the next week, and she was then dead. I then gave her 1s.6d., and she said, "That makes 3s.6d.; now I shall put your name down on the brief paper."

(To the reader. I don't put anything in my writings to boast of my little charities, but by setting an example it sometimes does good to others.)

Some of the tradesmen came and gave him 5s. because they saw my name on the paper, but the parish officials never gave him one penny - the man told me so himself. And yet the officials preach and beg twice or three times on a Sunday; and yet the church is standing within one hundred yards of the beerhouse, where the poor woman almost died for want of nourishment; and yet she was a good-hearted woman the whole of her lifetime, and would go to assist poor people, both by night and by day, as a midwife.

––––––––––

I think we ought to choose our own minister, for, as it is, the Church of England ministers are the greatest weeds the farmer has to contend with; and they don't assist the poor in any kind of way. There are some who have wolves' hearts and lambs' profession, dressed in sheep's clothing.

A man told me he had lost one of his little children, and it was buried in the Cranleigh churchyard, and the grave was covered up with the earth, and the parson's hens and fowls scratched the earth off from the grave, so he put some iron fencing around the grave which cost him 3s.6d. The managers of the churchyard did not let it stand a fortnight before they tore it up. I said, "You ought to have some crucifixes put on the irons and then they would let them alone."

The man then said, "I know they are Roman Catholics as near as they can be at Cranleigh."

This, is happy Cranleigh.

CHAPTER OF COMPLAINTS.

London Pickpockets on Epsom Racecourse on a Derby Day.

A farmer came into my house one day, and he had a glass of home-brewed beer, and he gave me some of his views, and he said he worked very hard with his horses through the summer to clear the land of rubbish, and for so doing he thought to raise his valuation, as the farmers had been farming out. Then the landlord employed a third valuer, and he could not get his valuation.

And he said, "Talk about the London pickpockets, and the blacklegs on the Epsom Race Course on a Derby Day, they never knew how to be half such rogues and vagabonds as these Lords, Dukes, and Squires, in making balls for the stewards to shoot us farmers down."

Then I came in contact with another farmer, and he told me he had just sold all his wheat for four hundred pounds, and he had one hundred to pay for tithes to the Church of England clergyman. And he told me that the clergyman had just had left him twenty-six thousand pounds, and then the clergyman had the cheek to send him a note to say the organ fund was in need of thirty shillings, and would he send him a subscription.

I said they are getting to be such a Popish, begging class of people, that they are causing more infidelity in the country - these old bachelors of arts - than any other class of beings. The country is too full of such miserable beings, they will never put their hands to the plough, nor the spade.

How the Widow and Two Daughters Multiplied by Three.

Then I came in contact with a tradesman. "And you think you know something about the evils of the game laws, but you don't say anything about what I knows."

"Well, and what do you know, then?"

"Well, I knew a squire who kept a keeper, and the keeper died and left a widow and two daughters, so the old gentleman paid his addresses to the widow, and the two sons paid their addresses to the two daughters. So they went on and multiplied by three. It appears that there were two other young men who paid their addresses to the two daughters, or wanted to, for one young man put an end to his existence through it, and the other crossed

229

the river over it."

I then said, "It is wonderful what the little legs will cause the big legs to do."

They are miserable if they go to sea,
Or if they put on the red coat they will miserable be,
Their consciences will never be at rest you see.
Then, I say, be true and just, and have a cistern of your own,
And then you will be able to keep a comfortable home.

Proper Way to Make a Will.

Then I had one of my customers - a widow lady. Her husband died and left a will, and because it was not worded just right she was like the mouse under the lion's paw; the lawyers were for everlasting worrying her about it. And I trust that there will be shortly a reform to make it better for the weaker sex.

If a person can't read or write, the most proper way to make a will is to get a lad about twelve years old and dictate to him everything that you wish, and then call in two witnesses, and sign your name in their presence, and also they sign their name in your presence, and there is no necessity of reading the will to any one; and therefore my advice is to see to it and get it done, as you won't die any sooner for it.

When you are in good health is the most proper time to do it. You could also get the boy who wrote your will to sign his name in your presence; you could then get an envelope and seal it up, and it would be an entire secret till after your death.

Then I paid a visit to an old bachelor, and he said that he had worked hard in his younger days, and he purchased a little property, and he added about two yards of the waste, and for so doing the clergyman's son visited him on a Sunday night, and the clergyman was there on the Monday morning, and they wanted him to throw it out again, and he had the lord of the manor to see him about it; and yet the squire could enclose the church tow-path, and also enclose land for the stag-park, where the poor man used to turn his cows and his pigs, which was a great help to him in bringing up his family.

They say it is a Christian country, but it is what a great many would call a crushing country, for he said it took one part out of four to pay the lawyers and the lords of the manor. Surely we need great reforms in our land laws;

surely it ought to be settled without so much going into the lawyer's and the lord of the manor's pockets.

The Irish are waking up in this direction, they are striving for Home Rule; and the United Kingdom will have to do the same thing, for as it is she is so much monopolised that she is becoming like a mass of rubbish, like a wilderness.

Mr. Gladstone has given us the privilege of the vote and also the privilege of the ballot, and I believe him to be the man who would cause the great wheel of industry to go working around.

———————

Mr. Plimsoll was a great and thoughtful man of his day, to prevent rotten ships being sent to sea. These I consider require great attention by our legislators as the sailors have oftentimes hardships to contend with, as they are sometimes neglected by our great merchants in the way of importing and exporting our great merchandise.

———————

Joseph Arch never Cheated the Labourers of a Brass Farthing.

Then, again, Joseph Arch, he has done a great deal of good for the benefit of the farm labourers. He was the means of the farm labourer getting a little more money for his work; he wanted to abolish the tithes and reduce the great landowners' rent roll; and for so doing a great number of people wanted to make him out as a dishonest man. But I am a constant reader of 'The English Labourers' Chronicle', and I don't believe he has cheated the labourers of a brass farthing as the Council have the paying of his salary.

Much credit is due, during the little time that he was in office as Member of Parliament, as he has given the farm labourer the privilege to brew his own beer free of taxation; also with the like of myself with the three acres and the cow. I think it is a great pity that there are not more men like Joseph Arch in the House of Commons. We want practical men who understand the nature of the soil, so that we might not have one foot of land to lay idle. God has given us good seed to sow but, through the monopoly, the weeds will multiply a hundredfold. It is a great crying question of the present day.

Then, I say, give the unemployed employment, so that they might be prosperous and have happy and healthy homes, and in employment they would have no time or inclination to stir up strife. Let us work permanently and intelligently on the land, and the adoption will then provide work for our workless workers, we shall have a prosperous, peaceful, and happy England.

The Little Farmer Thirty Years Ago.

I knew a little farmer about thirty years ago, he so happened to owe twelve pounds six shillings and five pence, and the farmer expected the lawyer to come, so they had got six pounds three shillings and five pence on Monday to pay him in part, and to pay the remainder on Friday.

And the lawyer said, 'All or none!' So they sold the little farmer out because he was a Dissenter. And this broke up their home; and the poor woman is still living, and, for selling some little boys some sweets on Sunday, the little children were ordered to boycott her, and two little boys lost their tickets because they did not obey the curate's orders.

THE CROYDON AND BASINGSTOKE SUBJECT.

In November, 1886, I saw a man and his wife with a baby in her arms, with a family of six children, and I said I thought he ought not to drag them about the country in that sort of way, getting wet through, making them so uncomfortable.

"Why don't you go to the Union with them?"

"You seem to know something; perhaps you can direct me a little. If I tell you the truth, my name is Blake, and I went into Croydon Union in 1884, when we had done hopping, and in less than three weeks I lost two of my dear children; and I went in again in 1885, and I then lost another child, and the porter told me I should lose the little girl that stands there. And when we go there I have to go one way, and my wife has to go another, and the little boys one way, and the little girls another."

He said it was a hardship, and the tears were running down his face when he told me his case. He said, "You see, I got a pair of trousers for that boy, and a pair of shoes for the other, out of the hopping money; and the other children wanted, but I could not get any more. I am a willing-minded man to work at anything, if I could only make a home for my wife and family.

We are almost ready to drop down for want of refreshment. But I can't go to Croydon Union. They that are fed to the full know not what a miserable

232

case it is to have a family of children hungry and thirsty, and to have no supply."

The Reverend Canon Blackley, at a meeting of agriculturists at Basingstoke, said that during the last eleven years 40 per cent. of his parishioners who died over the age of sixty years were consigned to a pauper's grave! A Hampshire village, in this year of grace, 1886!

The secretary of a Foresters' Court inquires the average wage in this locality. It is eleven shillings a week: eleven shillings a week to house, feed, and educate a family! And yet this experience is not singular, for there are many parishes in Hants and Dorset, Surrey and Sussex and Kent, where they receive no more than eleven shillings a week.

Notice the cottage gardens in this district; you will see some good vegetation. But the farmers ought not to have over one hundred acres, and the landowners ought to build cottages convenient to allow the labourer three or four acres to keep a cow, pigs, and poultry. Then the farmers would not have any poor-rates to pay.

We should study more to cultivate our minds. As a bird is known by its note, so is a man by his conversation. Then, I say, use the law of self, and don't use improper language, or it will oftentimes lead you away into temptation. Let the conscience be purified, that we may be ready for our future destination.

I don't trust in kings, nor princes, nor any such things,
But I do trust to my Maker good news for to bring;
I was brought up at my mother's breast on Nature's care;
And I wish to do good to everybody, everywhere.

The higher classes are brought up on goats' milk or asses' milk, and they intermarry, which is wrong, according to nature, I do declare. For if we could only get the finger of God in our mind, these angry passions would leave us, and we should be to each other just, true, and kind; and professors and ministers of religion would not like to see their neighbours plucked like a pigeon, for little children to go to school with empty stomachs and shoeless feet.

There will be one great doom. These professors and magistrates will have to meet. Woe to you. There will be weeping and wailing, and gnashing of teeth, for sending poor helpless people to prison for having nothing to eat. Your religion is all vanity, and I am afraid there will be no mercy shown at the great judgment-seat.

ESSEX AND CHELMSFORD MAGISTRATES.

February, 1889.

Charles Chapman, of Fye Green, whose aged father and mother, 84 and 85, became destitute, and had to go to the Union workhouse. Charles Chapman in grief protested that he would never have permitted his father and mother to become chargeable to the parish if he could have helped it, but he had not a farthing, and was up to his ears in debt, and he was a married man earning only ten shillings a week. His employment was a labourer; but the Chelmsford magistrates gave orders for him to pay one shilling per week - a bit of hard-heartedness on the magistrates' part.

How can two human beings feed, clothe, and house themselves for less than five shillings a week each? If cost of supporting our convicts be any guide, this is below the mark.

Surely it is a serious thing to send a man to prison when he has scarcely anything to exist on himself, and I trust that the M.P. will do something in building cottages and refuges, and that the poor might have a little more free access to the land, and the charity money belonging to the poor would be quite sufficient to build them if it was only put to work in the right channels; and we have millions of acres of land that are now lying dormant. It then could be worked upon self-supporting principles.

Then, I say, do away with monopoly, and let the masses of the people have the use of the great vineyard, as it is man's gift from his Maker.

THE QUEEN'S JUBILEE.

Sir, - There have been many schemes and plans devised to celebrate the Queen's Jubilee, but they are not of that kind and character which are calculated to benefit the working classes permanently, neither do they accord with the jubilee recorded in Scripture (see Leviticus XXV.).

I therefore propose that the Queen's Jubilee be commemorated by the restoration of half the common-land to the poor that has been taken away from them. This would give 500,000 labourers ten acres of land each, and as the Royal Family have received from this country over £25,000,000 in the last fifty years, I would humbly suggest that Her Majesty give £1,000,000 towards building cottages on this land so that the soldier could have from thirty to forty rod.

They would then have their own soil; it then would be neutralized on the land and would produce all kinds of vegetation, and the soldiers' wives would not be turned out of barracks, as they were a short time back - turned out on eight-pence a day!

THE PUBLICANS', BREWERS', AND GOVERNMENT SUBJECT.

The Publican on Jubilee Day.

The publican of my own parish once supplied a fête, and because the measures were not stamped he was summoned before the magistrates, and they forced him to pay five pounds; and then, again, on the Jubilee Day there by chance came a man on that day at twenty minutes past ten. Both the customer and the publican had to pay heavy fines.

The publicans are most always living in fear; the magistrates know but very little of their business, and they are often punished in the shape of heavy fines.

How they Rose the Publican's Licences.

The brewers purchase public-houses and beer-shops, and pay a good deal more than the value. I once knew a brewer who gave £1,700, when it was not worth more than £600, only it happened to have a public licence. Then I knew another brewer who purchased a beer-shop for £1,200 and the value of it was only £300, if it was not for the licence.

Then our legislators suggested, or are about to suggest, compensation to the brewers out of the taxpayers' pockets of the United Kingdom, which I consider would be very unjust. The masses of the people have no right to pay a brass farthing towards it.

I think that the brewers ought to pay the publicans a fair valuation, the same as when he took the house. The publican has no right to lose anything if the business of the house is abolished.

Publicans ought to be Independent Radicals.

I saw a publican, and he took the public-house in 1870, and he paid £5.15s. 5½d.; then they rose it to £8.5s.3d.; then they rose it to £11.15s.3d., the licence for the house. This house lies out in a little country hamlet, and there has been no improvement; only there has been a chapel and a church built on it.

He thought it was very unjust for him to keep raising his licence so, and he thought how much more convenient it would have been to build a school instead of the church after the chapel had been built, and that the land was going out of cultivation owing to the game laws in that district, and that trade was wonderfully dull.

I told him that the publicans would have to be more on the Radical side, as publicans were very much taken the advantage of by the brewers and by the government. The brewers will buy the property, and charge high rents to keep them in bondage, and the Government will billet their horses and soldiers on them, which is done at a great loss by the publican.

I think that publicans ought to be Radicals and Liberals. I don't see that there is any other tradesman that is more taken the advantage of, for they don't dare play a game of dominoes. For so doing they are brought before the magistrates, and have to pay heavy fines, but the club-houses are allowed to play all kinds of games at all hours at night.

A Receipt how to Brew our own Beer.

And my belief is, it is the most wholesome and the most genuine beverage of all drinks, and therefore I put a receipt for my readers to brew it the same as I do it myself, which is very easy to do.

For this purpose, get one bushel and a half of malt, and 1½ lbs. of hops, and 10lbs. of sugar, and that will make 40 gallons of good wholesome beer; and if brewed in March or October and put into good, clean tubs, it will keep any length of time.

The way to brew is to have 18 gallons of boiling water, and 4 gallons of cold water in the mash-tub with the boiling water, and put the whole of it into a mash-tub; then put up the malt, and let it stand for one hour; next draw it off, and boil it for one hour with the hops and 3lbs. of sugar; then strain it, and at night put in a little yeast. Put it in tub the next day.

Those who have not the convenience to brew this quantity of beer should brew in this way (the same as my little girl did; at ten years old she got up in the morning and brewed the beer): one gallon of malt, 1lb. of sugar, 2ozs. of hops.

They could do it with a pot to hold five gallons. Simmer it up steadily and then boil it for an hour, and then strain it off in a pan, and then, when it is cold as new milk, put a little yeast, and then the next day put it into a tub or bottle.

Surely if my little girl can brew this beer before she goes to school, if a man has got a wife that can wash his shirt and her own chemise, she will be able to brew her own beer.

I should think every working man would respect Joseph Arch for getting that great privilege through the House of Commons in the short space of time he was in office.

EXTRACT FROM THE MUTINY ACT.

The Innholder or other person on whom any soldier is billeted on the march in Great Britain, shall, if required, furnish him (but not exceeding two days when halted on the march) with one hot meal in each day, to consist of (but not exceeding) one pound and a quarter of meat, previous to being dressed, one pound of bread, one pound of potatoes, or other vegetables, two pints of small beer, vinegar, salt, and pepper, for which the sum of ten pence will be paid, and two pence halfpenny for a bed.

Soldiers not on the march, billeted on Innkeepers and others, instead of the hot meal, are entitled to a bed, candles, vinegar, salt, and the use of a fire, with the necessary utensils for dressing and eating their meat, in consideration for which the sum of four pence per diem, for each soldier, is to be paid.

Each horse belonging to Her Majesty's Forces, billeted in Great Britain, shall be supplied by the Innholder, or other person, daily, with ten pound of oats, twelve pounds of hay, and eight pounds of straw, for which the sum of one shilling and ninepence is to be paid.

Every Officer or Non-Commissioned Officer in charge should settle the just demands of the Innholder every four days, or before the soldiers quit their quarters, if they remain less than that time:- Appeals in default thereof to be made through resident magistrates.

International Court Arbitration.

There is a proposal to increase our military and naval expenditure. As far as lies in my power, I shall do all I can to lessen the expenditure.

Military system is the curse of Europe. It is the curse of mankind, and it takes the cream of the country to uphold it. Then, I say, stamp out this great evil, and adopt international means of doing so.

If England, France, Germany, Russia, America, Italy, and Austria, would agree that all disputes between nations should be settled by reason of argument and justice in an international court of arbitration, war would cease. I think my suggestion is perfectly feasible, and in less than a twelvemonth a system would be arranged which would do justice to every nation, and secure the rights of every party in case of a dispute arising, and would divert the attention and energies of every government from the arts of war to those of peace.

There is no necessity only to have one international army and navy kept for the purpose of meeting any emergency. Do that, and you will then put a stop to war and establish peace. I believe the thing is perfectly practicable, but it will have to come from the small powers. Look at the saving which this system would effect, besides the peace and comfort which it would bring to nations and peoples.

For a long time past there has been a party in England trying to create a war scare. They have persuaded themselves that England is not safe from invasion, and now they are trying to persuade other people to believe the same thing. They have persuaded the Government of it, and what do you think the sum of money it is proposed to spend? - £100,000,000! That is a sum which far exceeds my powers of comprehension. One hundred millions of money is a sum which cannot be comprehended by any. Now this money will have to be borrowed, and it will become a perpetual debt, and the interest will have to come out of the wages of the working classes.

There is an old proverb which says that, "He that goes a-borrowing goes a-sorrowing," and that is as true of a nation as it is of an individual; and I trust that God would transfer the money into a better position. God has given us the commandments to do unto others as you would be done by, and prefer others before ourselves.

I cannot help reminding my readers to think of our great Master, who said, "Peace and good-will towards mankind;" and always let this channel of love be running uppermost in your mind.

I have a great objection to spend millions of our hard-earned money for our military service. We one and all should do all we can to lessen the expenditure.

Some will say that the soldiers are the scum of the earth and they are sometimes treated as such, and very often die premature deaths.

A Stag-Hunt from Ewhurst to Forest Green.

February, 1886. - I was going from Ewhurst to Forest Green, and I met a buck on the road, and the dogs were hunting it along the road with its tongue hanging out of its mouth, and it ran up our Surrey hills, about two miles and a half, and then dropped dead, broken-hearted.

I went on the road about a quarter of a mile, and I met the horses with the hounds on their backs, and their navel was not very close to their backbone. They were rather tall and stout, like myself, weighing about fifteen stone.

My thought was that the horses' hearts were very much fatigued by the time they got where the stag dropped dead. They looked like Dorking five-claws, and the Ockley horse-pond dippers; and the rectors', and canons', and esquires' sons. The rectors and canons will administer sacrament on Sunday, and on Monday morning they go to this horrible, cruel, and destructive sport.

Then I met the farmer, and he said, "Just go and look at my wheat and swedes and tares; they just have galloped it into the ground. I wish you had been here and sold them some of your books." And I then drove on and come to a gate, and there they had drawn the staple out of the post, and thrown the lock one way and the staple another.

And the second farmer said, "My hogs are gone one way, and my colts are gone another, and the sheep and calves are gone another, and they will do as much damage as Wombwell's Menagerie let loose to-day."

"Yes," I said, "and if I drawed the staple and throwed the lock away, these same people would give me twelve months' hard labour."

Then the same day there were eighteen of their hounds rode over my three acres. I was not at home, or I think they would have had to pay the damages before they got out again.

Trip to Godalming, and the Cottage-Farmer.

On the 15th of April, 1889, I took a trip to Godalming thinking to hear and see Dr. Tanner, but, like many others, I was disappointed, as he did not put in an appearance; but they had a very clever speaker in the place of him, so that we were not so much disappointed after all.

I then called upon one of my friends to have a cup of tea, and they called my attention to some cottage property. They told me they had to pay 4s.6d. per week for a four-roomed cottage with a little back building and a w.c. attached to it, and about one rod of land for a garden.

The cottage-farmer had built himself a nice house on his piece of ground, and he had a large bow-window which looked out on his cottager's little out-building and the w.c., and there was rather an unpleasant smell from these earth-closets. I think we want a law to alter this unjust state of affairs, as these principles are carried out in almost every town throughout England by these cottage-farmers and builders.

Then I was told by my friend that Mr. Gosling had built some cottages that I see, and they were built very permanent with good large gardens, and not more than half the rent of the other cottages. We want more men like Mr. Gosling, as he is a good liberal-minded man.

Mr. Gosling at Ewhurst.

I once told Mr. Gosling at a public meeting held at Ewhurst that he would have to cut off his right arm and that he must give up stag-hunting as it did great damage to the tilling of the land, and because I told him in a plain sort of way the lawyer took hold of my round frock tail and pulled it for me to leave off telling him so plain. Mr. Gosling, being a gentleman, took my advice.

I am sure if he were to use a little perseverance he would be our representative at the next election for our Division in West Surrey.

DOG SMITH AND HIS CHARITIES.

A few particulars relating to a very remarkable man, whose history is little known, although thousands of our poorer countrymen annually participate in his benefactions, will, no doubt, be very interesting to my readers; I refer to Henry Smith, Esq., commonly designated 'Dog Smith'.

The materials for even an abstract of the history of this gentleman are very scanty. In Hone's Every Day and Year books we have a vast collection of curious customs and singular biographies, but there is no mention of Dog Smith. And in Horsfield's 'History of Sussex' we have simply a record of the charities which were bequeathed to a few of the parishes of our own county, by "one named Henry Smith, of London"; there is no further reference to the history of the liberal donor.

Mr. C. P. Gwilt, B.A., a descendant of the family, issued a book in 1836, for private circulation only, which contains much information respecting the pedigree, as well as the property, of Mr. Smith. It is from this work, which was kindly lent me by the Rector of Cowden, that the particulars for the present sketch have been chiefly taken.

Henry Smith was born at Wandsworth, Surrey, in May, 1548, and died in London, in January, 1627, having nearly reached his 79th year. From extensive researches it is pretty certain that he was a member of the family of Smith, of Camden, in Gloucestershire.

Of his early life little is known. Some have supposed that he was a silversmith, but there is no authority to support such a supposition. From certain deeds executed by him, as well as from other evidences, we learn that he was a citizen of London, residing in Silver Street, and that he belonged to the Salter's Company; the records of that company which would doubtless have thrown some light on his parentage were unfortunately destroyed in 1666, by the Great Fire of London.

On the 9th of February, 1608, Mr. Smith was elected alderman of the ward of Farringdon Without, in the room of Henry Vylett, but he never attained to higher civic honours. There exists no evidence to show by what means he acquired his great wealth.

Mankind in general surrender their property when they can no longer hold it, but to this common, though questionable, course of procedure, Mr. Smith's example was a noble exception, for his benevolence during his lifetime was almost boundless, and, until Mr. Peabody astonished the present generation by his princely bestowments, Mr. Smith's gifts to the poor had never, probably, been surpassed.

We find that his charitable intentions were first announced in 1620, when by deeds he conveyed in trust to the Earl of Essex, the Earl of Dorset, Sir Edward Francis, Mr. Richard Amherst, and others, "divers lands and tenements in the county of Sussex and elsewhere." The trustees were to devote the rents and profits to charitable uses.

In 1625, by another deed between himself of the one part, and the Earl of Essex, Sir Richard Nevill, and others of the other part, he declares the charitable uses to which he wished his estate to be applied, viz., the relief of poor prisoners, hurt and maimed soldiers, poor maids' marriages, setting up of poor apprentices, mending the highways, losses by fire and shipwreck.

In a subsequent deed, dated 1626, he specifies to his trustees the description of persons who were to receive assistance, such as poor or infirm persons, orphans, the aged, industrious men with large families, and for the education of poor children. No relief was to be given to bad characters, such as those addicted to drinking, whoremongers, swearers, idlers, pilferers, incorrigible disobedient vagabonds.

Mr. Smith's will is dated April 24th, 1627, and contains numerous bequests, from which the following are extracted:- "£10,000 to and for the purchasing and buying in of impropriations for the relief and maintenance of godly preachers, and the better furtherance of knowledge and religion."

"For buying a fellowship in Cambridge, or some college there, £500."

"The sum of £100, to be lent gratis for one half-year to deserving persons, in small parcels of £20, and when repaid to lend to others."

The estates of which Mr. Smith died seized, as far as can be ascertained, and those purchased by his trustees after his death, were situated in twelve counties, viz., Durham, Essex, Gloucestershire, Hampshire, Kent, Leicestershire, Middlesex, Shropshire, Staffordshire, Surrey, Sussex, and Worcestershire.

In 1641 the surviving trustees, by deeds, assigned the rents of the estates to the different parishes, and after bestowing a portion upon every parish in Surrey, gave what remained (which was very considerable) to divers parishes in other counties. The towns of Croydon, Kingston, Guildford, Dorking, Farnham, Reigate, and Richmond, all in Surrey, received £1,000 each; and Wandsworth, the birthplace of this bountiful donor, is enjoying £170 per annum.

In 1641 there were 81 parishes, selected from 23 counties (independent of Surrey), which participated in the rents and profits arising from this good man's bounty. The Sussex parishes are - Charlton, East Grinstead (£40 yearly), Fletching, Harting, Hurstpierpoint, Rotherfield, Singleton, Southover, Torant, Warbleton, Westbourne, Woolderton.

In front of the gallery in East Grinstead parish church there is the following record:- "Henry Smith, Esq., by deed of gift dated the 26th of January, 1626, gave proportion of rent arising from certain estates, to be expended annually on poor honest persons of good character in East Grinstead for ever."

The amount of the personality left in the hands of the trustees is unknown, but it must have been very considerable, to have enabled them to have purchased so many estates.

Mr. Smith was once married, but he had no issue; he was buried, at his own request, in the chancel of Wandsworth church; on the south side of the altar there is a mural monument with his effigy in the robes of an alderman, and on a tablet is an inscription setting forth his charitable bequests, &c.

Mr. Gwilt refers to a tradition which has come down even to our days, of Smith having travelled about the county of Surrey begging, accompanied by a dog, by which he obtained the appellation of Dog Smith.

The same tradition is current in Sussex, the version in this locality being as follows:- Dog Smith was a tramper, who wandered from place to place begging, attended by a faithful dog; that he took care of what was given him, and after awhile became possessed of a large fortune; on reaching the end of his vagrant life, having no relatives, he bequeathed all he had to the poor.

It is added that he left to the several parishes through which he used to beg, according to the amount of kindness which had been shown him, and to one parish (tradition says Worth), he bequeathed a horsewhip to be given away annually, because the authorities of that parish whipped him out of their boundaries.

This romantic story of Mr. Smith's vagrancy, Mr. Gwilt believes first appeared in print in Gibbon's Britannia (1695). The additions to Surrey were made by the celebrated John Evelyn, and he is the earliest authority it can be traced to.

Salmon, in his antiquities of Surrey (1736), embellishes the tale by adding, "he was whipped through Mitcham as a vagrant, for which that unfortunate place was doomed to be a sufferer, by not partaking of his bounty," but every parish in Surrey being in receipt of the charity, at once disproves the tale.

Mr. Gwilt sums up by observing that, "Smith, if the beggar and vagrant stated, must have been a curious associate of the Earls of Essex and Dorset, and others of the same rank with whom he was on terms of familiar intercourse. Moreover, it is not easy to believe that the inhabitants of Farringdon Without would have elected a dirty vagrant as alderman of their Ward, when there were three other competitors for the honour." These were Sir Stephen Soame, Sir Thomas Bennett, knights, and William Cokayne.

It is thought that Mr. Smith has been confounded with the Lambeth pedlar, the representation of whom, together with his dog, still remains in a painted window of Lambeth church, but this eccentric character lived long anterior to Smith.

A Letter from a Paper called 'The Echo'.

Though he was one of the earliest advocates of the 'Three Acres and a Cow' policy, the chief honour belongs to Mr. Impey, the Hon. Sec. of the Allotments Extension Association.

In point of date, however, Mr. Eli Hamshire, of Ewhurst, near Guildford, is still earlier. Several years ago Mr. Hamshire, who was a labourer, and is now a carrier, made a speech on the question, and subsequently advocated the policy by means of pamphlets.

He says in one of his pamphlets:- 'I told the meeting if we could get three or four cottages built upon every hundred acres of land, and two or three acres of land attached to each cottage, so that the labouring class could keep a cow and pigs, then there would be something for the women to do as well as the men.'

'The Echo'.

Extract from 'The West Surrey Times'.

Mr. Hamshire is warmly thanked for a copy of his interesting pamphlet which he has presented to us. The little political brochure is well worth perusal, and to those of our readers who enjoy unadulterated Radicalism of a strong type will be particularly entertaining. Mr. Hamshire has a practical knowledge of the state of the artizan and labouring classes, and many of his suggestions and proposals, more especially as to allotments, are of much value.

(We can testify also, thanks to the sample of butter kindly submitted by Mr. Hamshire, to the extreme excellence of one of the products of his application of the 'Three Acres and a Cow' system. - Ed. W.S.T.)

A Caution to Parents and Little Children and Nurses.

Never allow little children to over-excite themselves. I have known little children go into fits through it, and be subject to them all their lives.

I know a young man in Guildford, a shoeblack, whom I think ought to be better provided for, as I often see him have fits. He told me it was through being over-pleased at going by railway when a little boy.

Then I was speaking with a parent on the subject, and he told me he had a little girl twelve years old, and she was going to be examined at the School Board examination, and she excited herself so much that she died raving mad.

Therefore I would caution parents not to irritate their minds too much, and I would caution children never to imitate those people that stammer, as it is very catching.

I know a young lad who imitated an old man when he was a little boy, and he is now very much troubled to get his words out when he wants to speak to any one. He says it is a great denial to him.

A caution to nurses: I once knew a young woman who said when she went to church she went as a representative of the family, but when she went to chapel she said she went to hear what the parson said.

Now this young woman got married and had an increase, and done first-rate for a fortnight; then the nurse passed some remark about a young woman that she knew well, and the young woman died through the nurse speaking on the subject. It had such a chill on her system that she only lived a week afterwards. Therefore, always be careful what you say to people who are in a weak state of health, and more especially so to lying-in women.

I was at Eastbourne on June 3, 1889, when I came in contact with a gentleman who was a Radical in his views. He told me that he knew the land to be let at a low rent some few years back, but now three great locusts had got hold of it, and they charged enormous ground rents. He himself was away from home, in the shires, at the time, and as he owed about two pounds, the great locust sent him a threatening letter, a thing he had never received in all his life, and which seemed to aggravate his mind very much.

I asked him if he didn't think it served the Eastbourne, Surrey, and Sussex people right, because they have no representative in the House of

Commons. Surely the middle classes will come out of this route of Conservatism!

Then I came in contact with a working man who had purchased a piece of land, the measurement of which was twenty feet by thirty-five feet, and he told me that he made an application to make it freehold, but the great locust was going to charge him fifty pounds.

I myself, twenty years ago, made a piece of land about twice the size free, and the great locust then charged me two pounds fifteen shillings. Surely there must be something radically wrong in these unequal charges!

Therefore I ask every man who possesses a vote to send representatives to the House of Commons to alter this unequal and unjust state of things. To do this you must send unadulterated Radicals, who will not sell their birthrights for a mess of pottage.

Then I had a conversation, in Guildford, with a gentleman who had some property in Portsmouth twenty years ago, which was assessed at seven pounds per annum, but now they have raised it to twenty pounds per annum, although he has not improved it in any way.

It is a mystery to me, seeing the enormous number of new buildings throughout the country, why we are so heavily taxed. I trust the primrose dames will study some of my suggestions, so that we may get some of these wicked and unjust laws altered.

With the Author's hearty good wishes to every reader.

(The engraving on this page, and at the top of page 185, is taken from 'The Three Great Locusts'.)